BY NIGHT™

Volume One

BOOM! BOX™

APR 1 0 2019

BOOM! BOX™

BY NIGHT Volume One, March 2019. Published by BOOM! Box, a division of Boom
Entertainment, Inc. By Night is ™ & © 2019 John Allison. Originally published in single
magazine form as BY NIGHT No. 1-4. ™ & © 2018 John Allison. All rights reserved. BOOM!
Box™ and the BOOM! Box logo are trademarks of Boom Entertainment, Inc., registered
in various countries and categories. All characters, events, and institutions depicted herein
are fictional. Any similarity between any of the names, characters, persons, events, and/or
institutions in this publication to actual names, characters, and persons, whether living or dead,
events, and/or institutions is unintended and purely coincidental. BOOM! Box does not read
or accept unsolicited submissions of ideas, stories, or artwork.

For information regarding the CPSIA on this printed material, call: (203) 595-3636 and provide
reference #RICH – 825781.

BOOM! Studios, 5670 Wilshire Boulevard, Suite 400, Los Angeles, CA 90036-5679.
Printed in USA. First Printing.

ISBN: 978-1-68415-282-7, eISBN: 978-1-64144-144-5

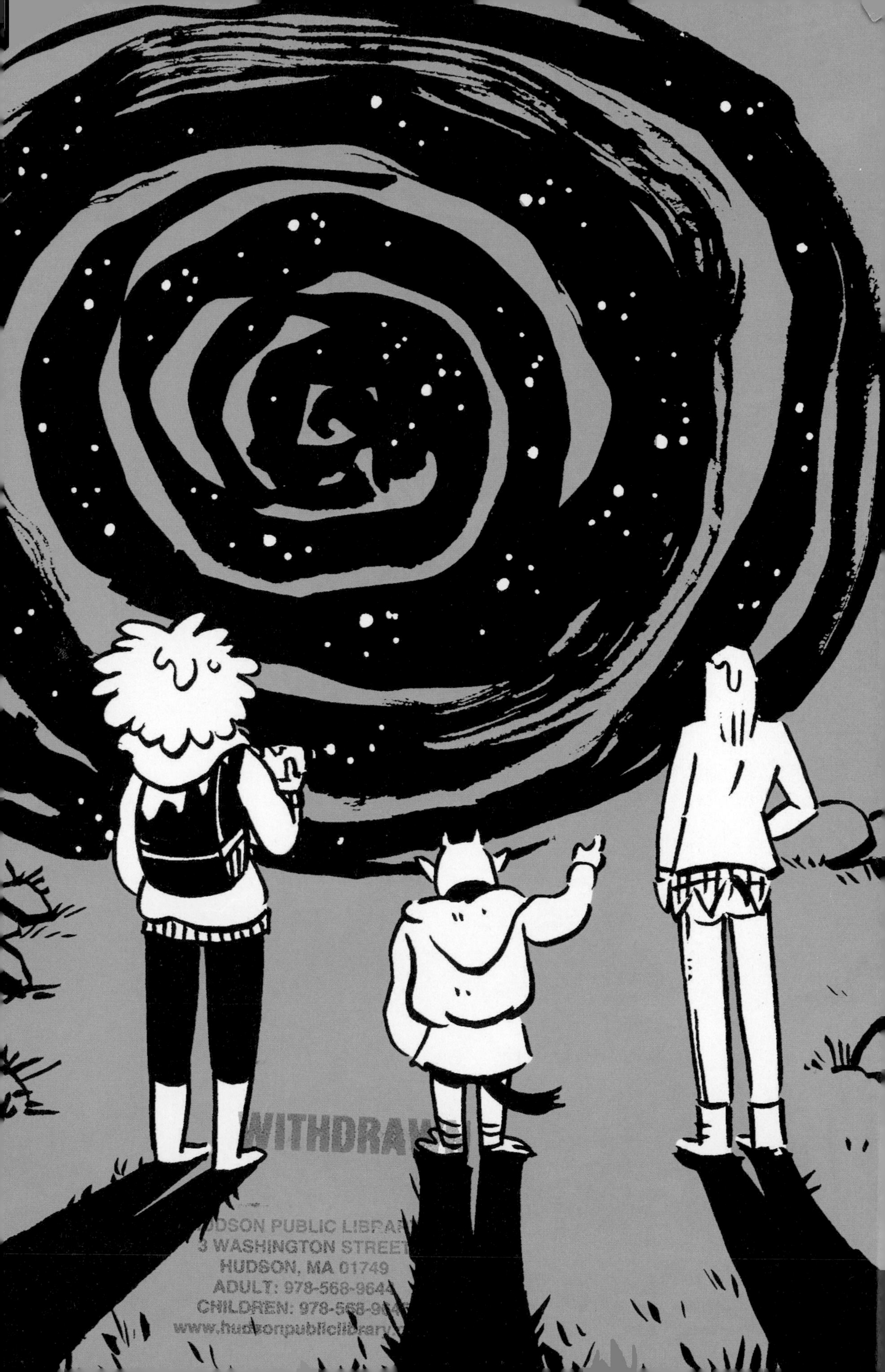

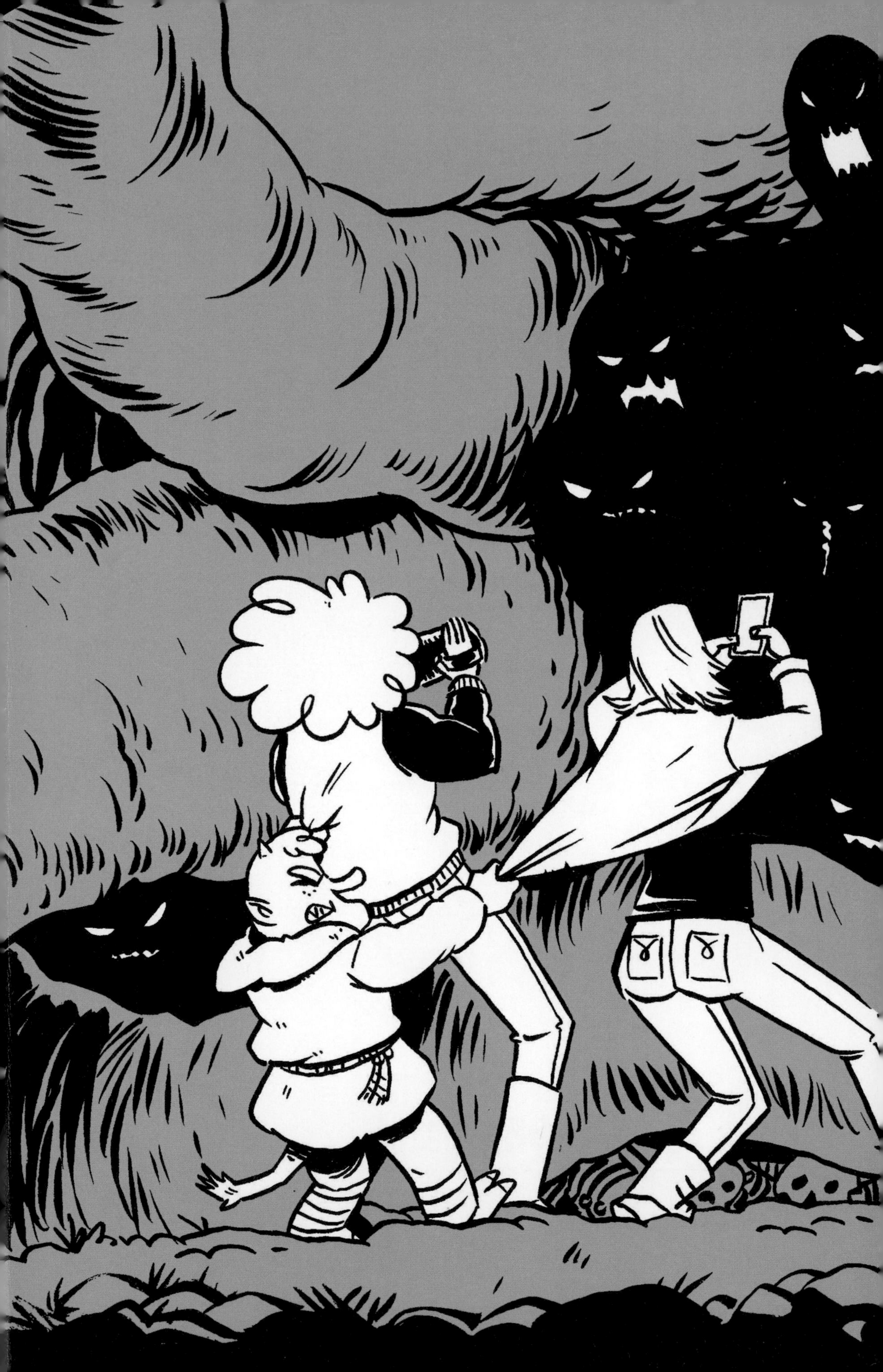

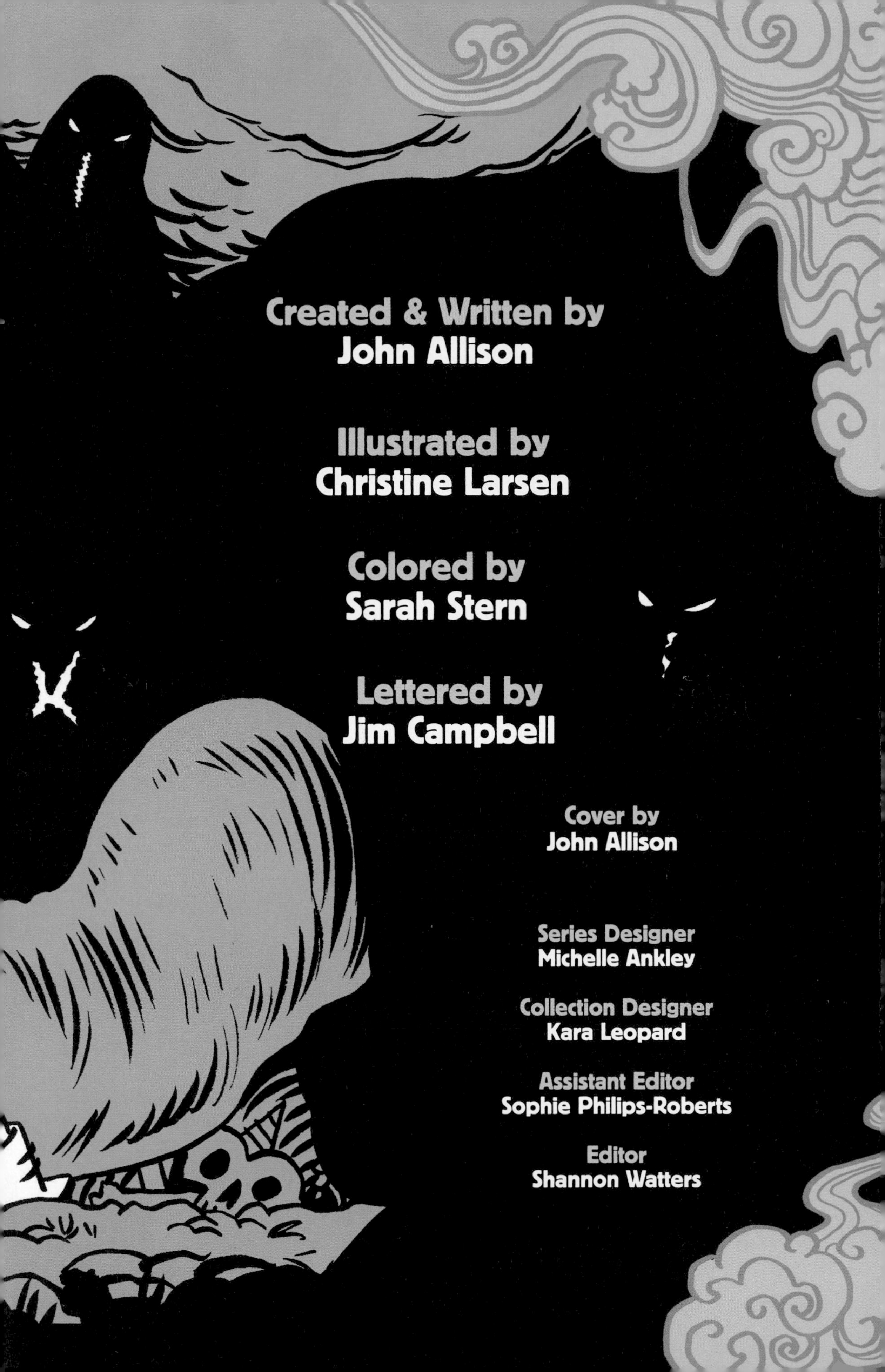

Created & Written by
John Allison

Illustrated by
Christine Larsen

Colored by
Sarah Stern

Lettered by
Jim Campbell

Cover by
John Allison

Series Designer
Michelle Ankley

Collection Designer
Kara Leopard

Assistant Editor
Sophie Philips-Roberts

Editor
Shannon Watters

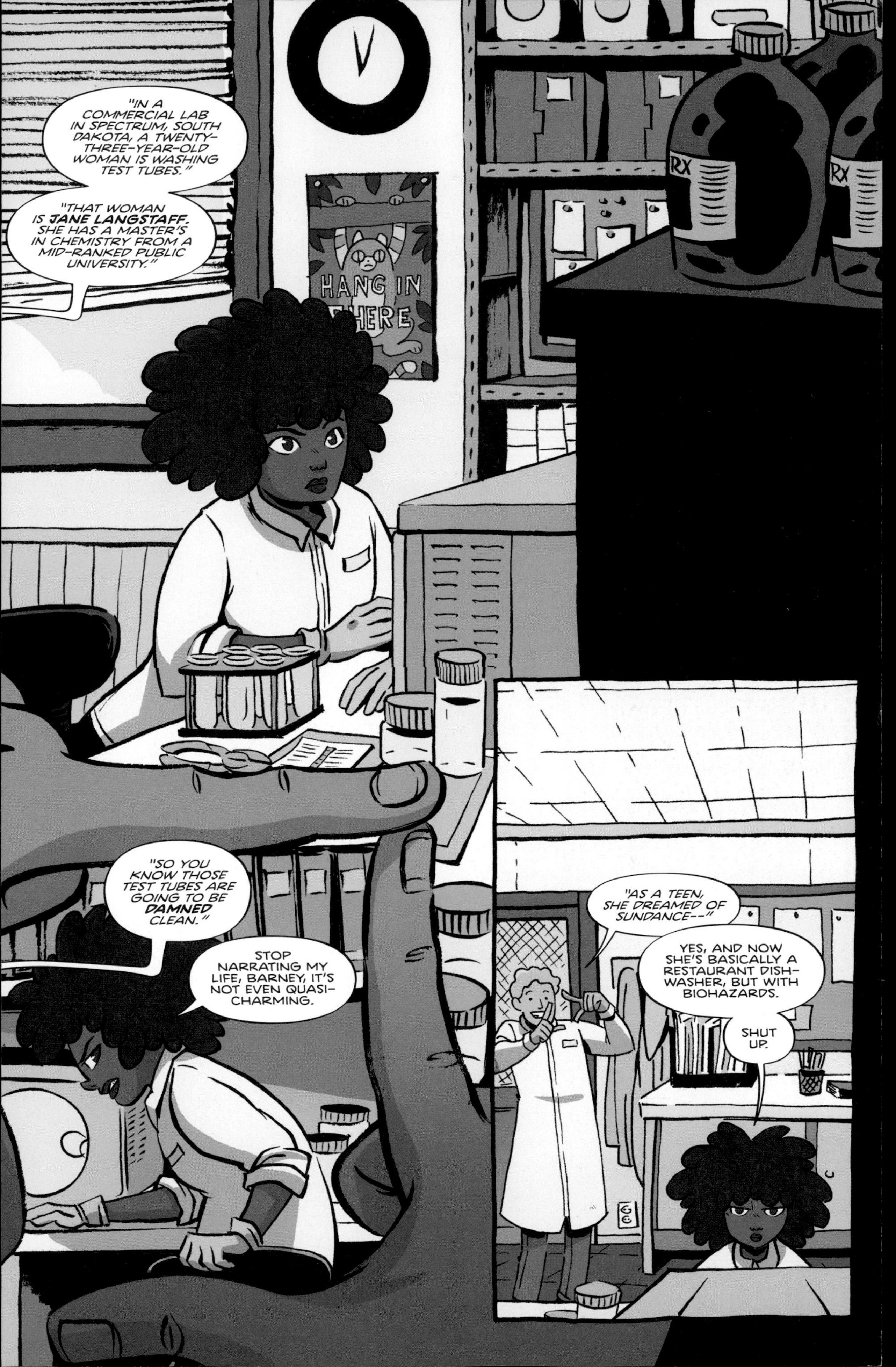
"IN A COMMERCIAL LAB IN SPECTRUM, SOUTH DAKOTA, A TWENTY-THREE-YEAR-OLD WOMAN IS WASHING TEST TUBES."
"THAT WOMAN IS JANE LANGSTAFF. SHE HAS A MASTER'S IN CHEMISTRY FROM A MID-RANKED PUBLIC UNIVERSITY."
HANG IN THERE
"SO YOU KNOW THOSE TEST TUBES ARE GOING TO BE DAMNED CLEAN."
STOP NARRATING MY LIFE, BARNEY, IT'S NOT EVEN QUASI-CHARMING.
"AS A TEEN, SHE DREAMED OF SUNDANCE--"
YES, AND NOW SHE'S BASICALLY A RESTAURANT DISH-WASHER, BUT WITH BIOHAZARDS.
SHUT UP.
RX
RX

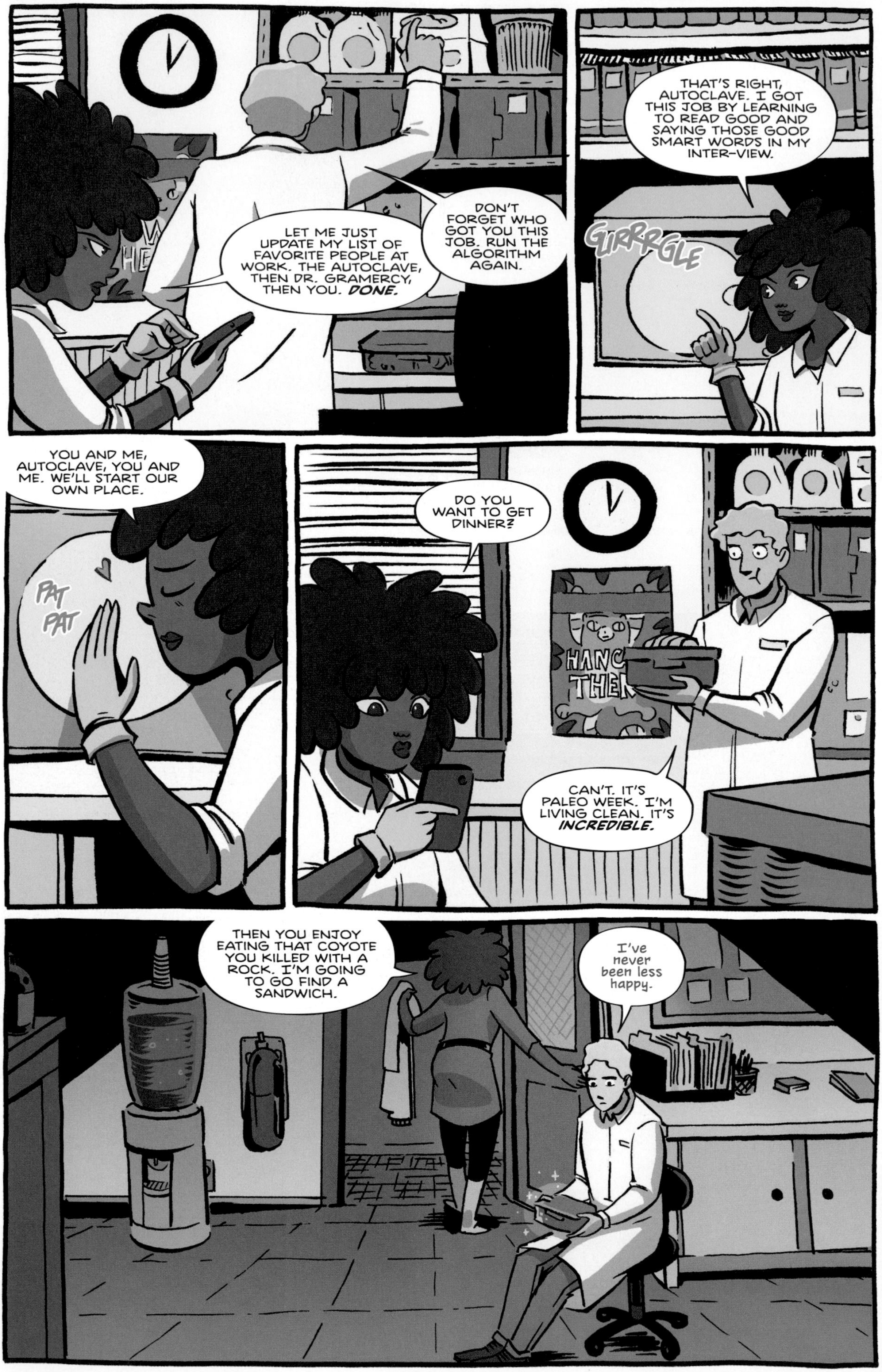
LET ME JUST UPDATE MY LIST OF FAVORITE PEOPLE AT WORK. THE AUTOCLAVE, THEN DR. GRAMERCY, THEN YOU. DONE.
DON'T FORGET WHO GOT YOU THIS JOB. RUN THE ALGORITHM AGAIN.
THAT'S RIGHT, AUTOCLAVE. I GOT THIS JOB BY LEARNING TO READ GOOD AND SAYING THOSE GOOD SMART WORDS IN MY INTER-VIEW.
GURRRGLE
YOU AND ME, AUTOCLAVE, YOU AND ME. WE'LL START OUR OWN PLACE.
PAT PAT
DO YOU WANT TO GET DINNER?
CAN'T. IT'S PALEO WEEK. I'M LIVING CLEAN. IT'S INCREDIBLE.
THEN YOU ENJOY EATING THAT COYOTE YOU KILLED WITH A ROCK. I'M GOING TO GO FIND A SANDWICH.
I've never been less happy.

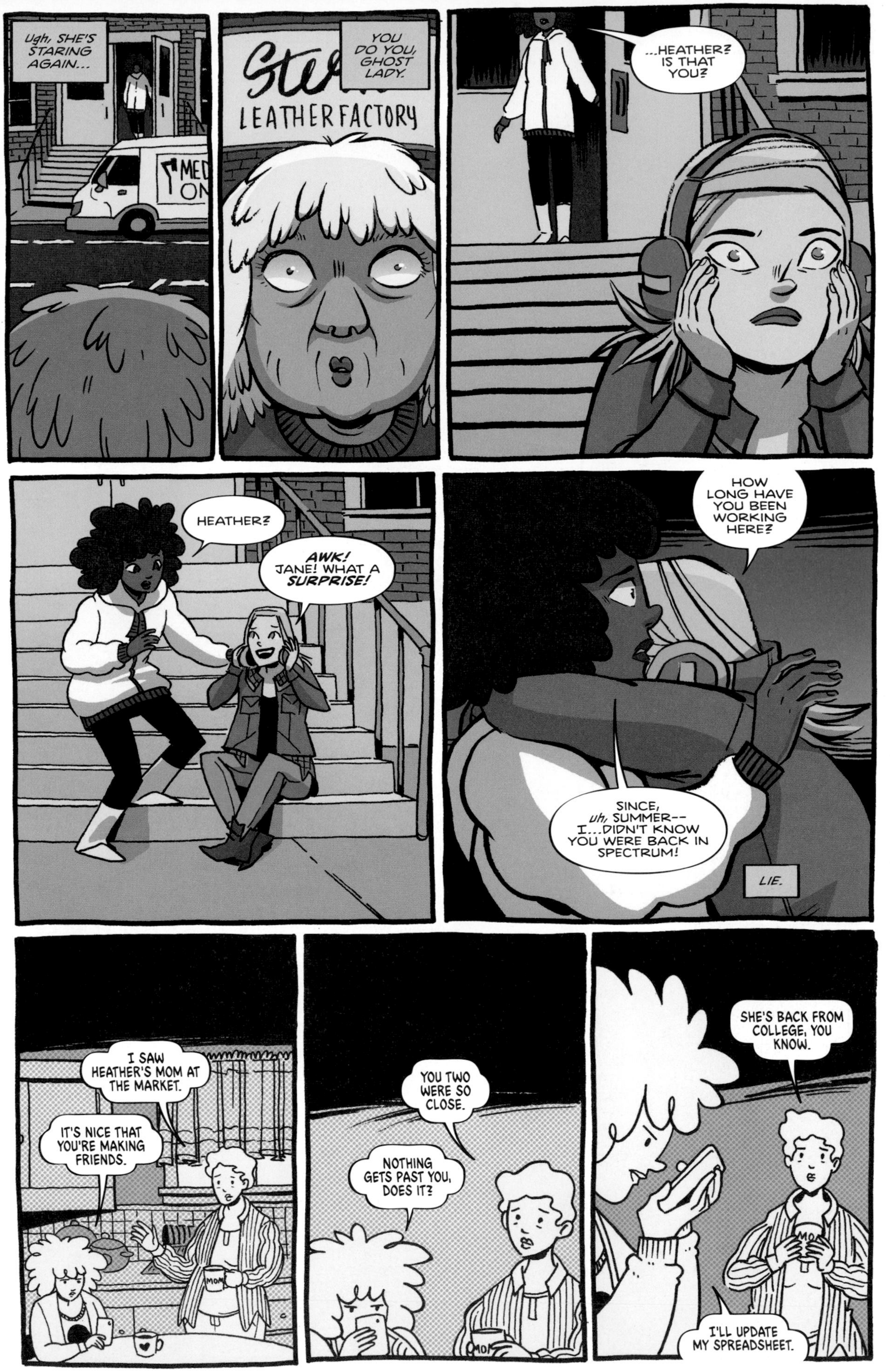
Ugh, SHE'S STARING AGAIN...
MED ON
YOU DO YOU, GHOST LADY.
LEATHER FACTORY
...HEATHER? IS THAT YOU?
HEATHER?
AWK! JANE! WHAT A SURPRISE!
HOW LONG HAVE YOU BEEN WORKING HERE?
SINCE, uh, SUMMER-- I...DIDN'T KNOW YOU WERE BACK IN SPECTRUM!
LIE.
I SAW HEATHER'S MOM AT THE MARKET.
IT'S NICE THAT YOU'RE MAKING FRIENDS.
YOU TWO WERE SO CLOSE.
NOTHING GETS PAST YOU, DOES IT?
SHE'S BACK FROM COLLEGE, YOU KNOW.
I'LL UPDATE MY SPREADSHEET.

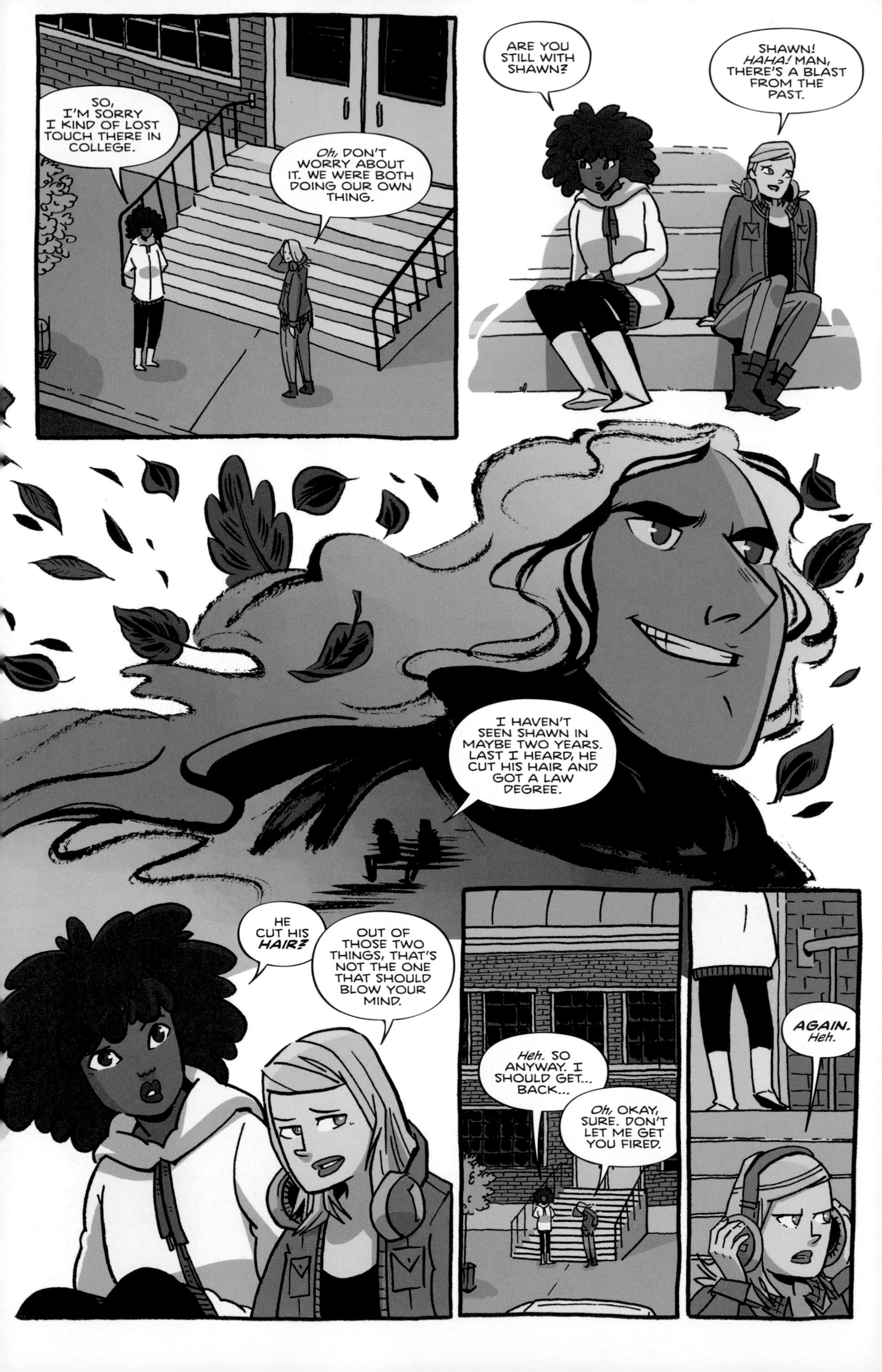
SO, I'M SORRY I KIND OF LOST TOUCH THERE IN COLLEGE.
Oh, DON'T WORRY ABOUT IT. WE WERE BOTH DOING OUR OWN THING.
ARE YOU STILL WITH SHAWN?
SHAWN! *HAHA!* MAN, THERE'S A BLAST FROM THE PAST.
I HAVEN'T SEEN SHAWN IN MAYBE TWO YEARS. LAST I HEARD, HE CUT HIS HAIR AND GOT A LAW DEGREE.
HE CUT HIS ***HAIR?***
OUT OF THOSE TWO THINGS, THAT'S NOT THE ONE THAT SHOULD BLOW YOUR MIND.
Heh. SO ANYWAY. I SHOULD GET... BACK...
Oh, OKAY, SURE. DON'T LET ME GET YOU FIRED.
AGAIN. *Heh.*

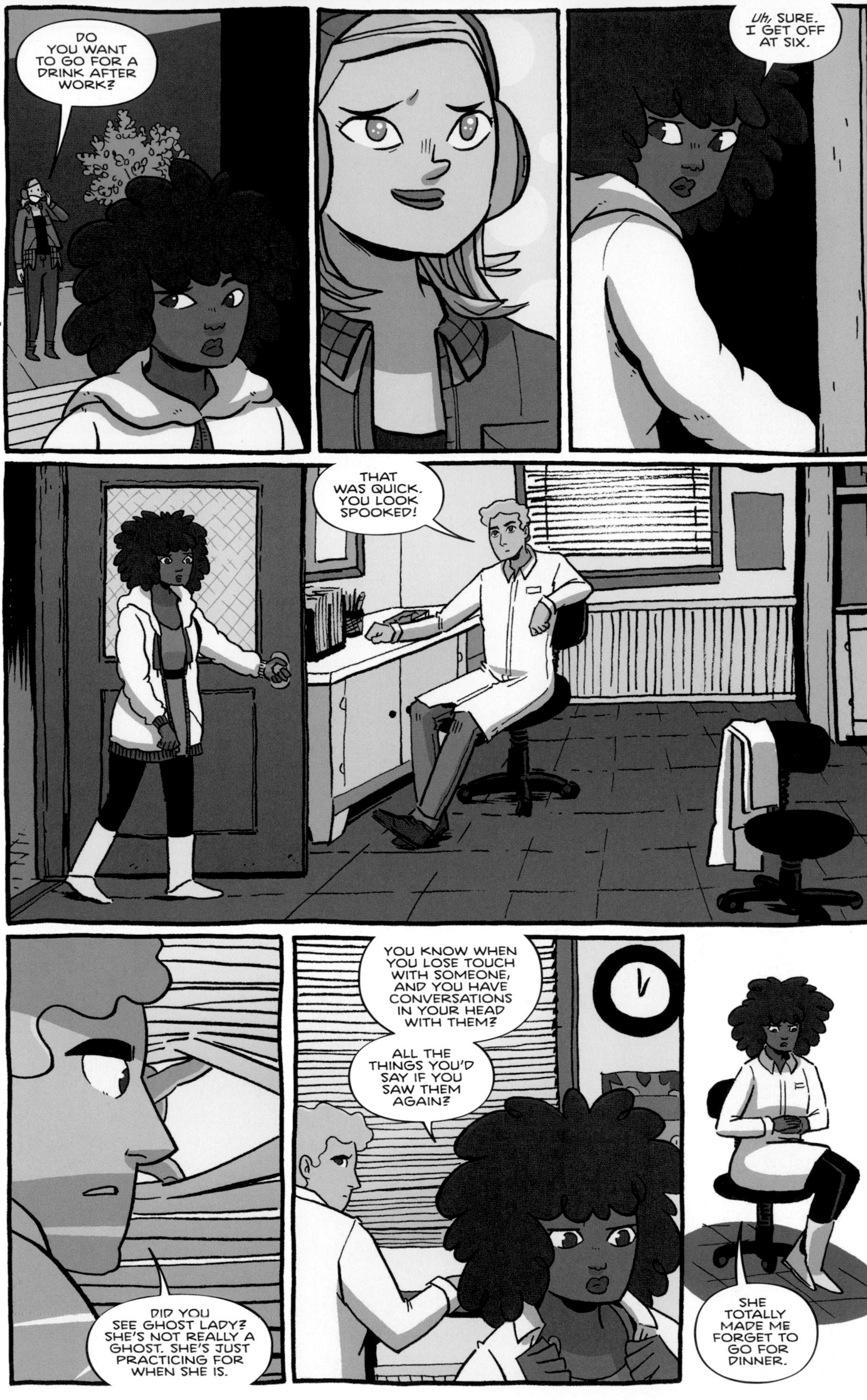
DO YOU WANT TO GO FOR A DRINK AFTER WORK?
Uh, SURE. I GET OFF AT SIX.
THAT WAS QUICK. YOU LOOK SPOOKED!
DID YOU SEE GHOST LADY? SHE'S NOT REALLY A GHOST. SHE'S JUST PRACTICING FOR WHEN SHE IS.
YOU KNOW WHEN YOU LOSE TOUCH WITH SOMEONE, AND YOU HAVE CONVERSATIONS IN YOUR HEAD WITH THEM?
ALL THE THINGS YOU'D SAY IF YOU SAW THEM AGAIN?
SHE TOTALLY MADE ME FORGET TO GO FOR DINNER.

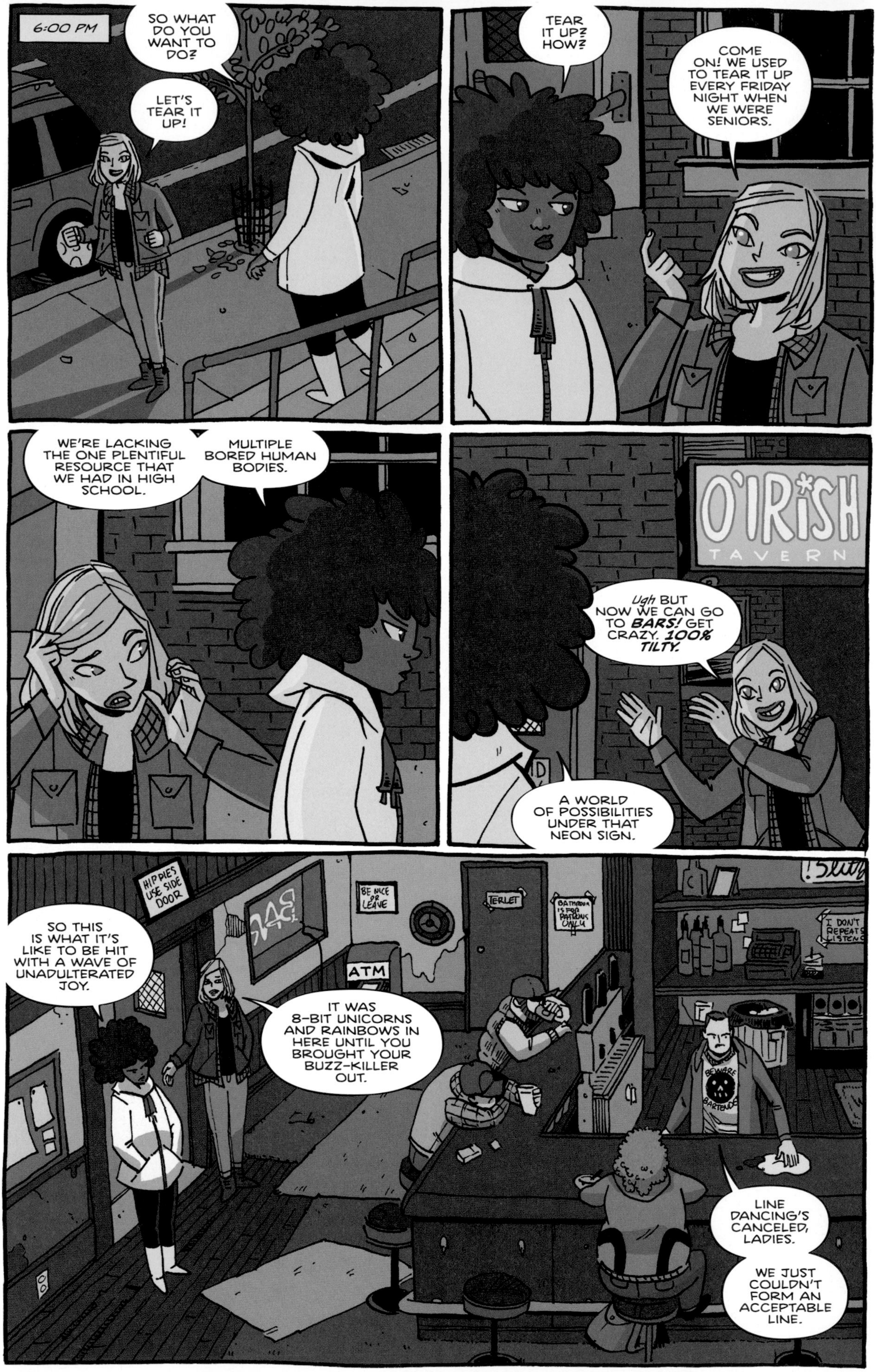
6:00 PM
SO WHAT DO YOU WANT TO DO?
LET'S TEAR IT UP!
TEAR IT UP? HOW?
COME ON! WE USED TO TEAR IT UP EVERY FRIDAY NIGHT WHEN WE WERE SENIORS.
WE'RE LACKING THE ONE PLENTIFUL RESOURCE THAT WE HAD IN HIGH SCHOOL.
MULTIPLE BORED HUMAN BODIES.
O'IRISH TAVERN
Ugh BUT NOW WE CAN GO TO ***BARS!*** GET CRAZY. ***100% TILTY.***
A WORLD OF POSSIBILITIES UNDER THAT NEON SIGN.
HIPPIES USE SIDE DOOR
BE NICE OR LEAVE
TERLET
ATM
SO THIS IS WHAT IT'S LIKE TO BE HIT WITH A WAVE OF UNADULTERATED JOY.
IT WAS 8-BIT UNICORNS AND RAINBOWS IN HERE UNTIL YOU BROUGHT YOUR BUZZ-KILLER OUT.
BEWARE BARTENDS
LINE DANCING'S CANCELED, LADIES.
WE JUST COULDN'T FORM AN ACCEPTABLE LINE.

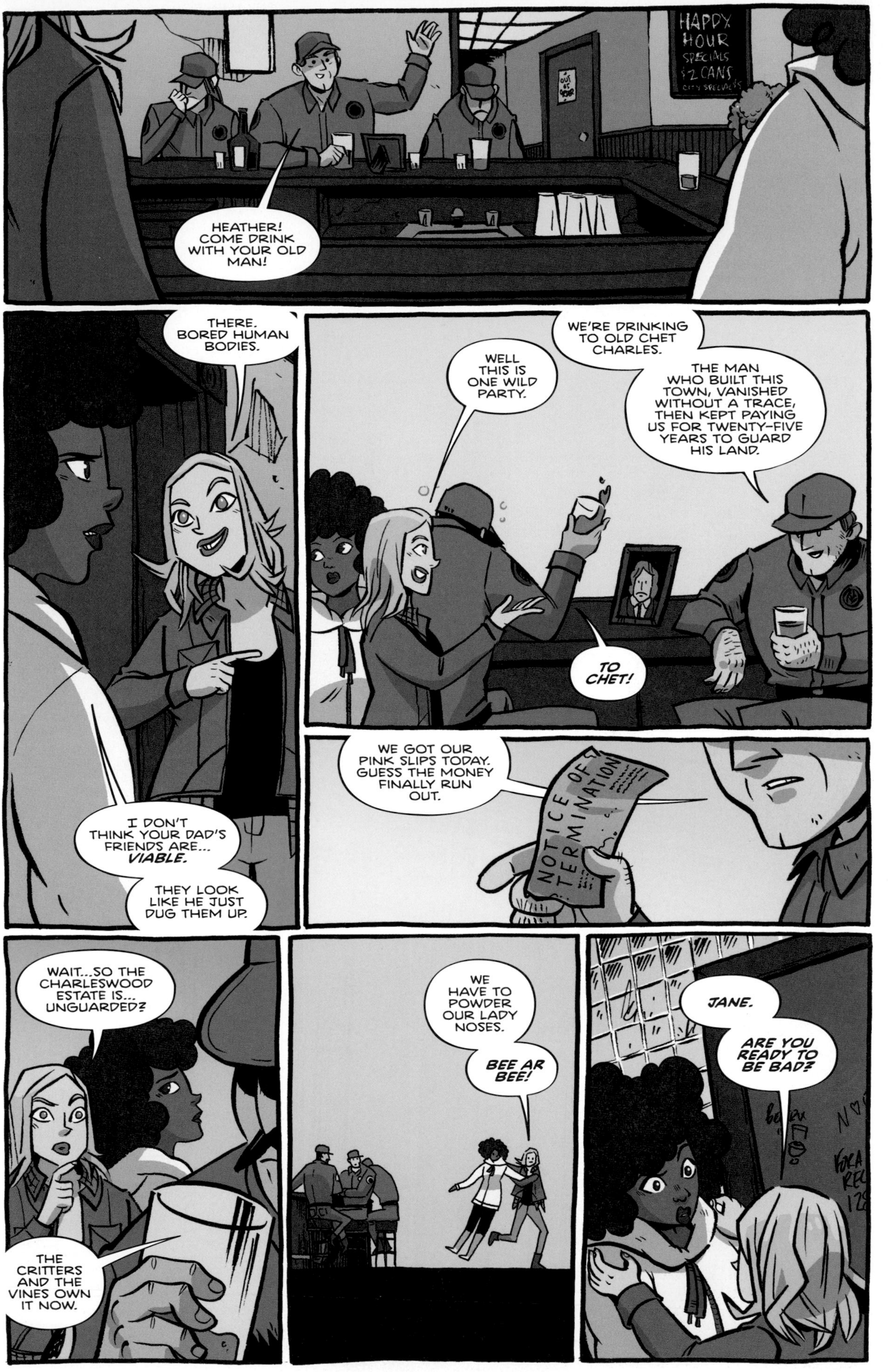
HAPPY HOUR SPECIALS $2 CANS
OUT OF ORDER
HEATHER! COME DRINK WITH YOUR OLD MAN!
THERE. BORED HUMAN BODIES.
I DON'T THINK YOUR DAD'S FRIENDS ARE... *VIABLE.*
THEY LOOK LIKE HE JUST DUG THEM UP.
WELL THIS IS ONE WILD PARTY.
WE'RE DRINKING TO OLD CHET CHARLES.
THE MAN WHO BUILT THIS TOWN, VANISHED WITHOUT A TRACE, THEN KEPT PAYING US FOR TWENTY-FIVE YEARS TO GUARD HIS LAND.
TO CHET!
WE GOT OUR PINK SLIPS TODAY. GUESS THE MONEY FINALLY RUN OUT.
NOTICE OF TERMINATION
WAIT...SO THE CHARLESWOOD ESTATE IS... UNGUARDED?
THE CRITTERS AND THE VINES OWN IT NOW.
WE HAVE TO POWDER OUR LADY NOSES.
BEE AR BEE!
JANE.
ARE YOU READY TO BE BAD?

ONE SECRET DISCUSSION LATER...

DON'T TOUCH THE WALL, DON'T TOUCH THE SEAT.

SO, IT WORKED, THEN, MY PLAN?

SHHHH DAD!

WHAT KINDA PLAN?

HEATHER HERE KNEW WHERE JANE WORKED, BUT THEY HADN'T SPOKEN IN YEARS. SO I SAID, JUST SIT ON THE STEPS AND WAIT. SHE'LL COME OUT EVENTUALLY.

THIS IMPLIES A CERTAIN *DESPERATION.*

HOUR SPECIALS $2 CANS

HELL, IT WASN'T LIKE SHE WAS DOING ANYTHING ELSE WITH HER LIFE RIGHT NOW.

I WISH I COULD PUT *MYSELF* IN THE AUTOCLAVE.

FLISHHHHH

I GOT A LOT OF VERY IMPORTANT THINKING DONE ON THAT STEP.

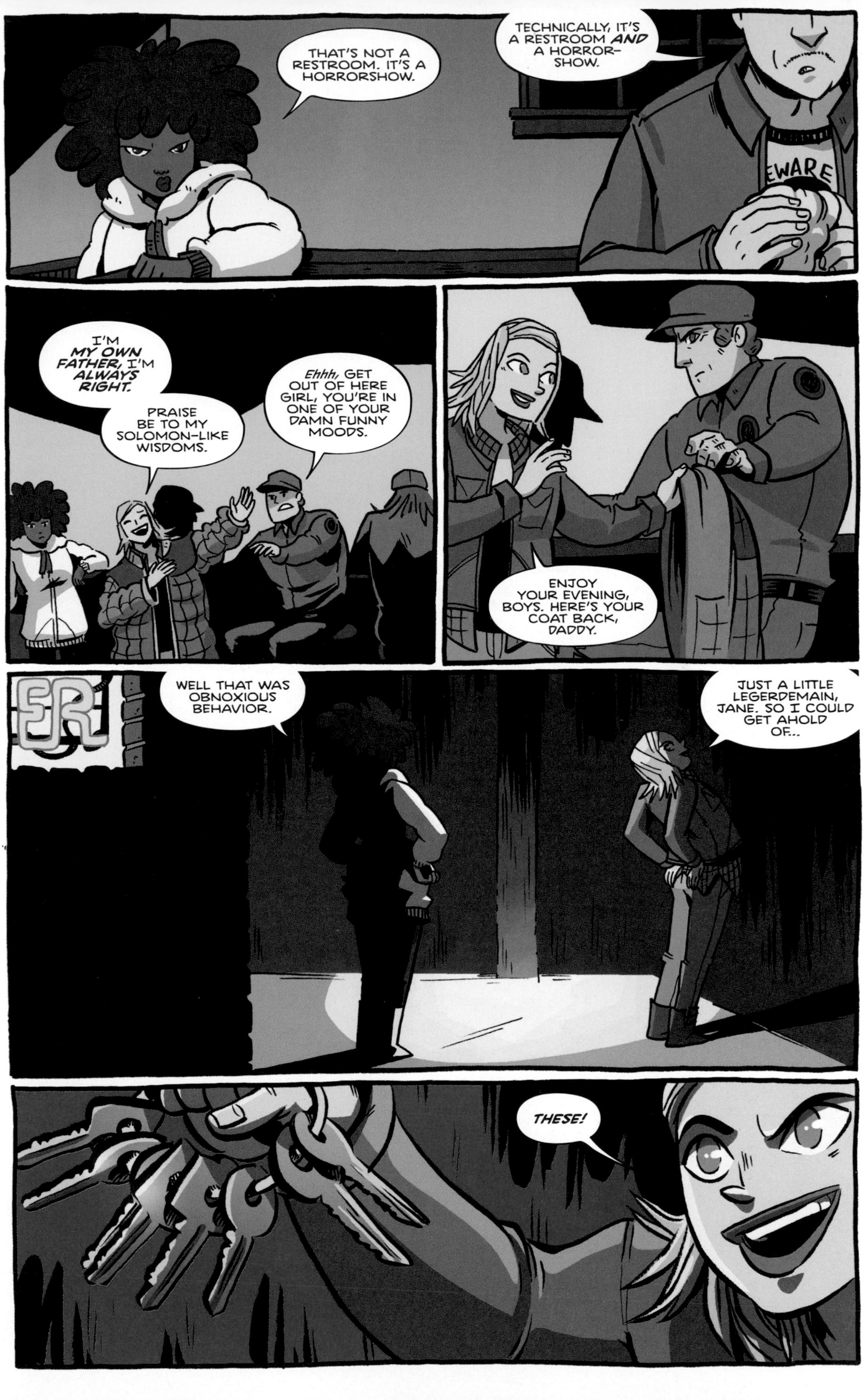
THAT'S NOT A RESTROOM. IT'S A HORRORSHOW.
TECHNICALLY, IT'S A RESTROOM AND A HORROR-SHOW.
EWARE
I'M MY OWN FATHER, I'M ALWAYS RIGHT.
PRAISE BE TO MY SOLOMON-LIKE WISDOMS.
Ehhh, GET OUT OF HERE GIRL, YOU'RE IN ONE OF YOUR DAMN FUNNY MOODS.
ENJOY YOUR EVENING, BOYS. HERE'S YOUR COAT BACK, DADDY.
WELL THAT WAS OBNOXIOUS BEHAVIOR.
JUST A LITTLE LEGERDEMAIN, JANE. SO I COULD GET AHOLD OF...
THESE!

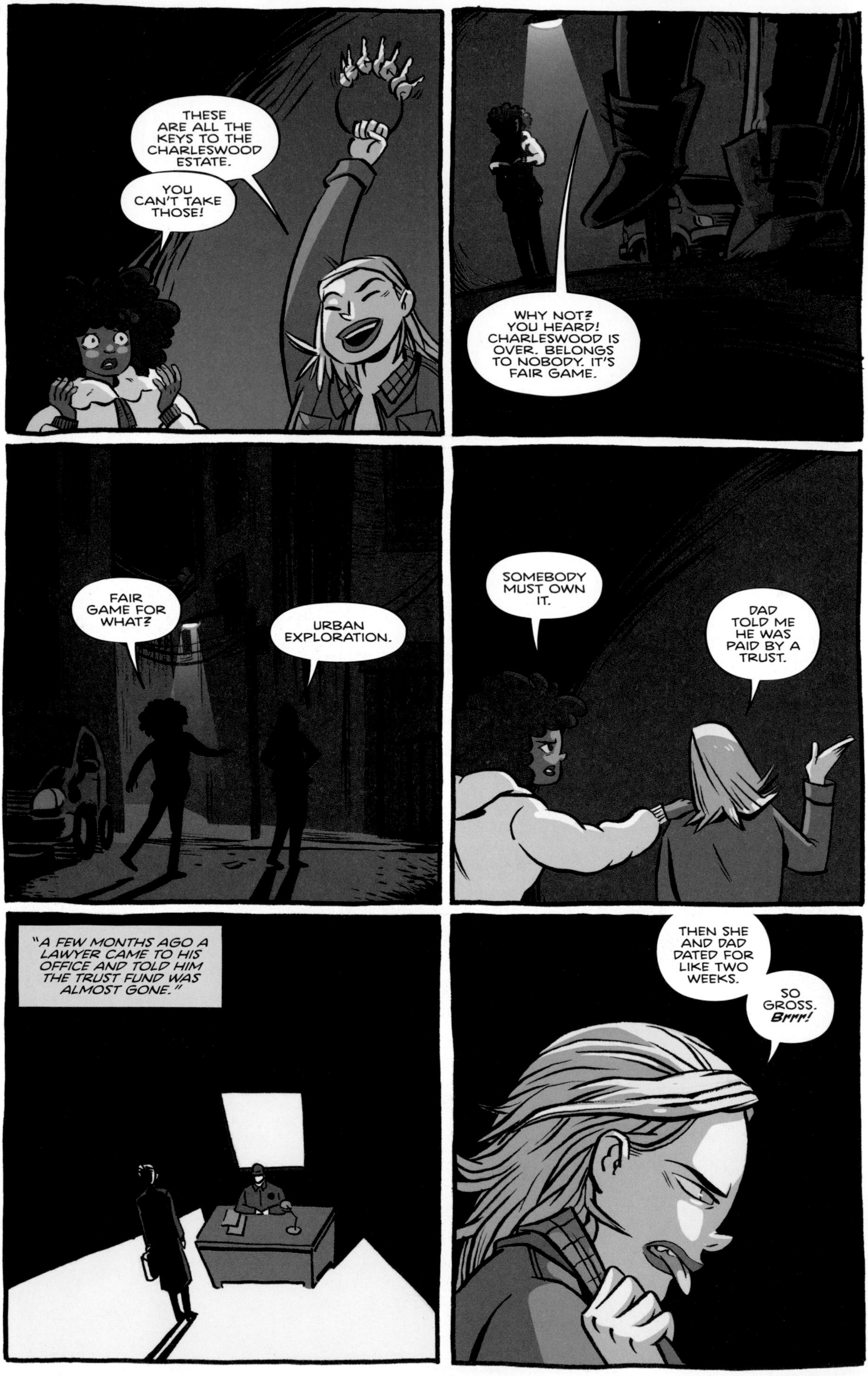

THESE ARE ALL THE KEYS TO THE CHARLESWOOD ESTATE.
YOU CAN'T TAKE THOSE!
WHY NOT? YOU HEARD! CHARLESWOOD IS OVER. BELONGS TO NOBODY. IT'S FAIR GAME.
FAIR GAME FOR WHAT?
URBAN EXPLORATION.
SOMEBODY MUST OWN IT.
DAD TOLD ME HE WAS PAID BY A TRUST.
"A FEW MONTHS AGO A LAWYER CAME TO HIS OFFICE AND TOLD HIM THE TRUST FUND WAS ALMOST GONE."
THEN SHE AND DAD DATED FOR LIKE TWO WEEKS.
SO GROSS. Brrr!

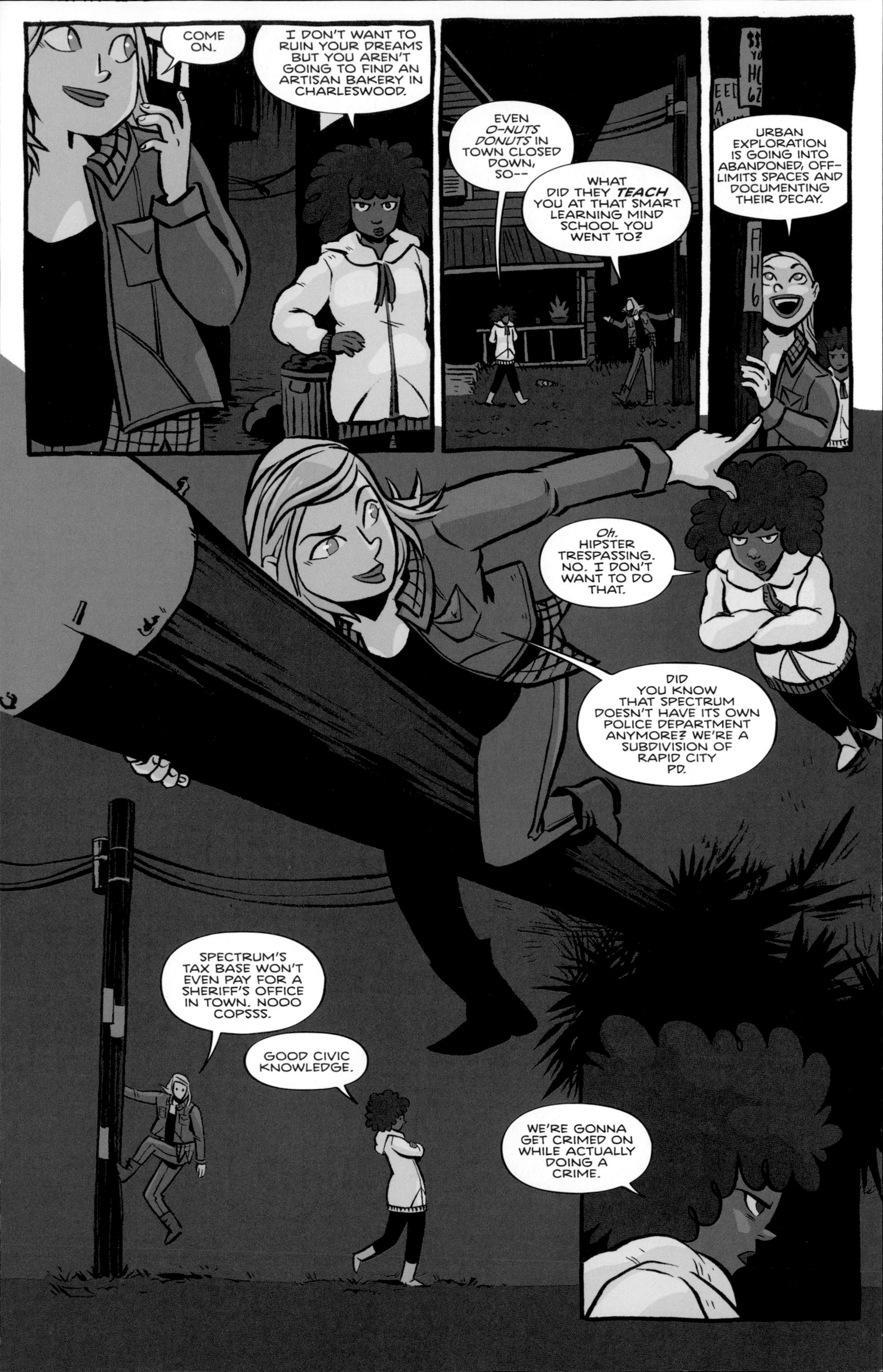
COME ON.
I DON'T WANT TO RUIN YOUR DREAMS BUT YOU AREN'T GOING TO FIND AN ARTISAN BAKERY IN CHARLESWOOD.
EVEN *O-NUTS DONUTS* IN TOWN CLOSED DOWN, SO--
WHAT DID THEY ***TEACH*** YOU AT THAT SMART LEARNING MIND SCHOOL YOU WENT TO?
URBAN EXPLORATION IS GOING INTO ABANDONED, OFF-LIMITS SPACES AND DOCUMENTING THEIR DECAY.
Oh. HIPSTER TRESPASSING. NO. I DON'T WANT TO DO THAT.
DID YOU KNOW THAT SPECTRUM DOESN'T HAVE ITS OWN POLICE DEPARTMENT ANYMORE? WE'RE A SUBDIVISION OF RAPID CITY PD.
SPECTRUM'S TAX BASE WON'T EVEN PAY FOR A SHERIFF'S OFFICE IN TOWN. NOOO COPSSS.
GOOD CIVIC KNOWLEDGE.
WE'RE GONNA GET CRIMED ON WHILE ACTUALLY DOING A CRIME.

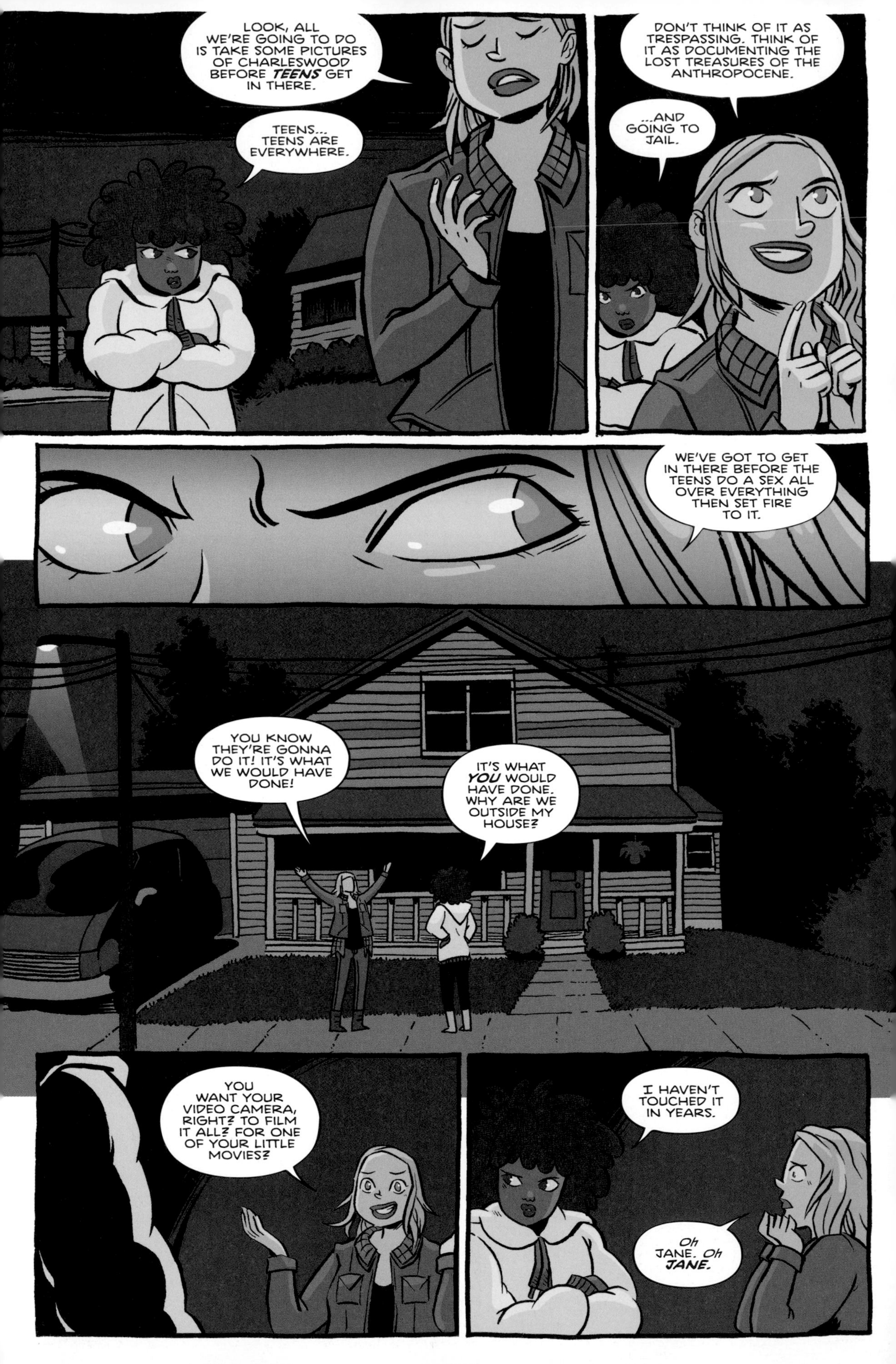
LOOK, ALL WE'RE GOING TO DO IS TAKE SOME PICTURES OF CHARLESWOOD BEFORE *TEENS* GET IN THERE.
TEENS... TEENS ARE EVERYWHERE.
DON'T THINK OF IT AS TRESPASSING. THINK OF IT AS DOCUMENTING THE LOST TREASURES OF THE ANTHROPOCENE.
...AND GOING TO JAIL.
WE'VE GOT TO GET IN THERE BEFORE THE TEENS DO A SEX ALL OVER EVERYTHING THEN SET FIRE TO IT.
YOU KNOW THEY'RE GONNA DO IT! IT'S WHAT WE WOULD HAVE DONE!
IT'S WHAT *YOU* WOULD HAVE DONE. WHY ARE WE OUTSIDE MY HOUSE?
YOU WANT YOUR VIDEO CAMERA, RIGHT? TO FILM IT ALL? FOR ONE OF YOUR LITTLE MOVIES?
I HAVEN'T TOUCHED IT IN YEARS.
Oh JANE. *Oh* ***JANE.***

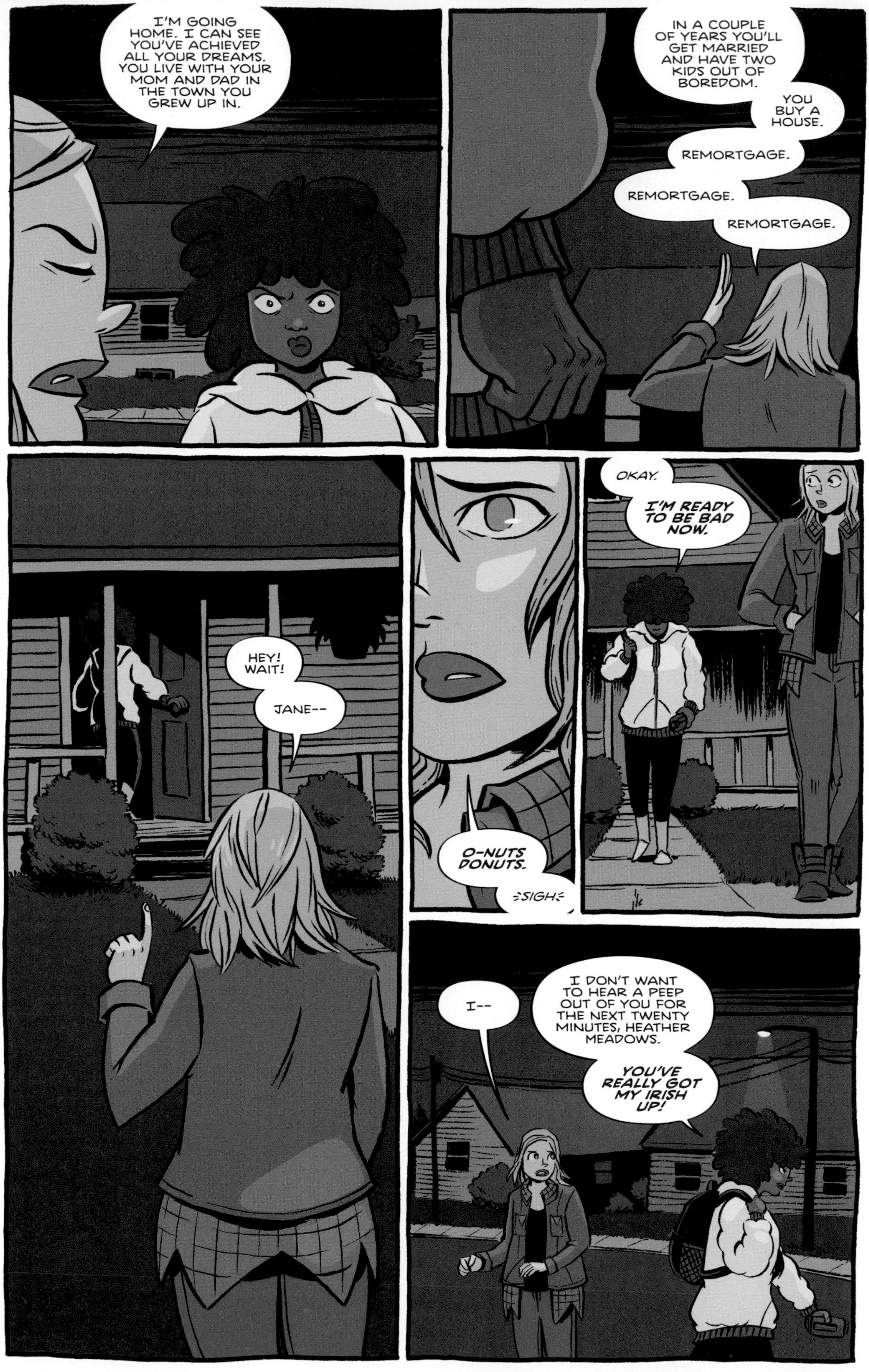
I'M GOING HOME. I CAN SEE YOU'VE ACHIEVED ALL YOUR DREAMS. YOU LIVE WITH YOUR MOM AND DAD IN THE TOWN YOU GREW UP IN.
IN A COUPLE OF YEARS YOU'LL GET MARRIED AND HAVE TWO KIDS OUT OF BOREDOM.
YOU BUY A HOUSE.
REMORTGAGE.
REMORTGAGE.
REMORTGAGE.
HEY! WAIT!
JANE--
O-NUTS DONUTS.
SIGH
OKAY.
I'M READY TO BE BAD NOW.
I--
I DON'T WANT TO HEAR A PEEP OUT OF YOU FOR THE NEXT TWENTY MINUTES, HEATHER MEADOWS.
YOU'VE REALLY GOT MY IRISH UP!

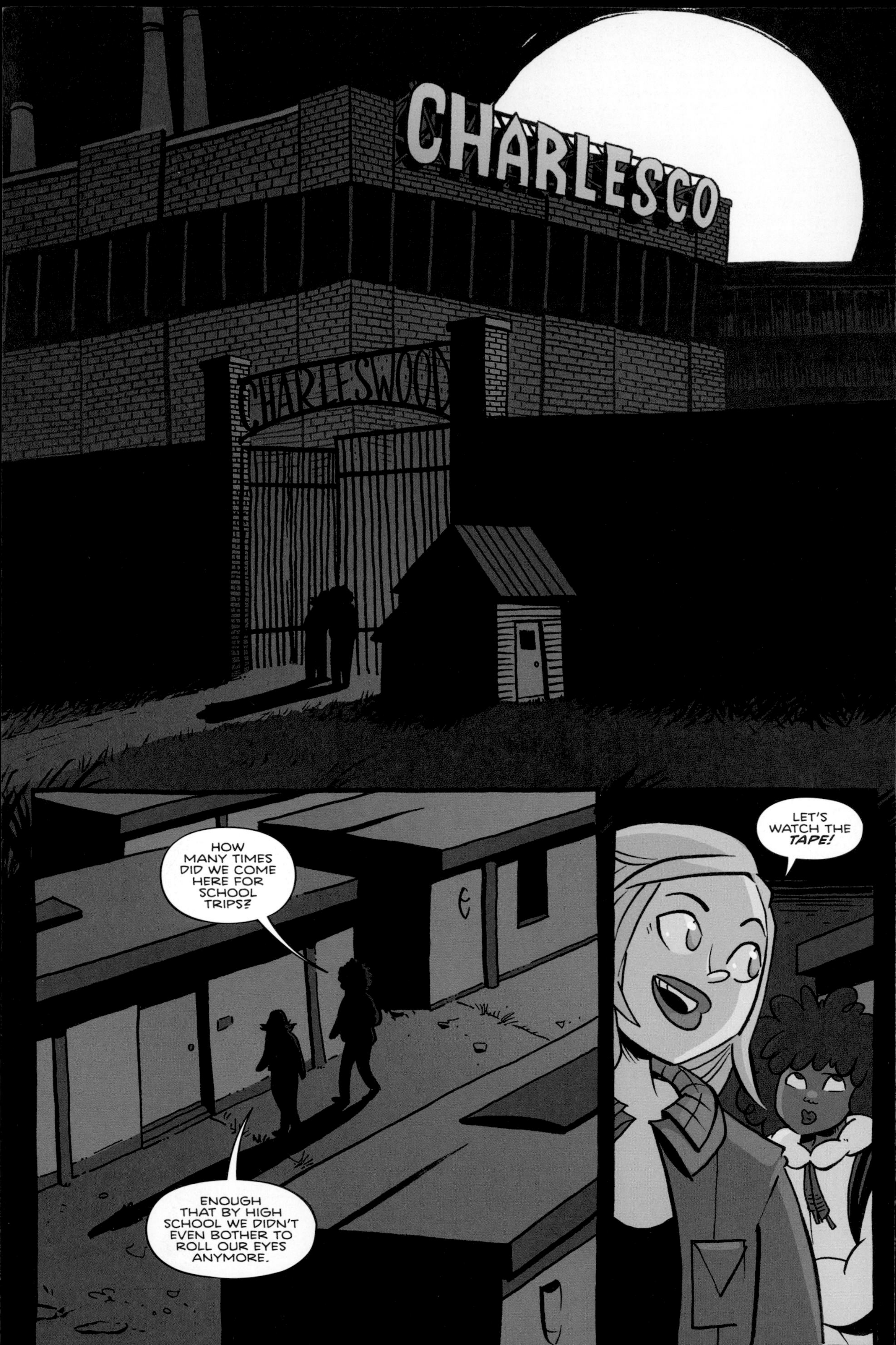
CHARLESCO
CHARLESWOOD
HOW MANY TIMES DID WE COME HERE FOR SCHOOL TRIPS?
ENOUGH THAT BY HIGH SCHOOL WE DIDN'T EVEN BOTHER TO ROLL OUR EYES ANYMORE.
LET'S WATCH THE *TAPE!*

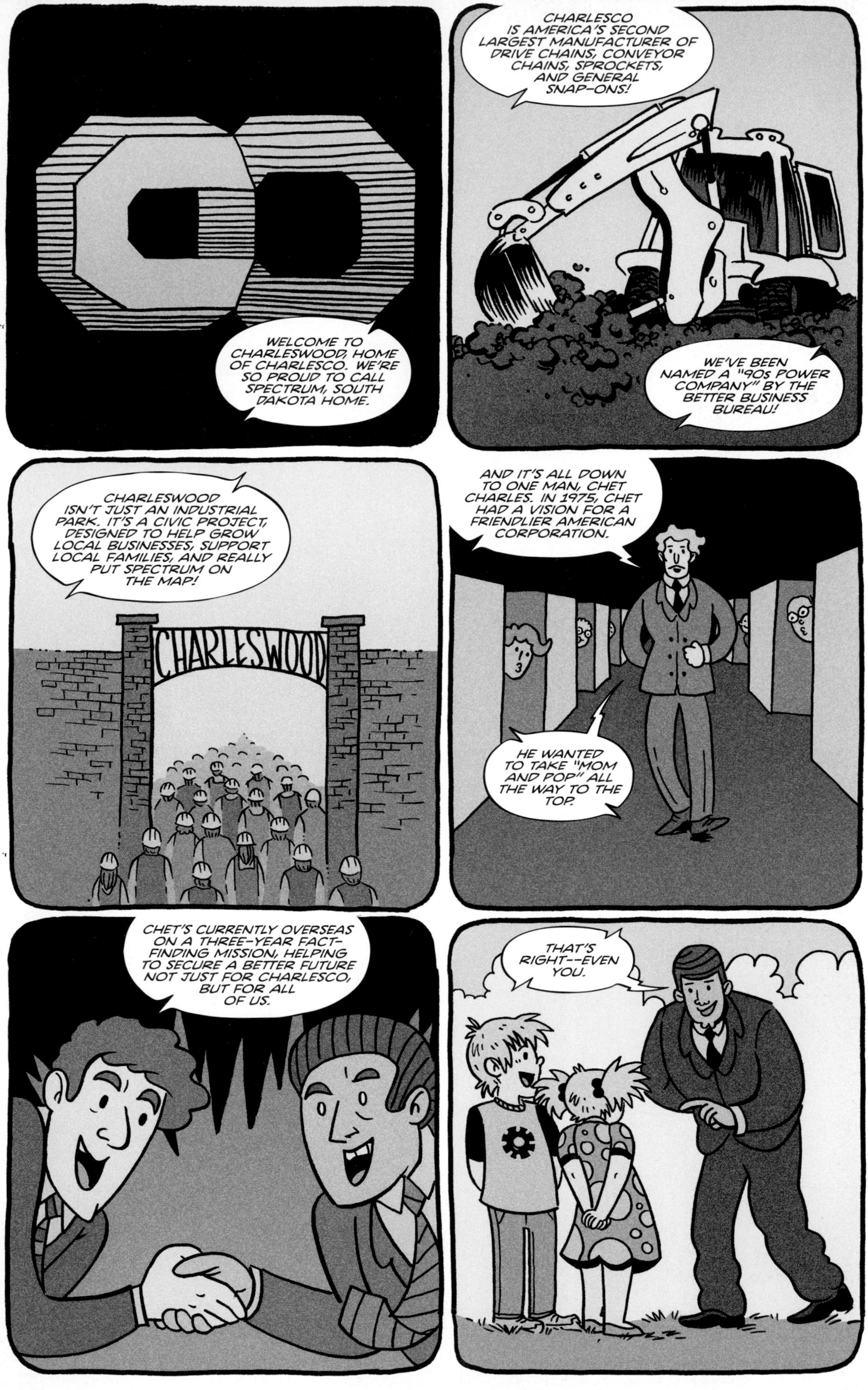
WELCOME TO CHARLESWOOD, HOME OF CHARLESCO. WE'RE SO PROUD TO CALL SPECTRUM, SOUTH DAKOTA HOME.
CHARLESCO IS AMERICA'S SECOND LARGEST MANUFACTURER OF DRIVE CHAINS, CONVEYOR CHAINS, SPROCKETS, AND GENERAL SNAP-ONS!
WE'VE BEEN NAMED A "90s POWER COMPANY" BY THE BETTER BUSINESS BUREAU!
CHARLESWOOD ISN'T JUST AN INDUSTRIAL PARK. IT'S A CIVIC PROJECT, DESIGNED TO HELP GROW LOCAL BUSINESSES, SUPPORT LOCAL FAMILIES, AND REALLY PUT SPECTRUM ON THE MAP!
CHARLESWOOD
AND IT'S ALL DOWN TO ONE MAN, CHET CHARLES. IN 1975, CHET HAD A VISION FOR A FRIENDLIER AMERICAN CORPORATION.
HE WANTED TO TAKE "MOM AND POP" ALL THE WAY TO THE TOP.
CHET'S CURRENTLY OVERSEAS ON A THREE-YEAR FACT-FINDING MISSION, HELPING TO SECURE A BETTER FUTURE NOT JUST FOR CHARLESCO, BUT FOR ALL OF US.
THAT'S RIGHT--EVEN YOU.

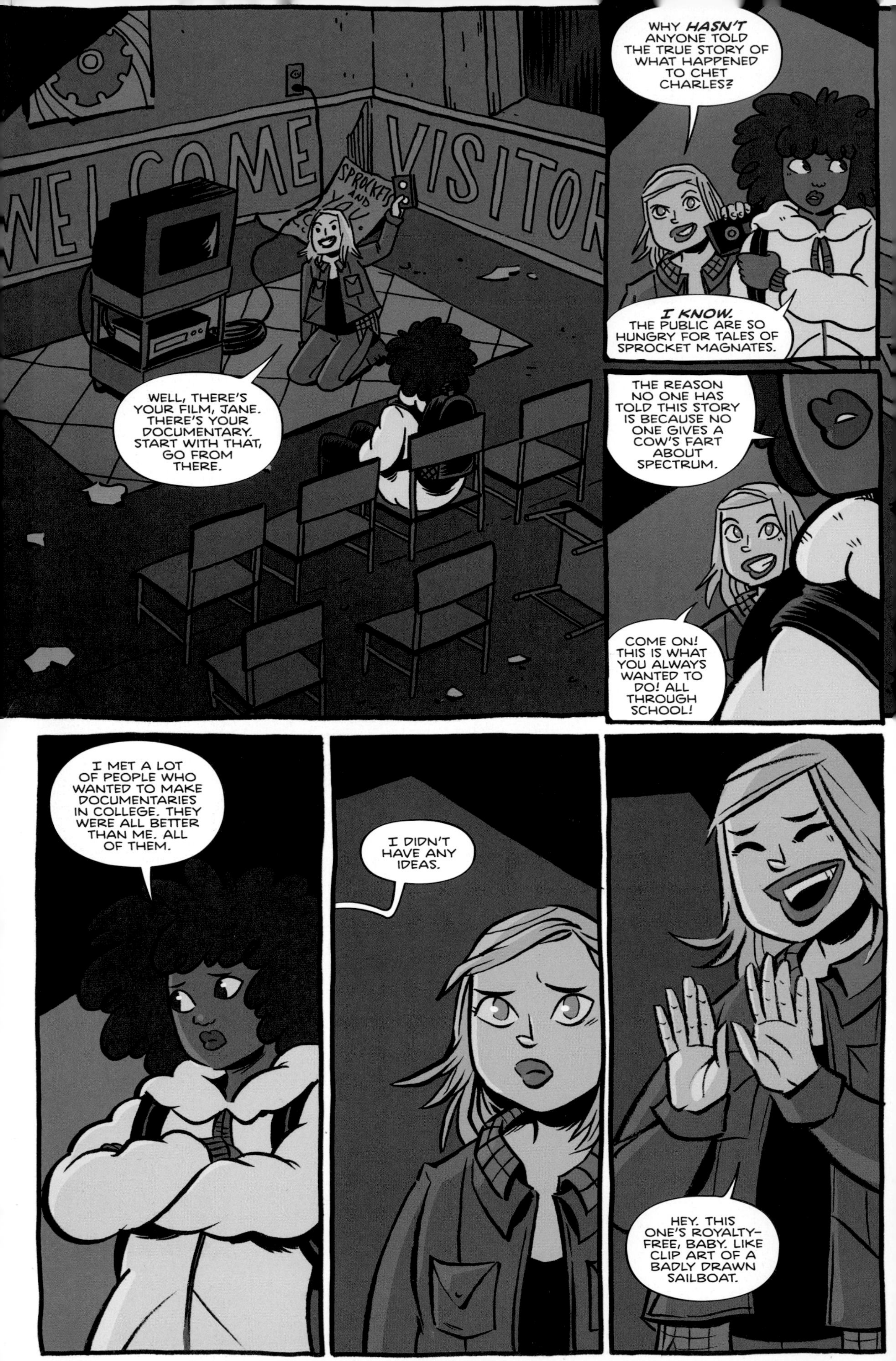
WELCOME VISITOR
SPROCKETS AND
WELL, THERE'S YOUR FILM, JANE. THERE'S YOUR DOCUMENTARY. START WITH THAT, GO FROM THERE.
WHY HASN'T ANYONE TOLD THE TRUE STORY OF WHAT HAPPENED TO CHET CHARLES?
I KNOW. THE PUBLIC ARE SO HUNGRY FOR TALES OF SPROCKET MAGNATES.
THE REASON NO ONE HAS TOLD THIS STORY IS BECAUSE NO ONE GIVES A COW'S FART ABOUT SPECTRUM.
COME ON! THIS IS WHAT YOU ALWAYS WANTED TO DO! ALL THROUGH SCHOOL!
I MET A LOT OF PEOPLE WHO WANTED TO MAKE DOCUMENTARIES IN COLLEGE. THEY WERE ALL BETTER THAN ME. ALL OF THEM.
I DIDN'T HAVE ANY IDEAS.
HEY. THIS ONE'S ROYALTY-FREE, BABY. LIKE CLIP ART OF A BADLY DRAWN SAILBOAT.

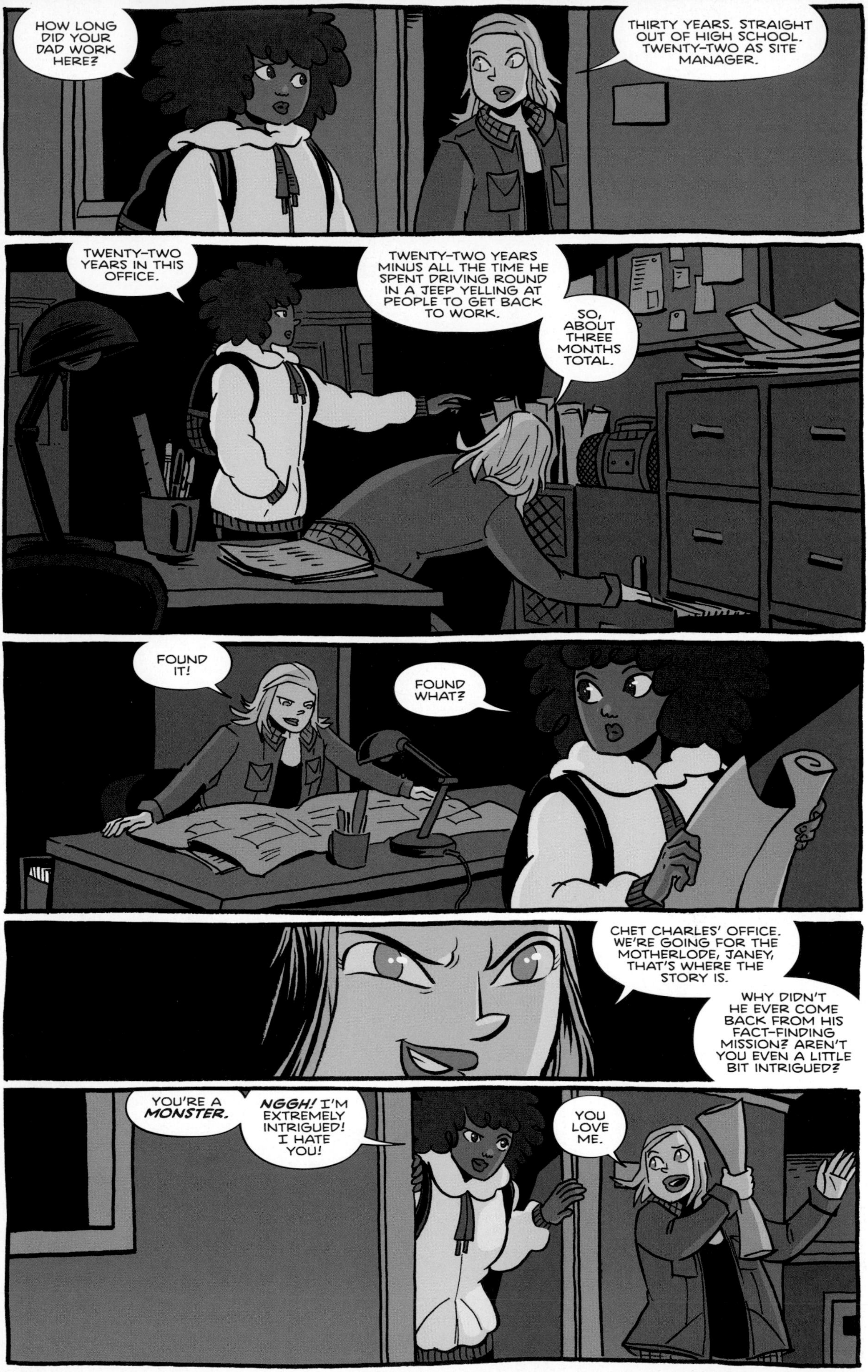
HOW LONG DID YOUR DAD WORK HERE?
THIRTY YEARS. STRAIGHT OUT OF HIGH SCHOOL. TWENTY-TWO AS SITE MANAGER.
TWENTY-TWO YEARS IN THIS OFFICE.
TWENTY-TWO YEARS MINUS ALL THE TIME HE SPENT DRIVING ROUND IN A JEEP YELLING AT PEOPLE TO GET BACK TO WORK.
SO, ABOUT THREE MONTHS TOTAL.
FOUND IT!
FOUND WHAT?
CHET CHARLES' OFFICE. WE'RE GOING FOR THE MOTHERLODE, JANEY, THAT'S WHERE THE STORY IS.
WHY DIDN'T HE EVER COME BACK FROM HIS FACT-FINDING MISSION? AREN'T YOU EVEN A LITTLE BIT INTRIGUED?
YOU'RE A ***MONSTER.***
NGGH! I'M EXTREMELY INTRIGUED! I HATE YOU!
YOU LOVE ME.

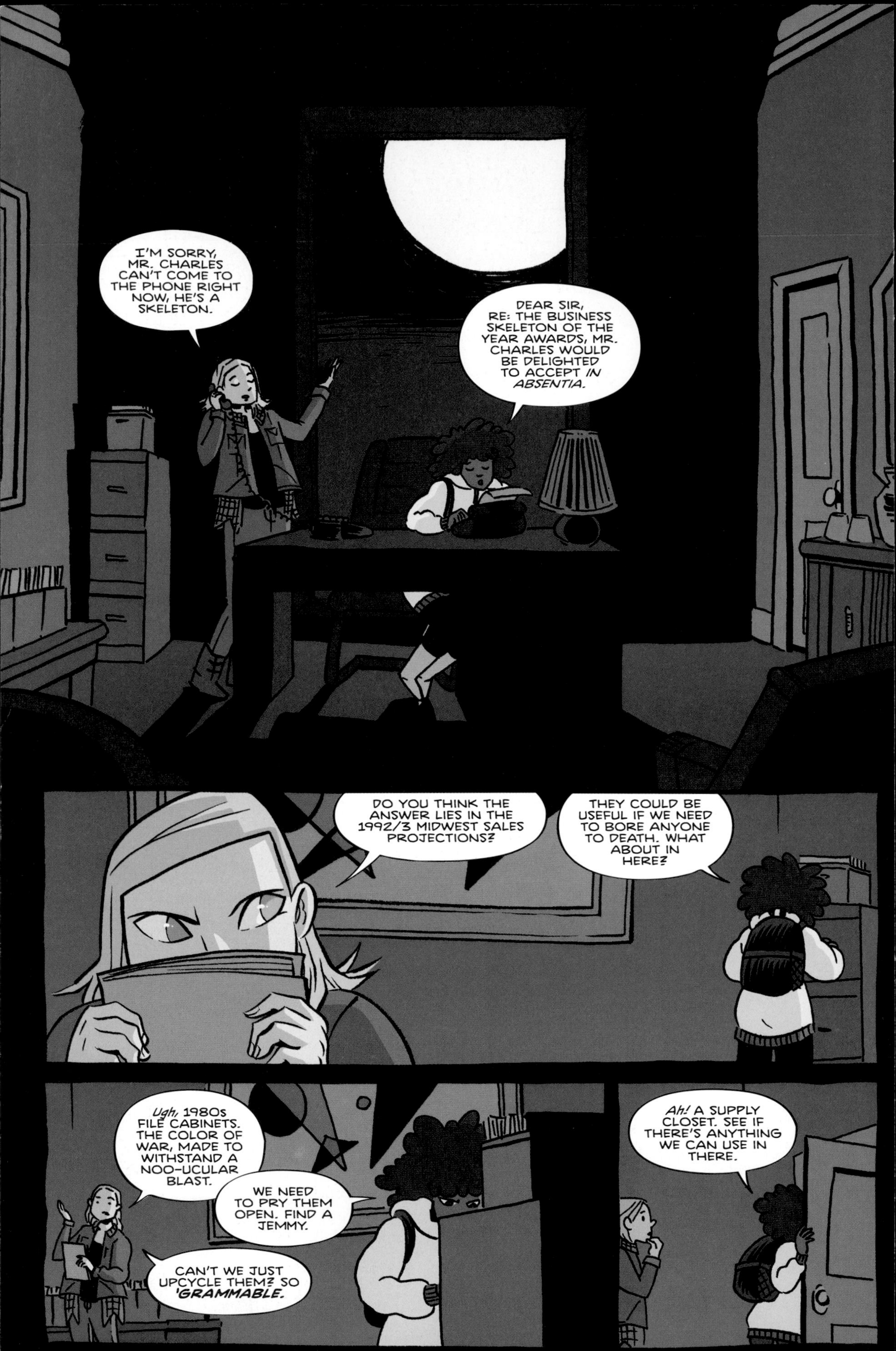
I'M SORRY, MR. CHARLES CAN'T COME TO THE PHONE RIGHT NOW, HE'S A SKELETON.
DEAR SIR, RE: THE BUSINESS SKELETON OF THE YEAR AWARDS, MR. CHARLES WOULD BE DELIGHTED TO ACCEPT *IN ABSENTIA.*
DO YOU THINK THE ANSWER LIES IN THE 1992/3 MIDWEST SALES PROJECTIONS?
THEY COULD BE USEFUL IF WE NEED TO BORE ANYONE TO DEATH. WHAT ABOUT IN HERE?
Ugh, 1980s FILE CABINETS. THE COLOR OF WAR, MADE TO WITHSTAND A NOO-UCULAR BLAST.
WE NEED TO PRY THEM OPEN. FIND A JEMMY.
CAN'T WE JUST UPCYCLE THEM? SO *'GRAMMABLE.*
Ah! A SUPPLY CLOSET. SEE IF THERE'S ANYTHING WE CAN USE IN THERE.

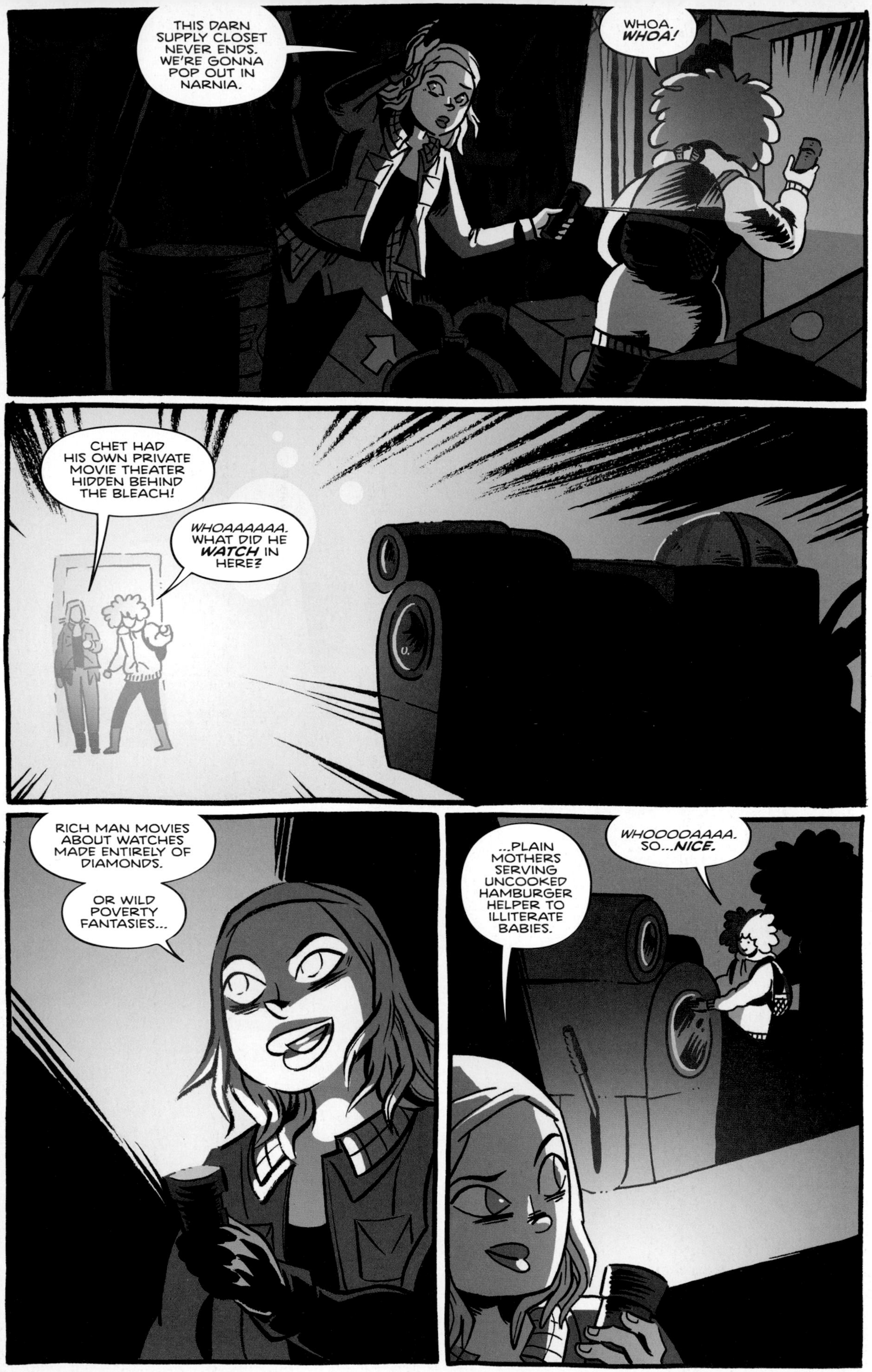
THIS DARN SUPPLY CLOSET NEVER ENDS. WE'RE GONNA POP OUT IN NARNIA.
WHOA. ***WHOA!***
CHET HAD HIS OWN PRIVATE MOVIE THEATER HIDDEN BEHIND THE BLEACH!
WHOAAAAAAA. WHAT DID HE ***WATCH*** IN HERE?
RICH MAN MOVIES ABOUT WATCHES MADE ENTIRELY OF DIAMONDS.
OR WILD POVERTY FANTASIES...
...PLAIN MOTHERS SERVING UNCOOKED HAMBURGER HELPER TO ILLITERATE BABIES.
WHOOOOAAAA. SO...***NICE.***

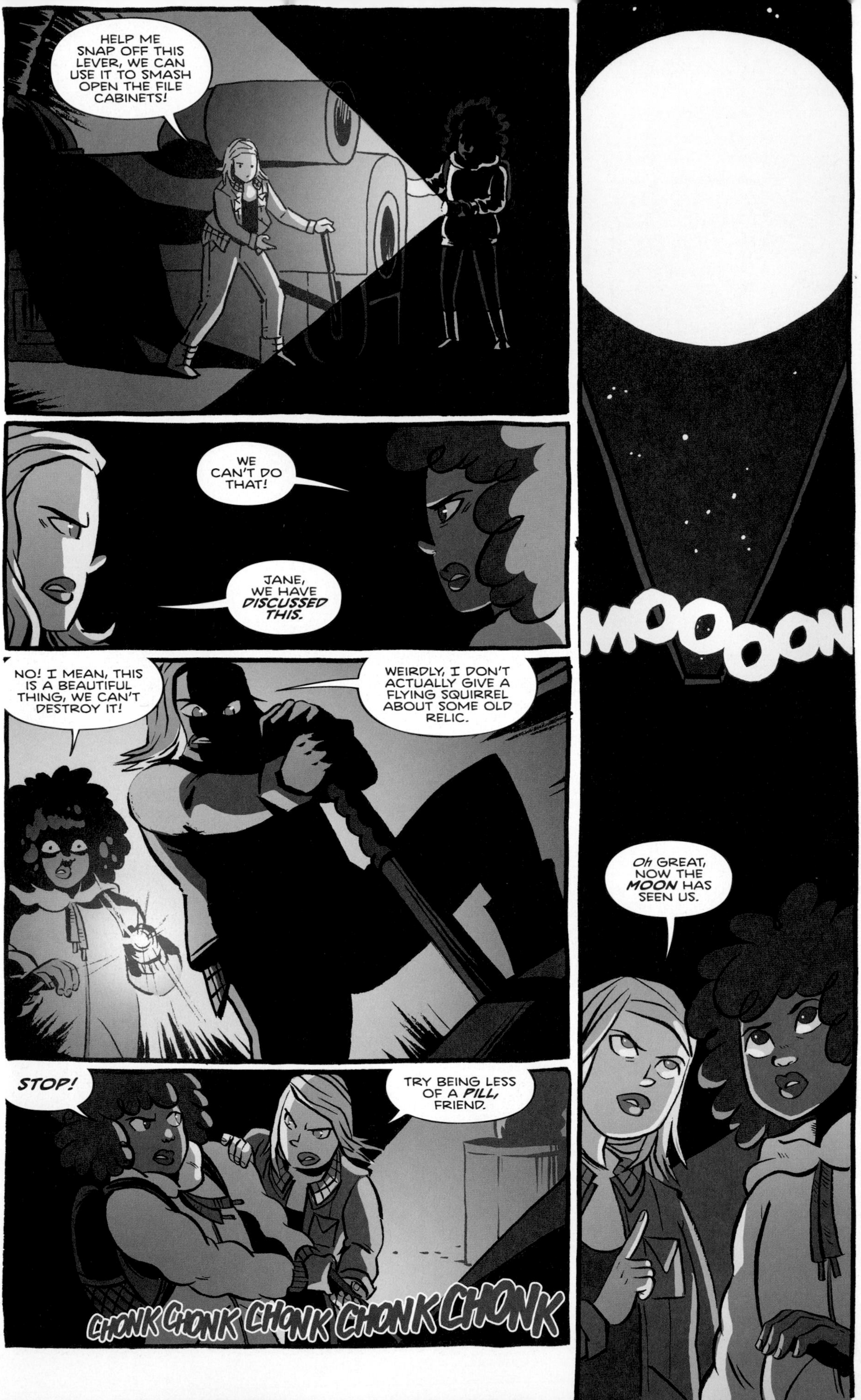
HELP ME SNAP OFF THIS LEVER, WE CAN USE IT TO SMASH OPEN THE FILE CABINETS!
WE CAN'T DO THAT!
JANE, WE HAVE *DISCUSSED* THIS.
NO! I MEAN, THIS IS A BEAUTIFUL THING, WE CAN'T DESTROY IT!
WEIRDLY, I DON'T ACTUALLY GIVE A FLYING SQUIRREL ABOUT SOME OLD RELIC.
STOP!
TRY BEING LESS OF A *PILL,* FRIEND.
CHONK CHONK CHONK CHONK CHONK
MOOOOON
Oh GREAT, NOW THE *MOON* HAS SEEN US.

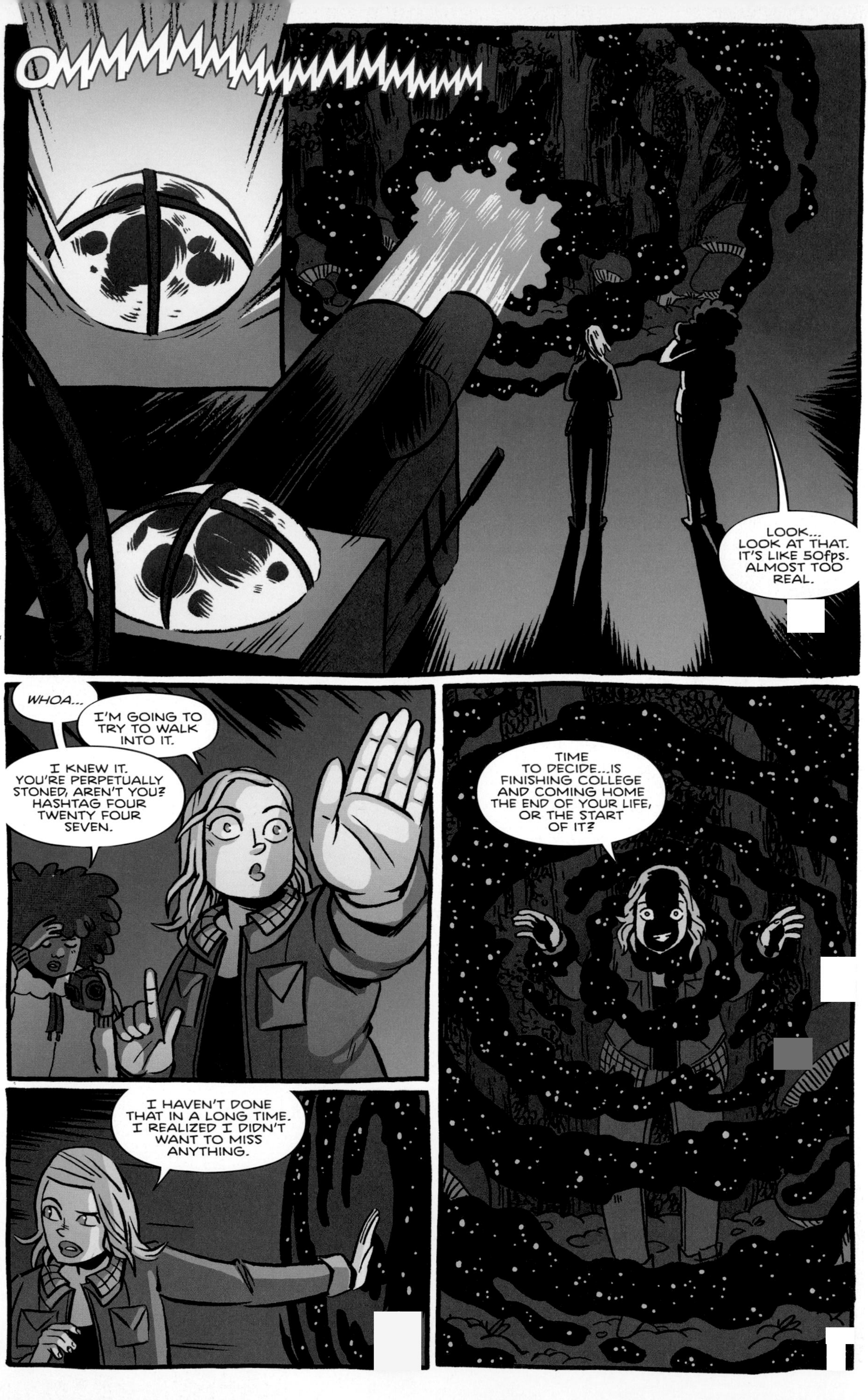
OMMMMMMMMMMMMMM
LOOK... LOOK AT THAT. IT'S LIKE 50fps. ALMOST TOO REAL.
WHOA...
I'M GOING TO TRY TO WALK INTO IT.
I KNEW IT. YOU'RE PERPETUALLY STONED, AREN'T YOU? HASHTAG FOUR TWENTY FOUR SEVEN.
I HAVEN'T DONE THAT IN A LONG TIME. I REALIZED I DIDN'T WANT TO MISS ANYTHING.
TIME TO DECIDE...IS FINISHING COLLEGE AND COMING HOME THE END OF YOUR LIFE, OR THE START OF IT?

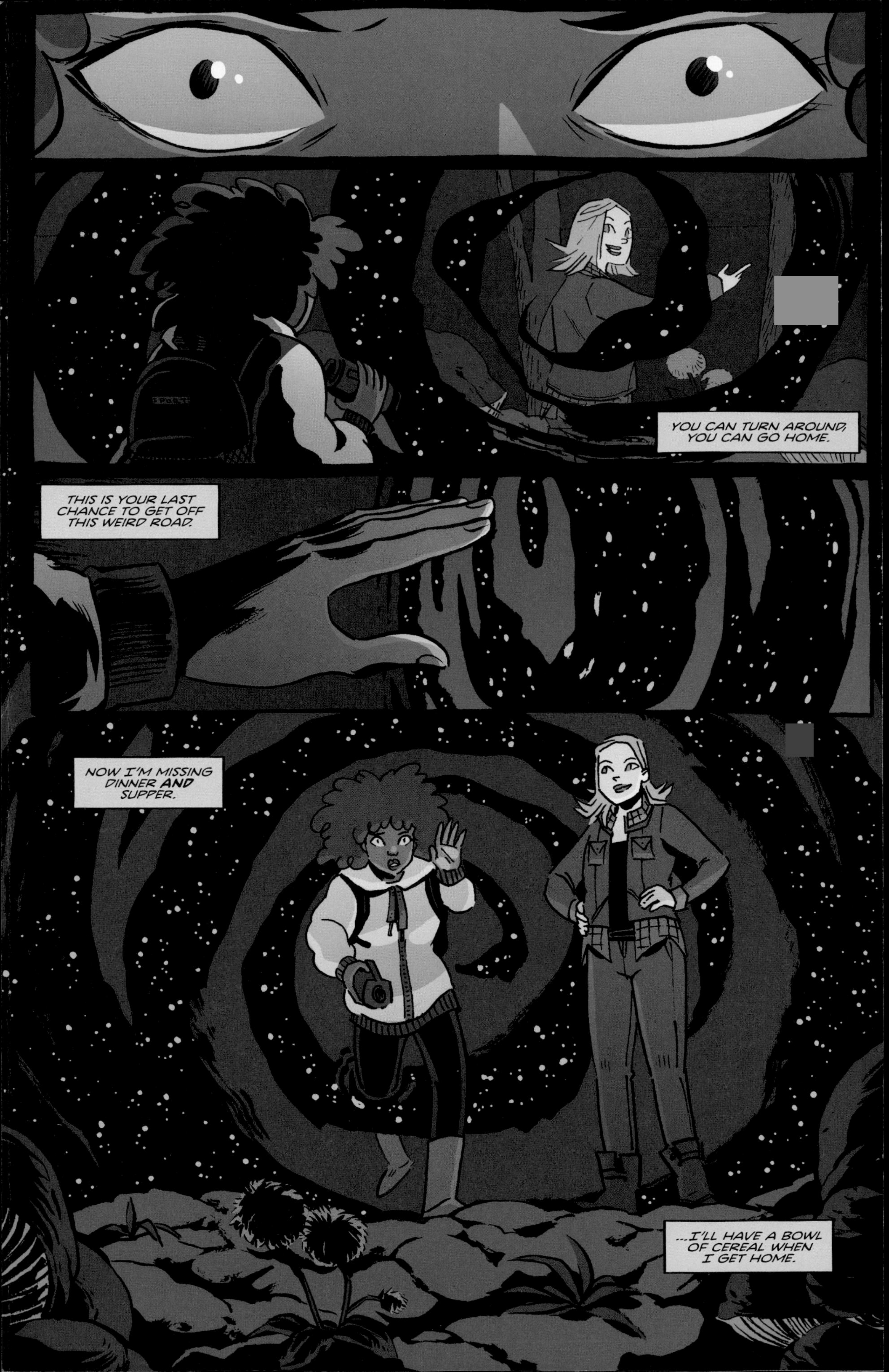
YOU CAN TURN AROUND, YOU CAN GO HOME.
THIS IS YOUR LAST CHANCE TO GET OFF THIS WEIRD ROAD.
NOW I'M MISSING DINNER **AND** SUPPER.
...I'LL HAVE A BOWL OF CEREAL WHEN I GET HOME.

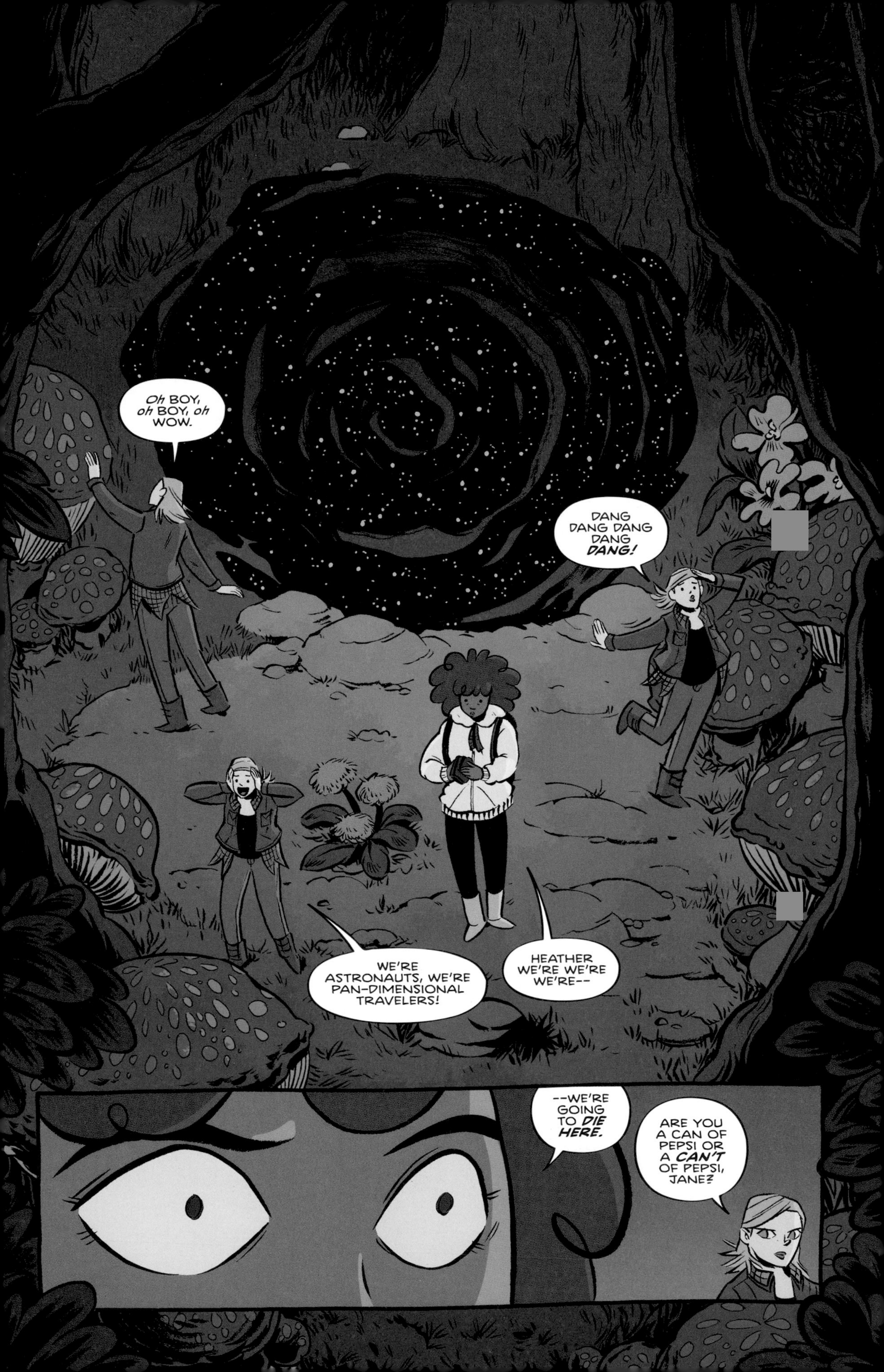
Oh BOY, oh BOY, oh WOW.
DANG DANG DANG DANG DANG!
WE'RE ASTRONAUTS, WE'RE PAN-DIMENSIONAL TRAVELERS!
HEATHER WE'RE WE'RE WE'RE--
--WE'RE GOING TO DIE HERE.
ARE YOU A CAN OF PEPSI OR A CAN'T OF PEPSI, JANE?

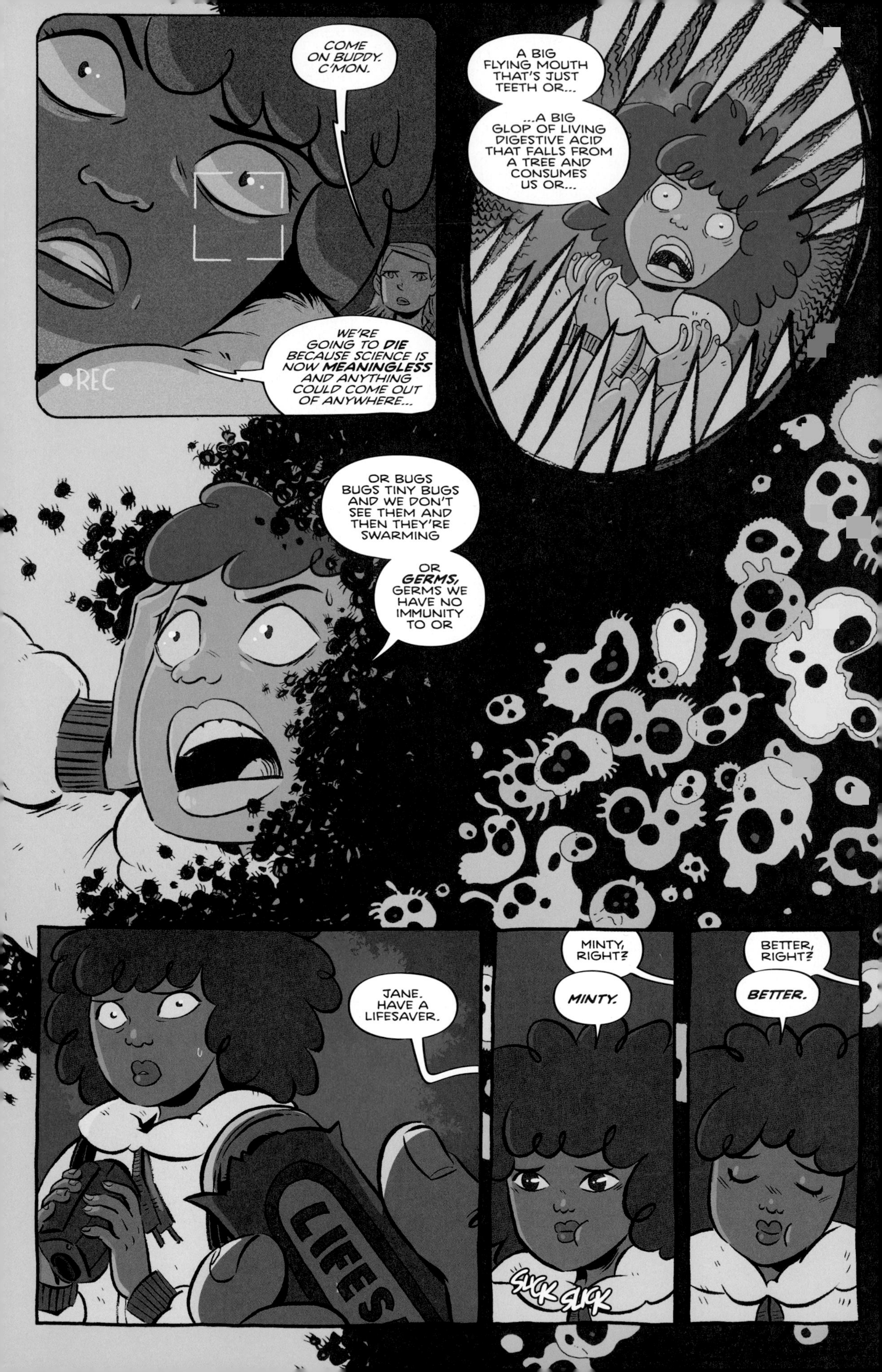
COME ON BUDDY. C'MON.
●REC
WE'RE GOING TO DIE BECAUSE SCIENCE IS NOW MEANINGLESS AND ANYTHING COULD COME OUT OF ANYWHERE...
A BIG FLYING MOUTH THAT'S JUST TEETH OR...
...A BIG GLOP OF LIVING DIGESTIVE ACID THAT FALLS FROM A TREE AND CONSUMES US OR...
OR BUGS BUGS TINY BUGS AND WE DON'T SEE THEM AND THEN THEY'RE SWARMING
OR GERMS, GERMS WE HAVE NO IMMUNITY TO OR
JANE. HAVE A LIFESAVER.
LIFES
MINTY, RIGHT?
MINTY.
SUCK SUCK
BETTER, RIGHT?
BETTER.

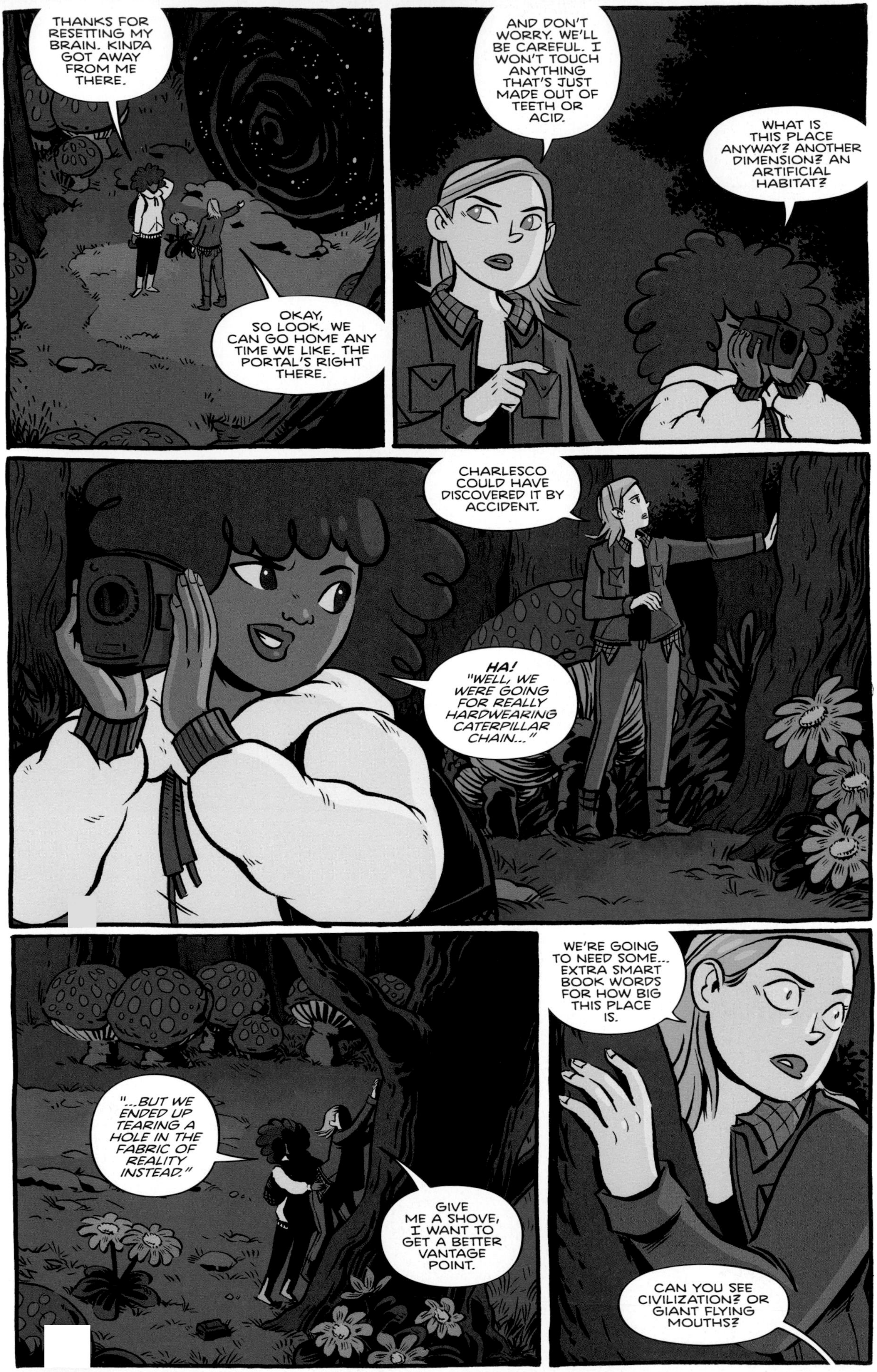
THANKS FOR RESETTING MY BRAIN. KINDA GOT AWAY FROM ME THERE.
OKAY, SO LOOK. WE CAN GO HOME ANY TIME WE LIKE. THE PORTAL'S RIGHT THERE.
AND DON'T WORRY. WE'LL BE CAREFUL. I WON'T TOUCH ANYTHING THAT'S JUST MADE OUT OF TEETH OR ACID.
WHAT IS THIS PLACE ANYWAY? ANOTHER DIMENSION? AN ARTIFICIAL HABITAT?
CHARLESCO COULD HAVE DISCOVERED IT BY ACCIDENT.
HA! "WELL, WE WERE GOING FOR REALLY HARDWEARING CATERPILLAR CHAIN..."
"...BUT WE ENDED UP TEARING A HOLE IN THE FABRIC OF REALITY INSTEAD."
GIVE ME A SHOVE, I WANT TO GET A BETTER VANTAGE POINT.
WE'RE GOING TO NEED SOME... EXTRA SMART BOOK WORDS FOR HOW BIG THIS PLACE IS.
CAN YOU SEE CIVILIZATION? OR GIANT FLYING MOUTHS?

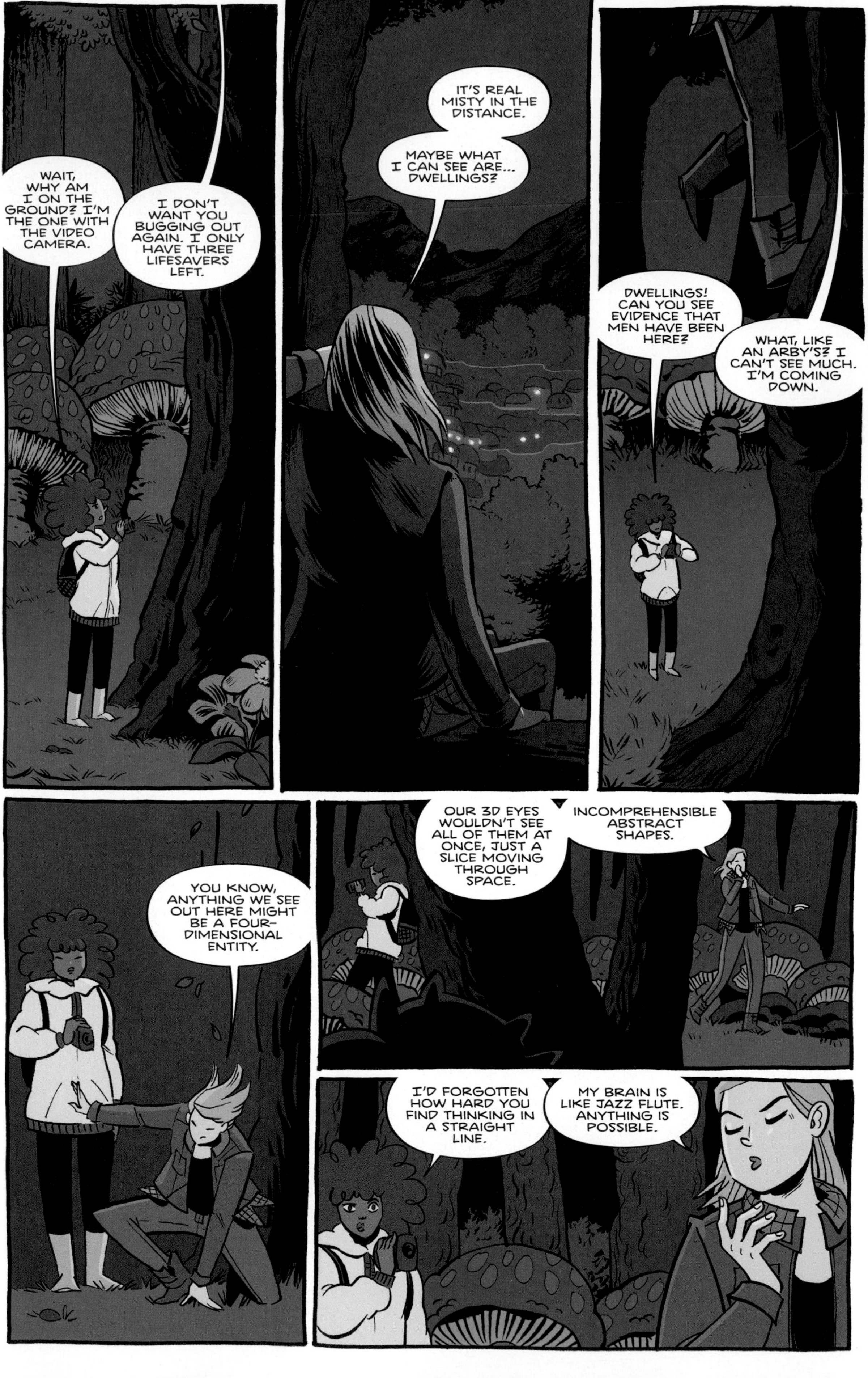
WAIT, WHY AM I ON THE GROUND? I'M THE ONE WITH THE VIDEO CAMERA.
I DON'T WANT YOU BUGGING OUT AGAIN. I ONLY HAVE THREE LIFESAVERS LEFT.
IT'S REAL MISTY IN THE DISTANCE.
MAYBE WHAT I CAN SEE ARE... DWELLINGS?
DWELLINGS! CAN YOU SEE EVIDENCE THAT MEN HAVE BEEN HERE?
WHAT, LIKE AN ARBY'S? I CAN'T SEE MUCH. I'M COMING DOWN.
YOU KNOW, ANYTHING WE SEE OUT HERE MIGHT BE A FOUR-DIMENSIONAL ENTITY.
OUR 3D EYES WOULDN'T SEE ALL OF THEM AT ONCE, JUST A SLICE MOVING THROUGH SPACE.
INCOMPREHENSIBLE ABSTRACT SHAPES.
I'D FORGOTTEN HOW HARD YOU FIND THINKING IN A STRAIGHT LINE.
MY BRAIN IS LIKE JAZZ FLUTE. ANYTHING IS POSSIBLE.

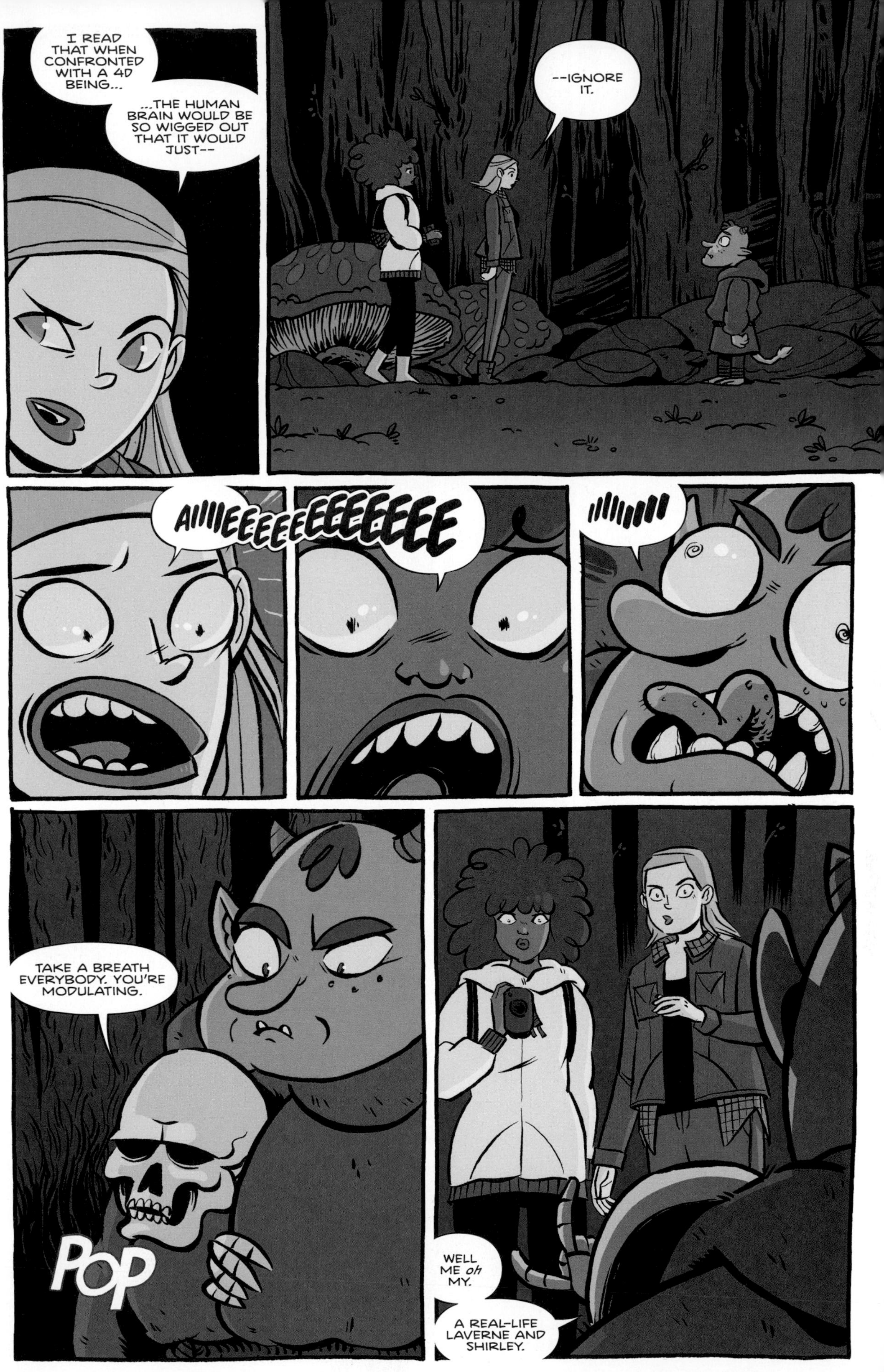
I READ THAT WHEN CONFRONTED WITH A 4D BEING...
...THE HUMAN BRAIN WOULD BE SO WIGGED OUT THAT IT WOULD JUST--
--IGNORE IT.
AIIIIEEEEEEEEEEEEE
IIIIIII
TAKE A BREATH EVERYBODY. YOU'RE MODULATING.
POP
WELL ME *oh* MY.
A REAL-LIFE LAVERNE AND SHIRLEY.

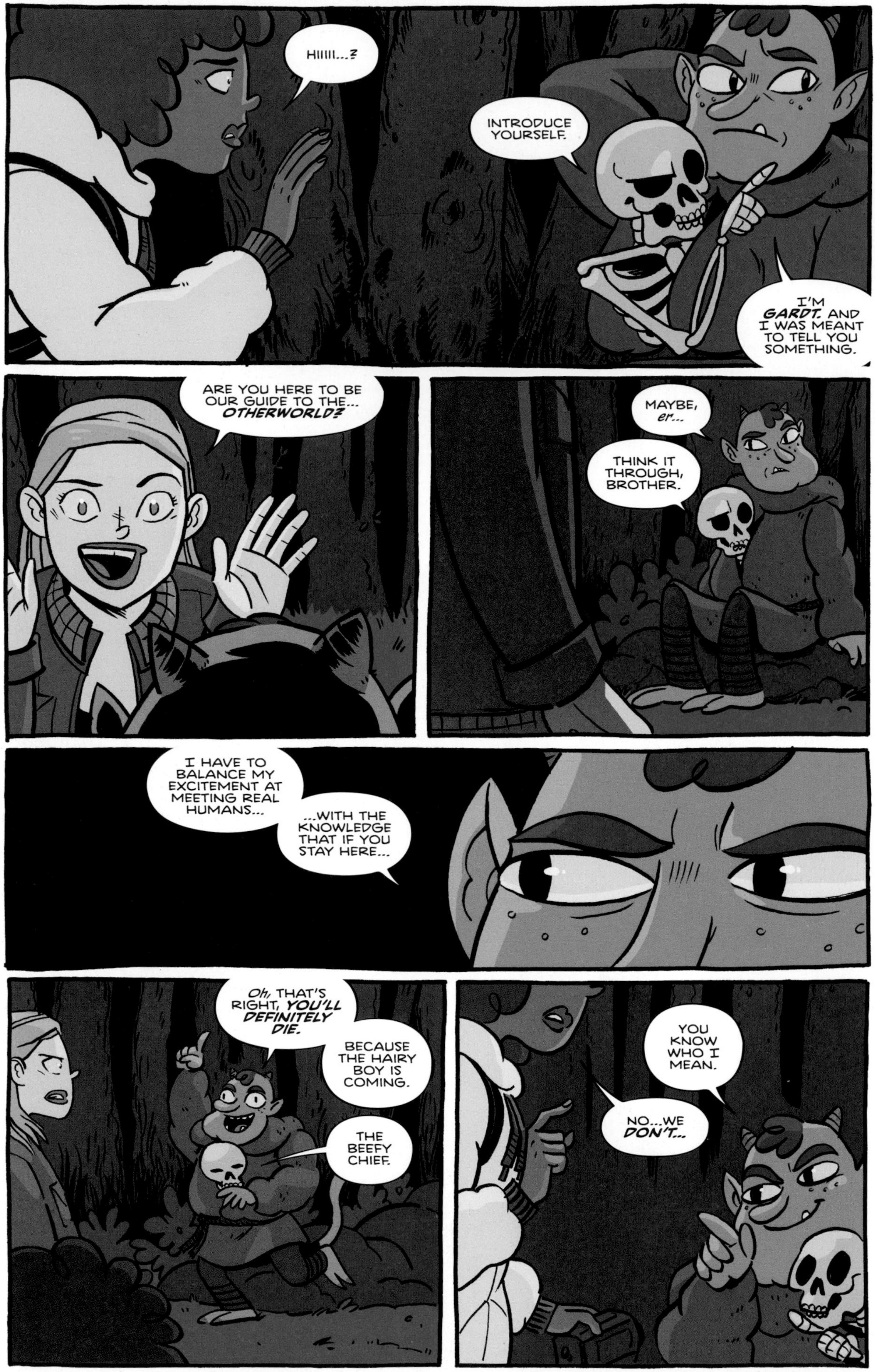
HIIIII...?
INTRODUCE YOURSELF.
I'M GARDT. AND I WAS MEANT TO TELL YOU SOMETHING.
ARE YOU HERE TO BE OUR GUIDE TO THE... OTHERWORLD?
MAYBE, er...
THINK IT THROUGH, BROTHER.
I HAVE TO BALANCE MY EXCITEMENT AT MEETING REAL HUMANS...
...WITH THE KNOWLEDGE THAT IF YOU STAY HERE...
Oh, THAT'S RIGHT, YOU'LL DEFINITELY DIE.
BECAUSE THE HAIRY BOY IS COMING.
THE BEEFY CHIEF.
YOU KNOW WHO I MEAN.
NO...WE DON'T...

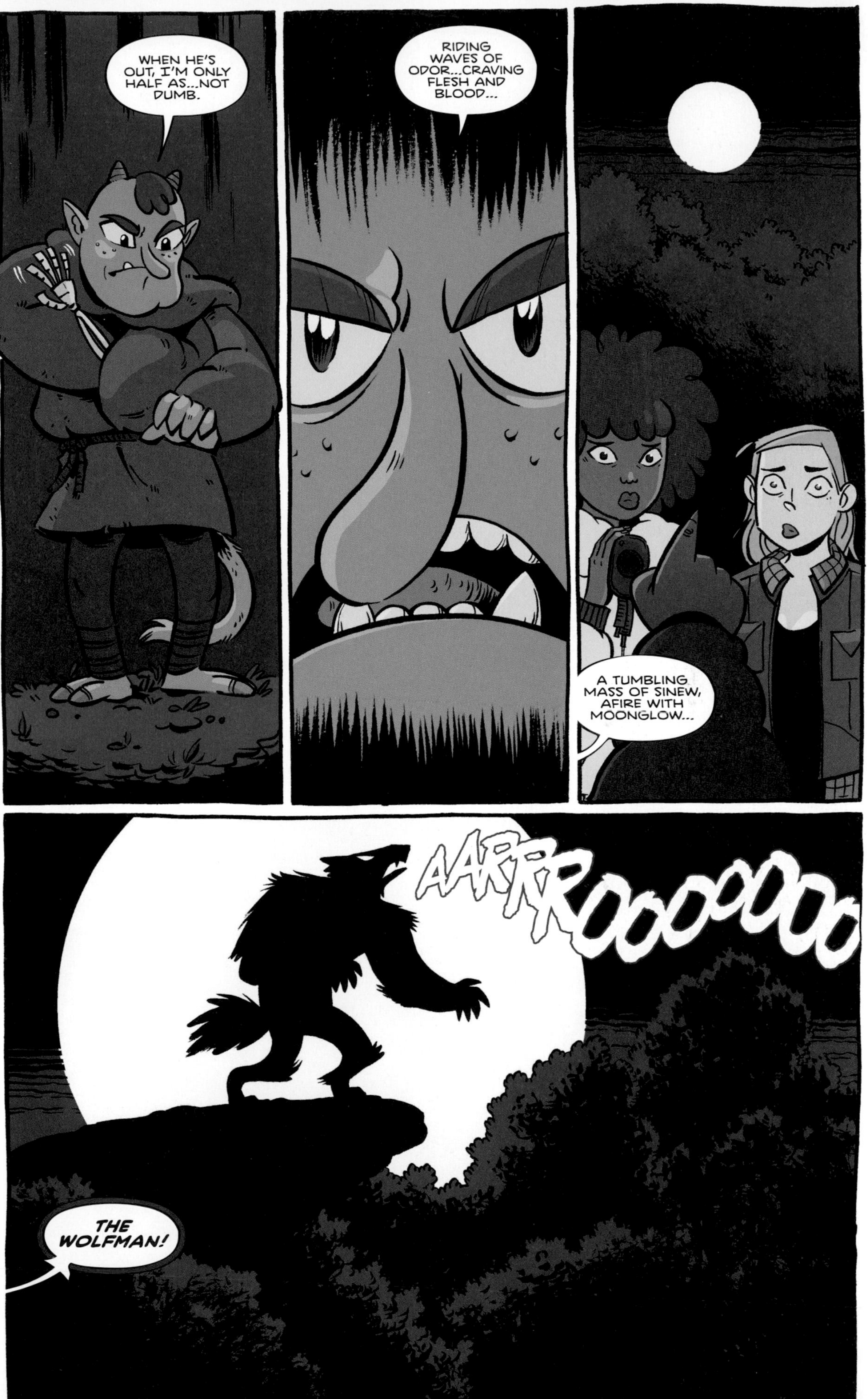

WHEN HE'S OUT, I'M ONLY HALF AS...NOT DUMB.
RIDING WAVES OF ODOR...CRAVING FLESH AND BLOOD...
A TUMBLING MASS OF SINEW, AFIRE WITH MOONGLOW...
AARRROOOOOOO
THE WOLFMAN!

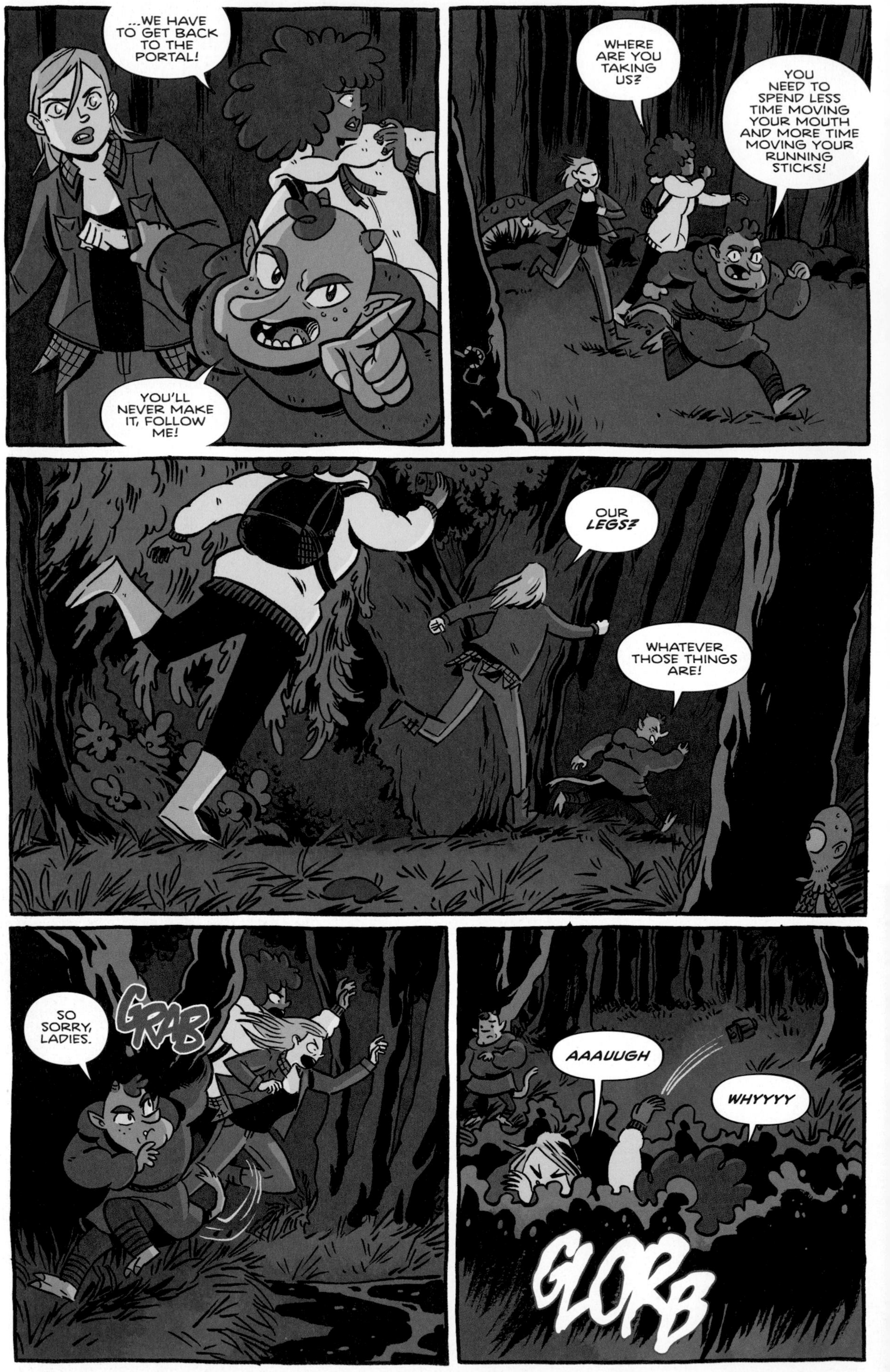
...WE HAVE TO GET BACK TO THE PORTAL!
YOU'LL NEVER MAKE IT, FOLLOW ME!
WHERE ARE YOU TAKING US?
YOU NEED TO SPEND LESS TIME MOVING YOUR MOUTH AND MORE TIME MOVING YOUR RUNNING STICKS!
OUR *LEGS?*
WHATEVER THOSE THINGS ARE!
SO SORRY, LADIES.
GRAB
AAAUUGH
WHYYYY
GLORB

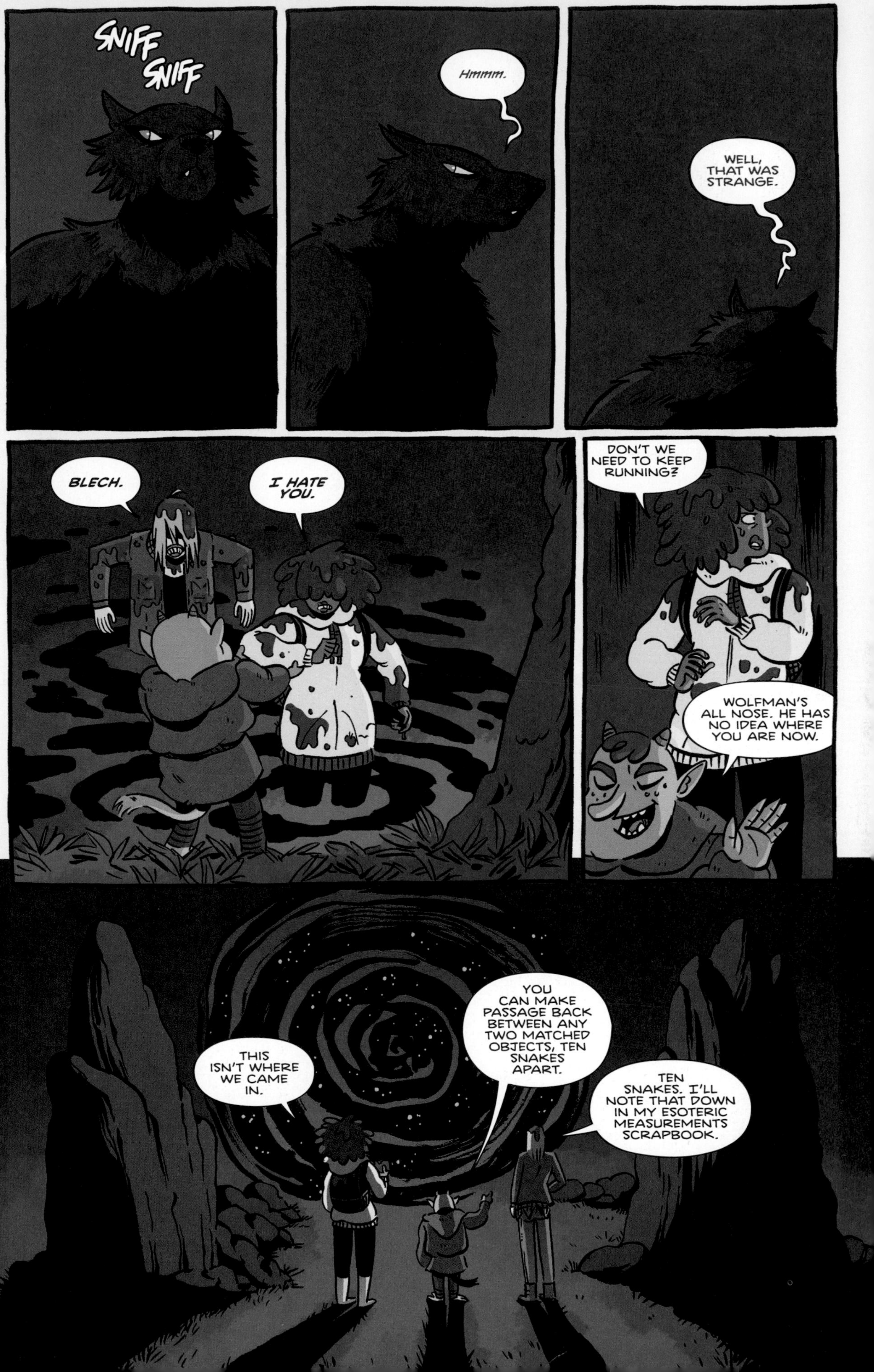
SNIFF SNIFF
Hmmm.
WELL, THAT WAS STRANGE.
BLECH.
I HATE YOU.
DON'T WE NEED TO KEEP RUNNING?
WOLFMAN'S ALL NOSE. HE HAS NO IDEA WHERE YOU ARE NOW.
THIS ISN'T WHERE WE CAME IN.
YOU CAN MAKE PASSAGE BACK BETWEEN ANY TWO MATCHED OBJECTS, TEN SNAKES APART.
TEN SNAKES. I'LL NOTE THAT DOWN IN MY ESOTERIC MEASUREMENTS SCRAPBOOK.

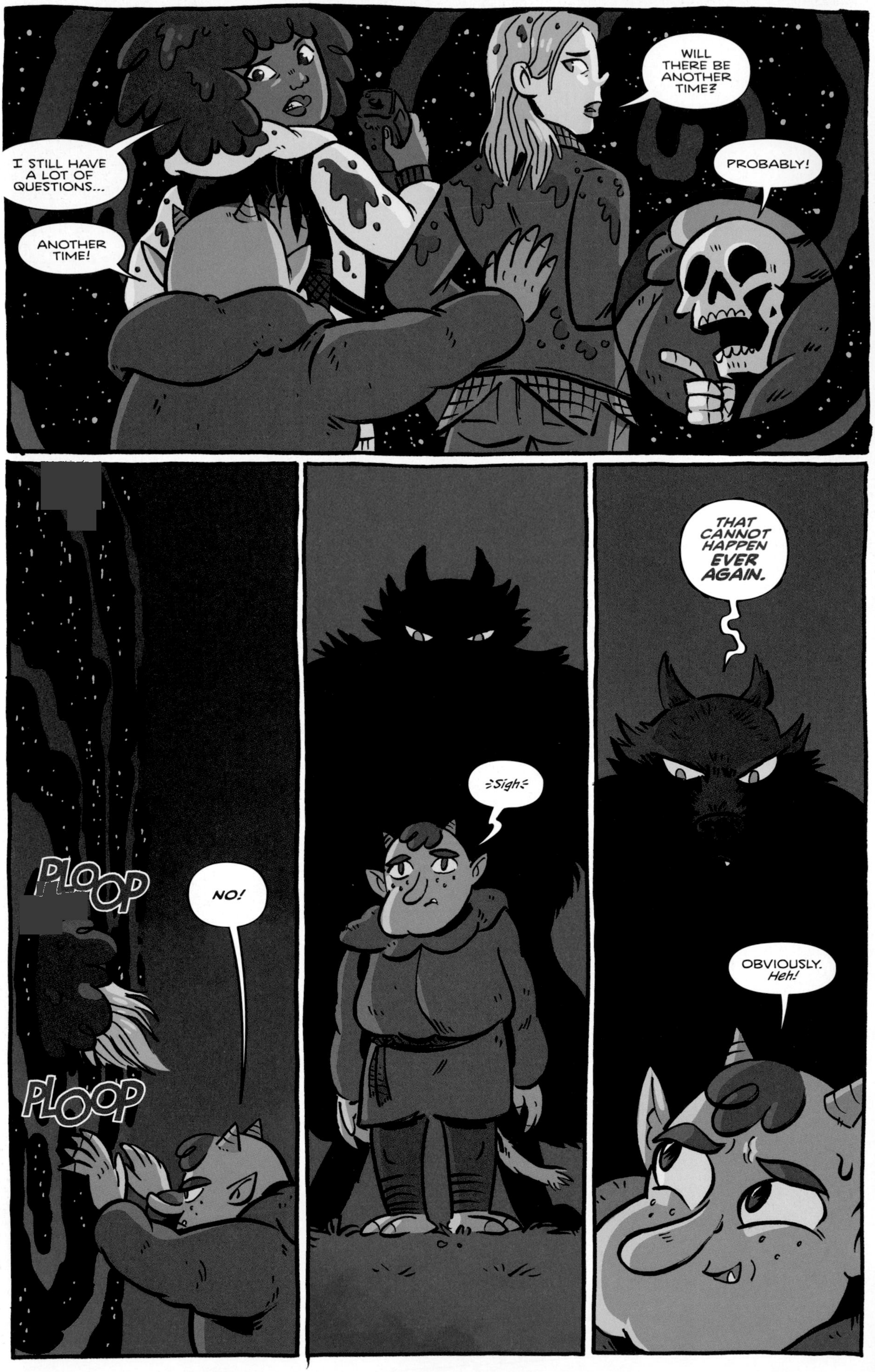

I STILL HAVE A LOT OF QUESTIONS...
ANOTHER TIME!
WILL THERE BE ANOTHER TIME?
PROBABLY!
PLOOP
PLOOP
NO!
Sigh
THAT CANNOT HAPPEN *EVER AGAIN.*
OBVIOUSLY. *Heh!*

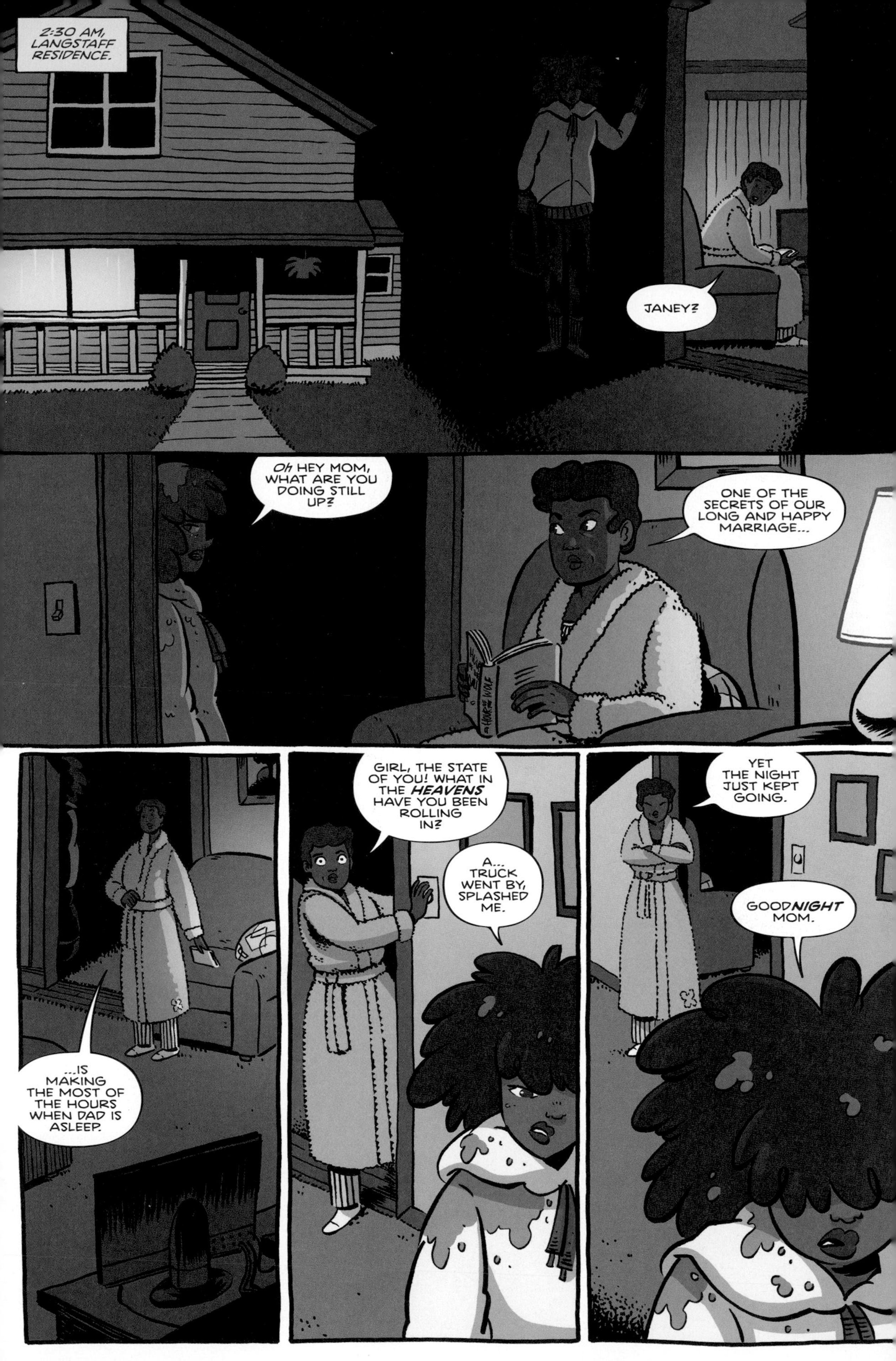
2:30 AM, LANGSTAFF RESIDENCE.
JANEY?
Oh HEY MOM, WHAT ARE YOU DOING STILL UP?
ONE OF THE SECRETS OF OUR LONG AND HAPPY MARRIAGE...
...IS MAKING THE MOST OF THE HOURS WHEN DAD IS ASLEEP.
GIRL, THE STATE OF YOU! WHAT IN THE HEAVENS HAVE YOU BEEN ROLLING IN?
A... TRUCK WENT BY, SPLASHED ME.
YET THE NIGHT JUST KEPT GOING.
GOODNIGHT MOM.

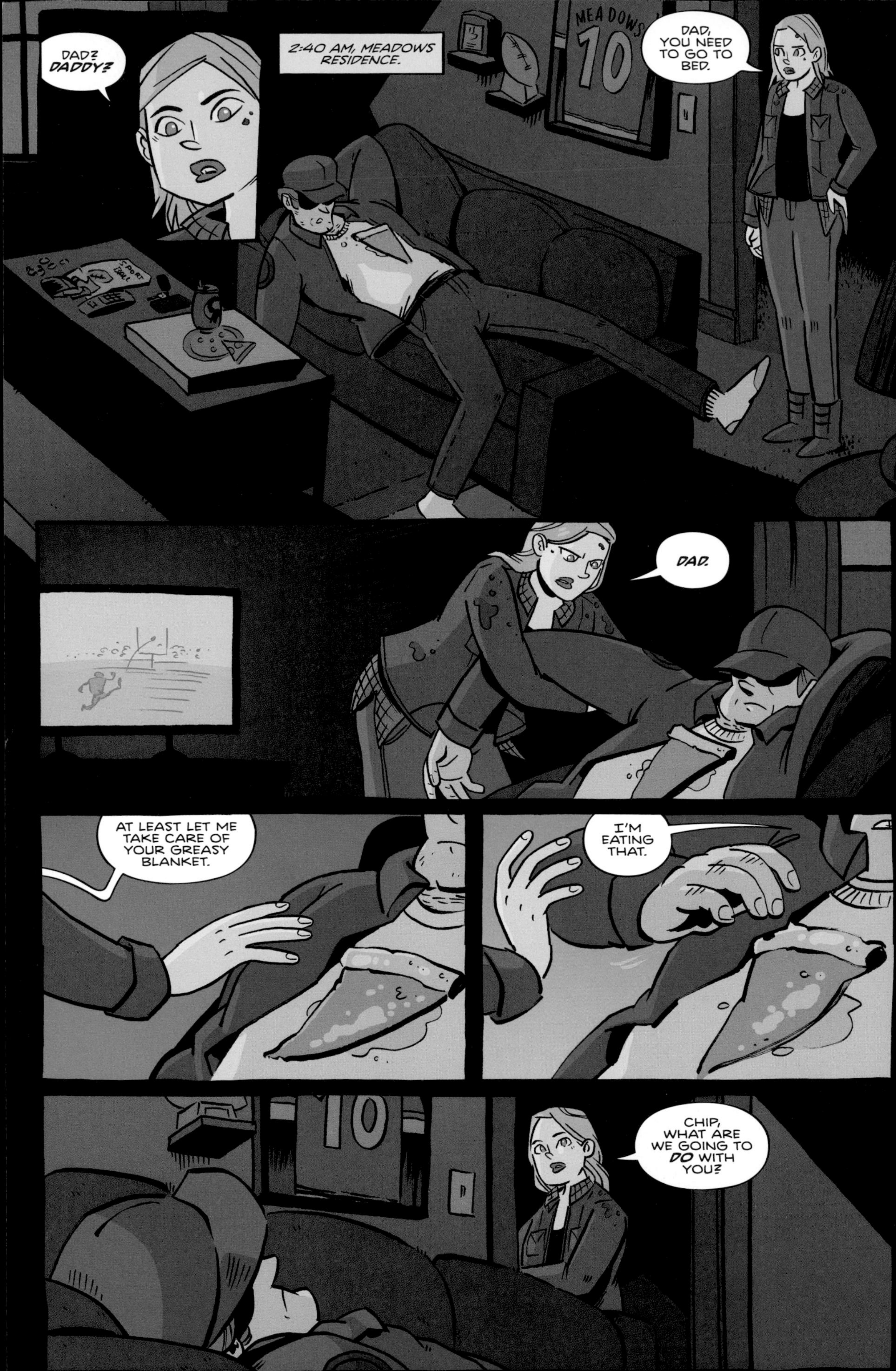
DAD? DADDY?
2:40 AM, MEADOWS RESIDENCE.
MEADOWS 10
DAD, YOU NEED TO GO TO BED.
DAD.
AT LEAST LET ME TAKE CARE OF YOUR GREASY BLANKET.
I'M EATING THAT.
10
CHIP, WHAT ARE WE GOING TO DO WITH YOU?

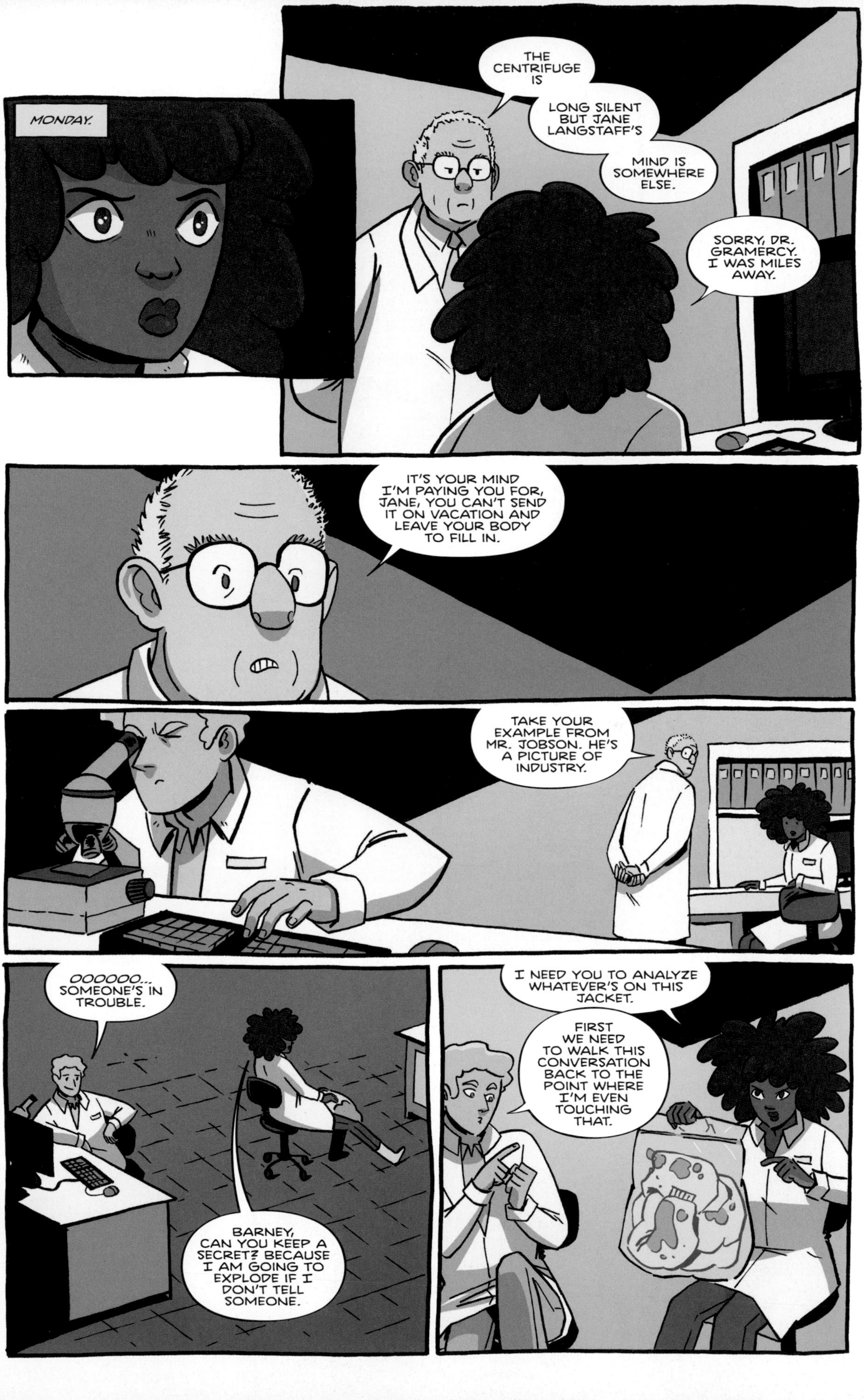
MONDAY.
THE CENTRIFUGE IS
LONG SILENT BUT JANE LANGSTAFF'S
MIND IS SOMEWHERE ELSE.
SORRY, DR. GRAMERCY. I WAS MILES AWAY.
IT'S YOUR MIND I'M PAYING YOU FOR, JANE, YOU CAN'T SEND IT ON VACATION AND LEAVE YOUR BODY TO FILL IN.
TAKE YOUR EXAMPLE FROM MR. JOBSON. HE'S A PICTURE OF INDUSTRY.
OOOOOO... SOMEONE'S IN TROUBLE.
BARNEY, CAN YOU KEEP A SECRET? BECAUSE I AM GOING TO EXPLODE IF I DON'T TELL SOMEONE.
I NEED YOU TO ANALYZE WHATEVER'S ON THIS JACKET.
FIRST WE NEED TO WALK THIS CONVERSATION BACK TO THE POINT WHERE I'M EVEN TOUCHING THAT.

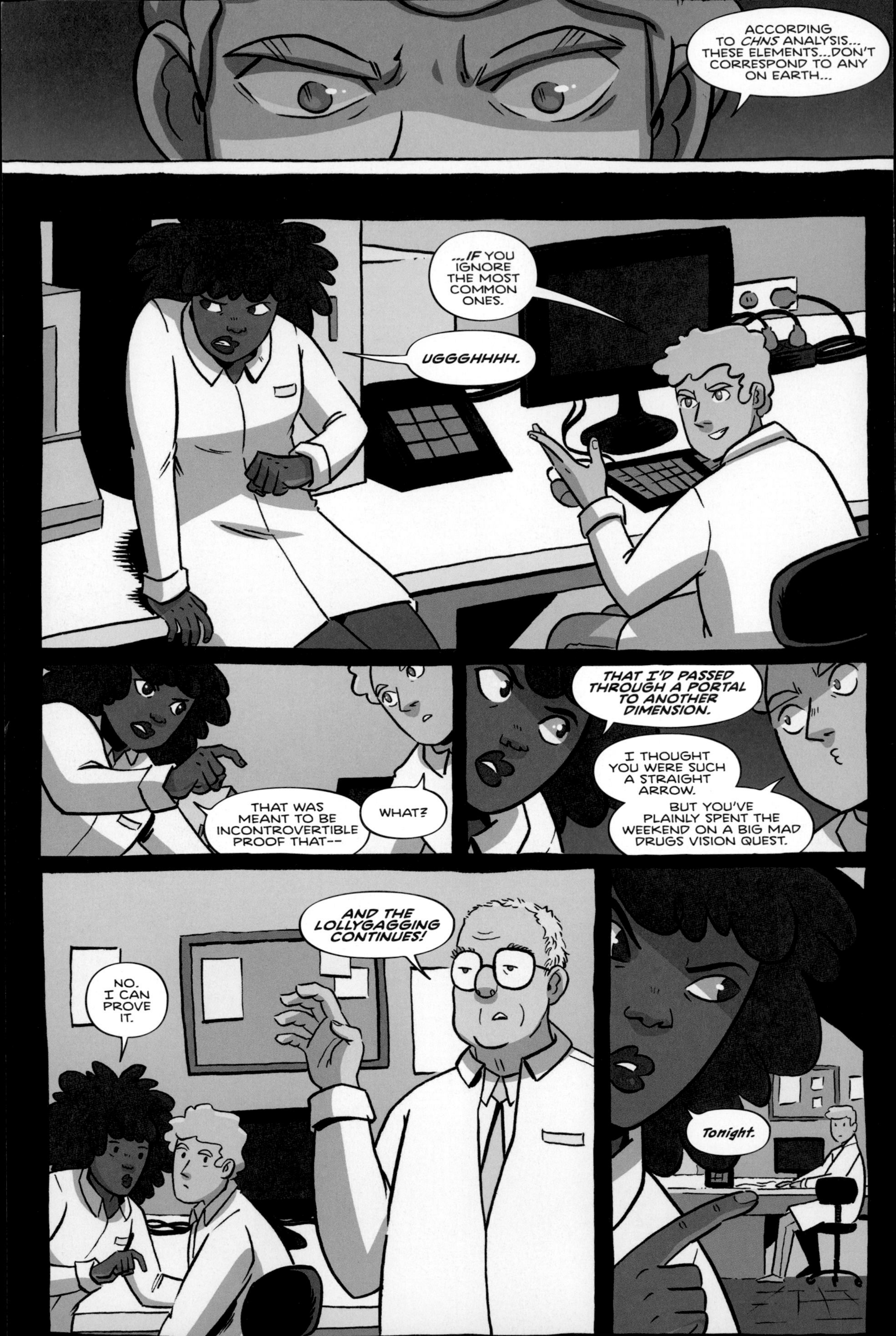
ACCORDING TO CHNS ANALYSIS... THESE ELEMENTS...DON'T CORRESPOND TO ANY ON EARTH...
...IF YOU IGNORE THE MOST COMMON ONES.
UGGGHHHH.
THAT WAS MEANT TO BE INCONTROVERTIBLE PROOF THAT--
WHAT?
THAT I'D PASSED THROUGH A PORTAL TO ANOTHER DIMENSION.
I THOUGHT YOU WERE SUCH A STRAIGHT ARROW.
BUT YOU'VE PLAINLY SPENT THE WEEKEND ON A BIG MAD DRUGS VISION QUEST.
NO. I CAN PROVE IT.
AND THE LOLLYGAGGING CONTINUES!
Tonight.

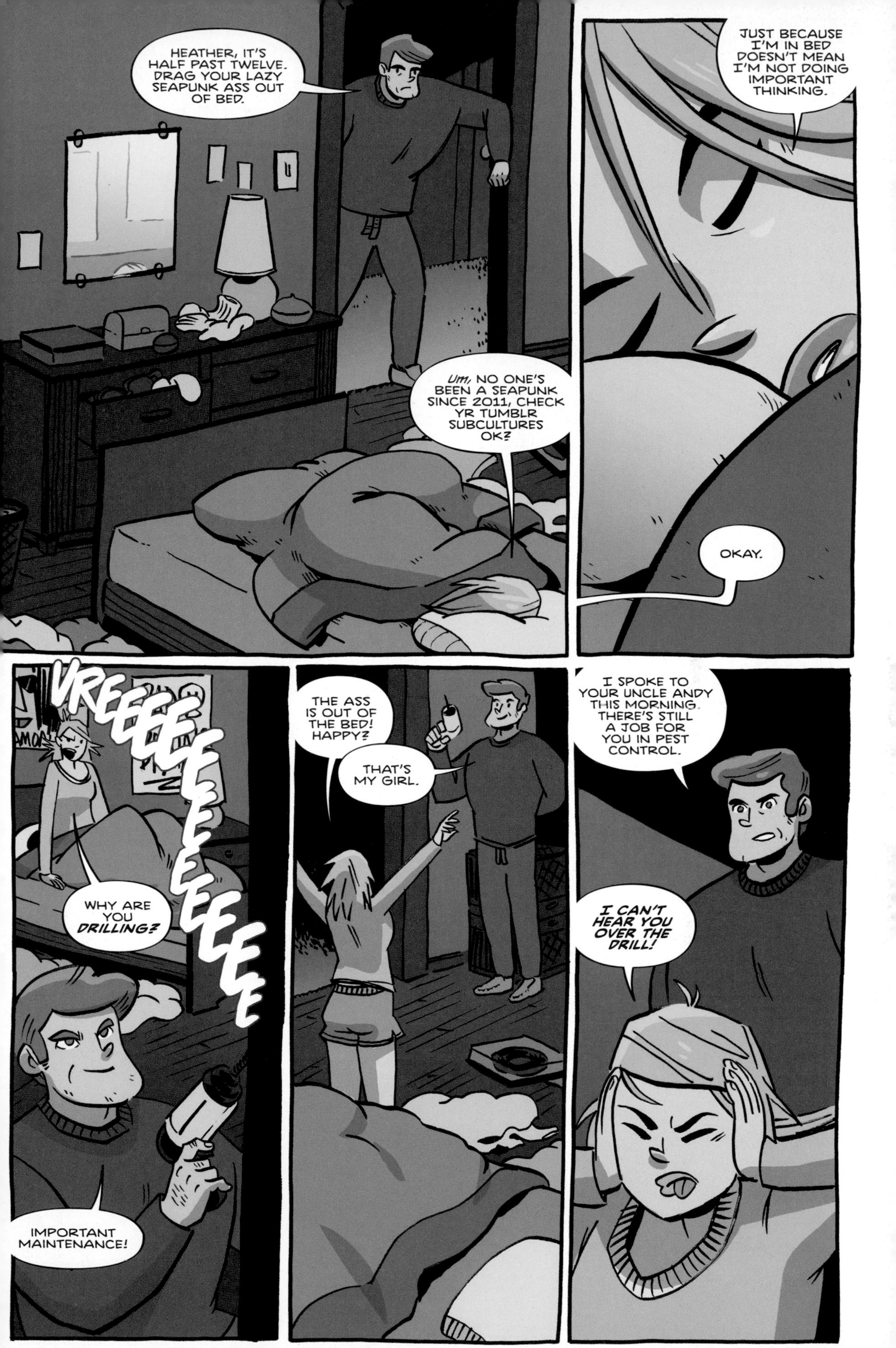
HEATHER, IT'S HALF PAST TWELVE. DRAG YOUR LAZY SEAPUNK ASS OUT OF BED.
UM, NO ONE'S BEEN A SEAPUNK SINCE 2011, CHECK YR TUMBLR SUBCULTURES OK?
JUST BECAUSE I'M IN BED DOESN'T MEAN I'M NOT DOING IMPORTANT THINKING.
OKAY.
VREEEEEEEEEEEEEEE
WHY ARE YOU *DRILLING?*
IMPORTANT MAINTENANCE!
THE ASS IS OUT OF THE BED! HAPPY?
THAT'S MY GIRL.
I SPOKE TO YOUR UNCLE ANDY THIS MORNING. THERE'S STILL A JOB FOR YOU IN PEST CONTROL.
I CAN'T HEAR YOU OVER THE DRILL!

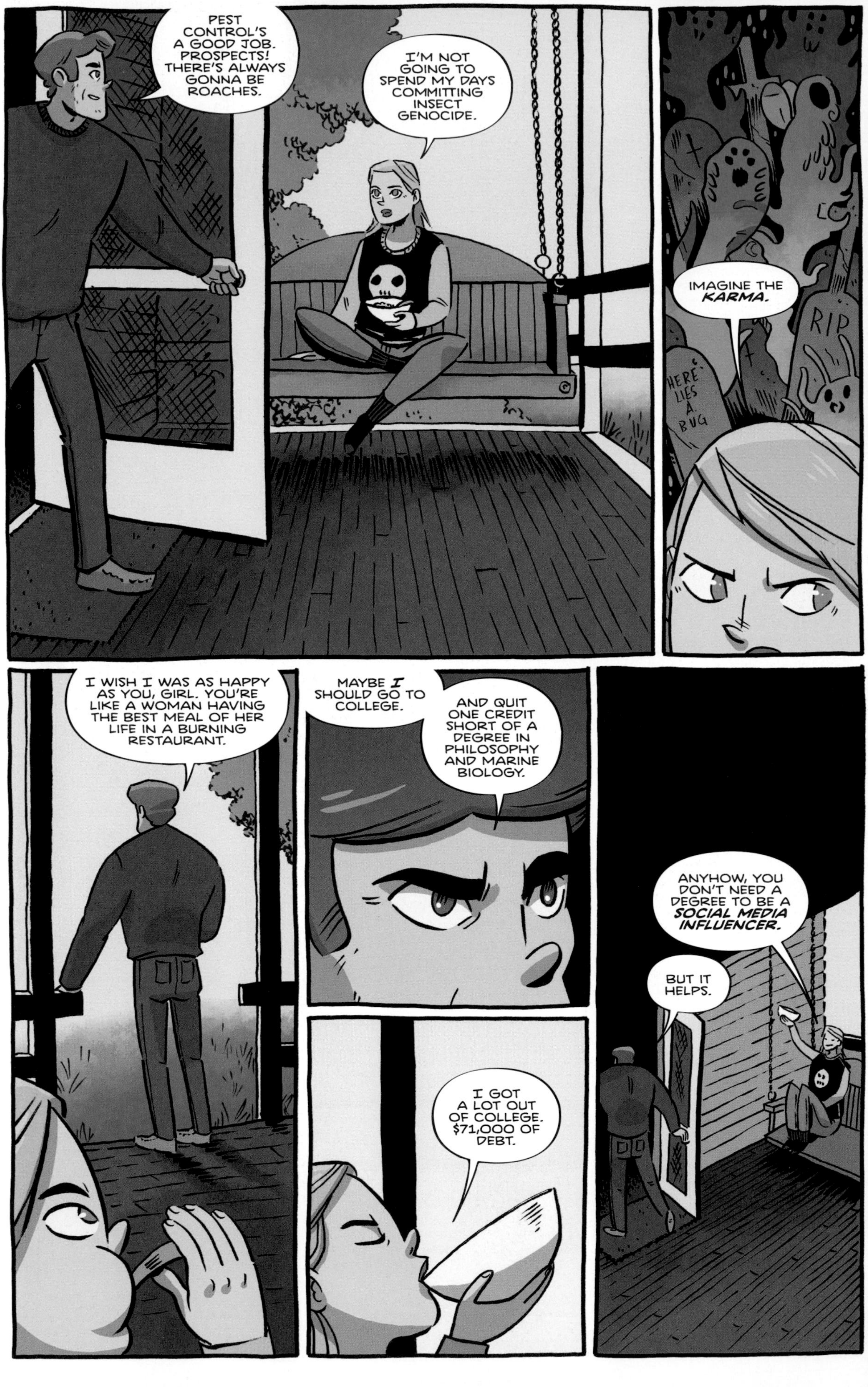
PEST CONTROL'S A GOOD JOB. PROSPECTS! THERE'S ALWAYS GONNA BE ROACHES.
I'M NOT GOING TO SPEND MY DAYS COMMITTING INSECT GENOCIDE.
IMAGINE THE *KARMA.*
RIP
HERE LIES A BUG
I WISH I WAS AS HAPPY AS YOU, GIRL. YOU'RE LIKE A WOMAN HAVING THE BEST MEAL OF HER LIFE IN A BURNING RESTAURANT.
MAYBE *I* SHOULD GO TO COLLEGE.
AND QUIT ONE CREDIT SHORT OF A DEGREE IN PHILOSOPHY AND MARINE BIOLOGY.
I GOT A LOT OUT OF COLLEGE. $71,000 OF DEBT.
ANYHOW, YOU DON'T NEED A DEGREE TO BE A ***SOCIAL MEDIA INFLUENCER.***
BUT IT HELPS.

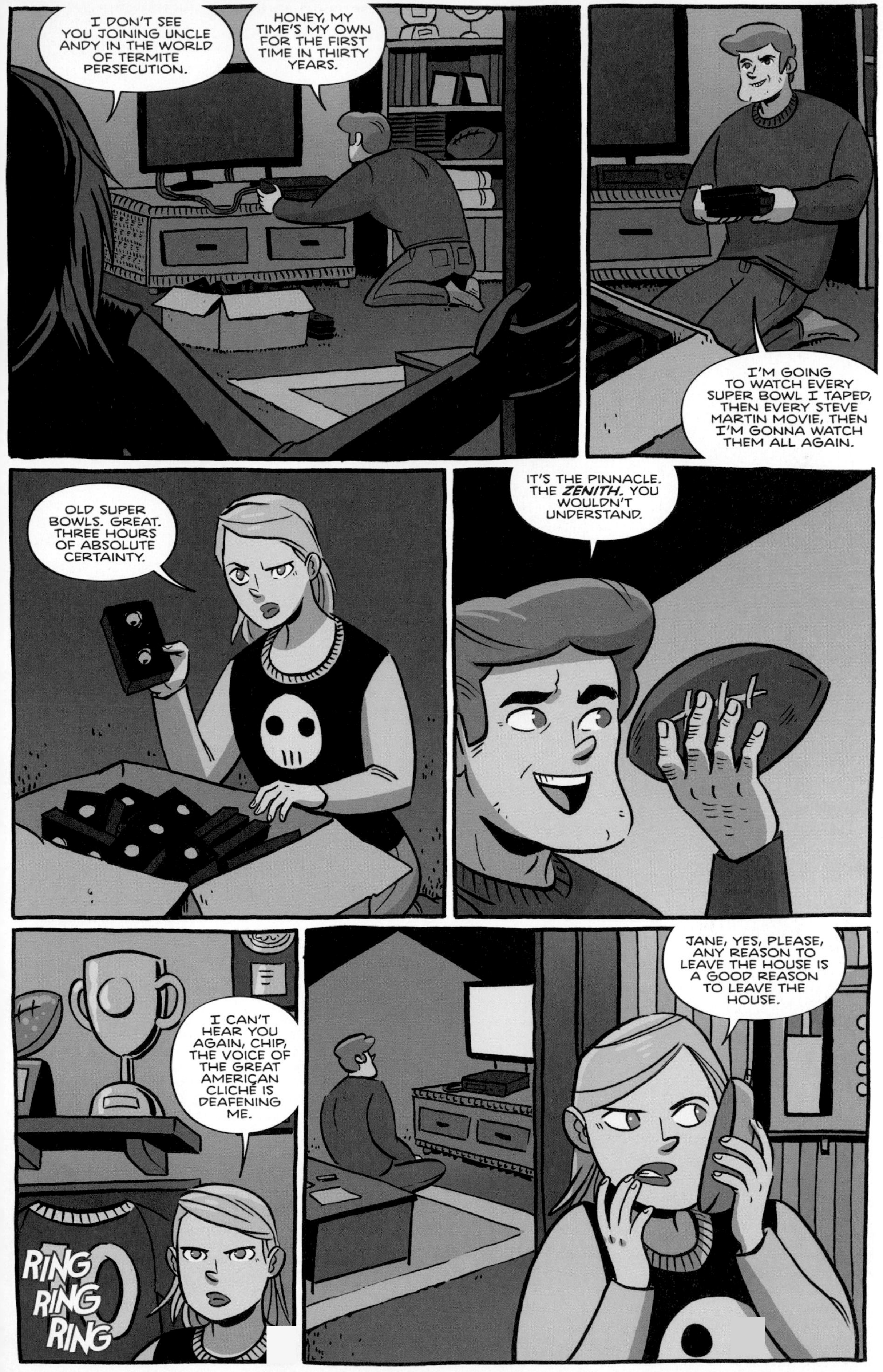
I DON'T SEE YOU JOINING UNCLE ANDY IN THE WORLD OF TERMITE PERSECUTION.
HONEY, MY TIME'S MY OWN FOR THE FIRST TIME IN THIRTY YEARS.
I'M GOING TO WATCH EVERY SUPER BOWL I TAPED, THEN EVERY STEVE MARTIN MOVIE, THEN I'M GONNA WATCH THEM ALL AGAIN.
OLD SUPER BOWLS. GREAT. THREE HOURS OF ABSOLUTE CERTAINTY.
IT'S THE PINNACLE. THE *ZENITH.* YOU WOULDN'T UNDERSTAND.
I CAN'T HEAR YOU AGAIN, CHIP, THE VOICE OF THE GREAT AMERICAN CLICHÉ IS DEAFENING ME.
RING RING RING
JANE, YES, PLEASE, ANY REASON TO LEAVE THE HOUSE IS A GOOD REASON TO LEAVE THE HOUSE.

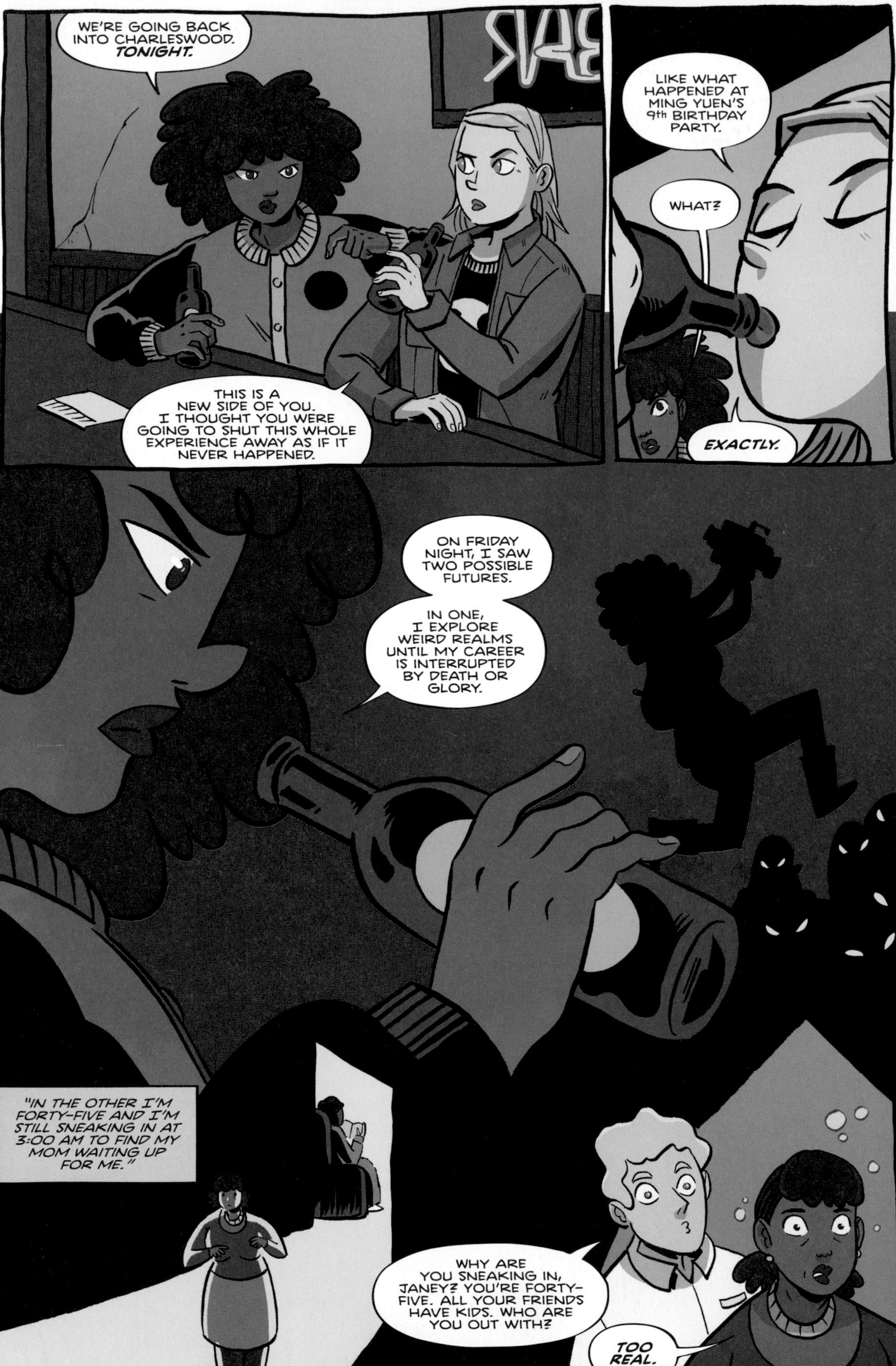
WE'RE GOING BACK INTO CHARLESWOOD. *TONIGHT.*
THIS IS A NEW SIDE OF YOU. I THOUGHT YOU WERE GOING TO SHUT THIS WHOLE EXPERIENCE AWAY AS IF IT NEVER HAPPENED.
LIKE WHAT HAPPENED AT MING YUEN'S 9th BIRTHDAY PARTY.
WHAT?
EXACTLY.
ON FRIDAY NIGHT, I SAW TWO POSSIBLE FUTURES.
IN ONE, I EXPLORE WEIRD REALMS UNTIL MY CAREER IS INTERRUPTED BY DEATH OR GLORY.
"IN THE OTHER I'M FORTY-FIVE AND I'M STILL SNEAKING IN AT 3:00 AM TO FIND MY MOM WAITING UP FOR ME."
WHY ARE YOU SNEAKING IN, JANEY? YOU'RE FORTY-FIVE. ALL YOUR FRIENDS HAVE KIDS. WHO ARE YOU OUT WITH?
TOO REAL.

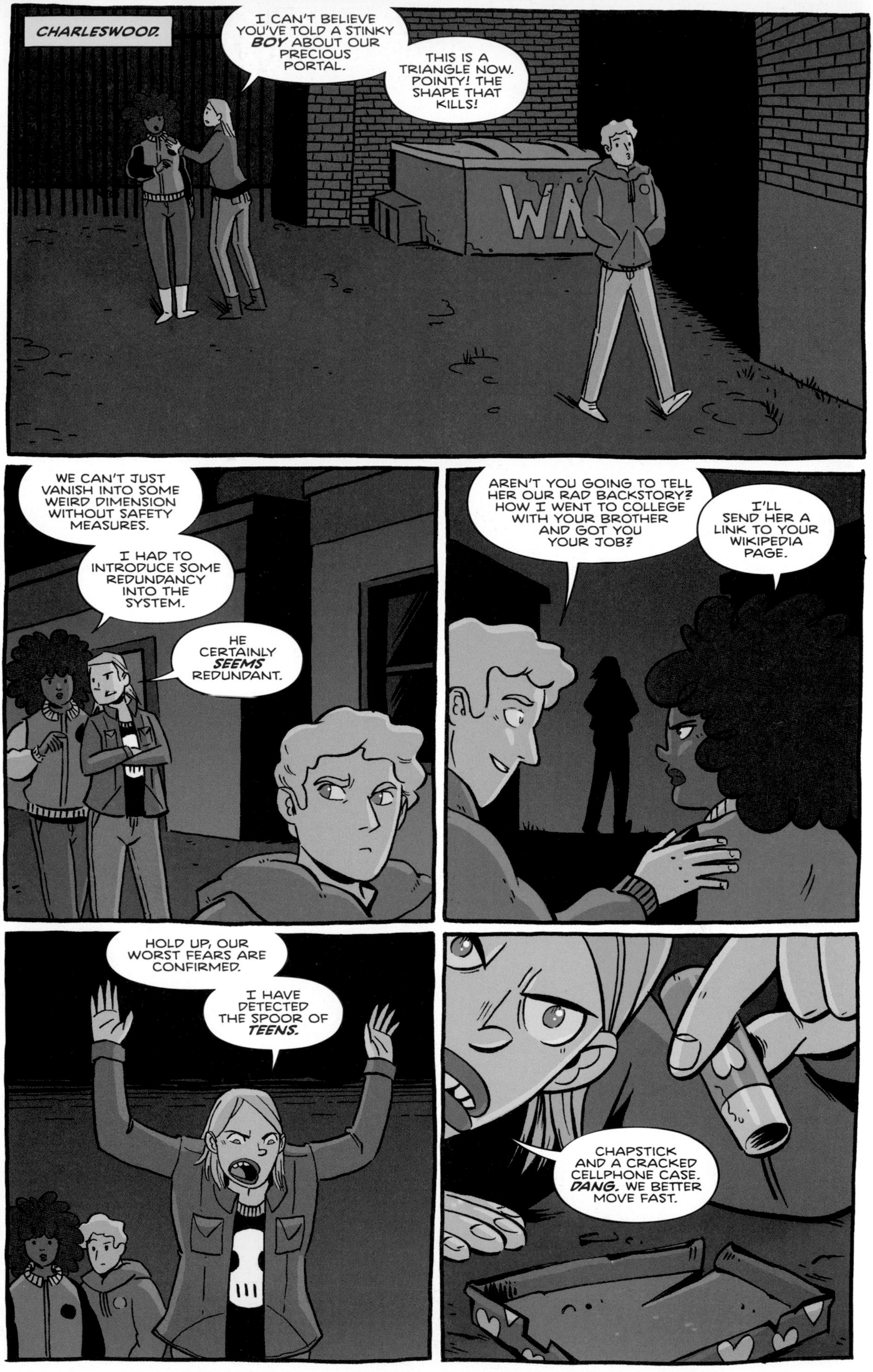
CHARLESWOOD.
I CAN'T BELIEVE YOU'VE TOLD A STINKY *BOY* ABOUT OUR PRECIOUS PORTAL.
THIS IS A TRIANGLE NOW. POINTY! THE SHAPE THAT KILLS!
WA
WE CAN'T JUST VANISH INTO SOME WEIRD DIMENSION WITHOUT SAFETY MEASURES.
I HAD TO INTRODUCE SOME REDUNDANCY INTO THE SYSTEM.
HE CERTAINLY *SEEMS* REDUNDANT.
AREN'T YOU GOING TO TELL HER OUR RAD BACKSTORY? HOW I WENT TO COLLEGE WITH YOUR BROTHER AND GOT YOU YOUR JOB?
I'LL SEND HER A LINK TO YOUR WIKIPEDIA PAGE.
HOLD UP, OUR WORST FEARS ARE CONFIRMED.
I HAVE DETECTED THE SPOOR OF *TEENS.*
CHAPSTICK AND A CRACKED CELLPHONE CASE. *DANG.* WE BETTER MOVE FAST.

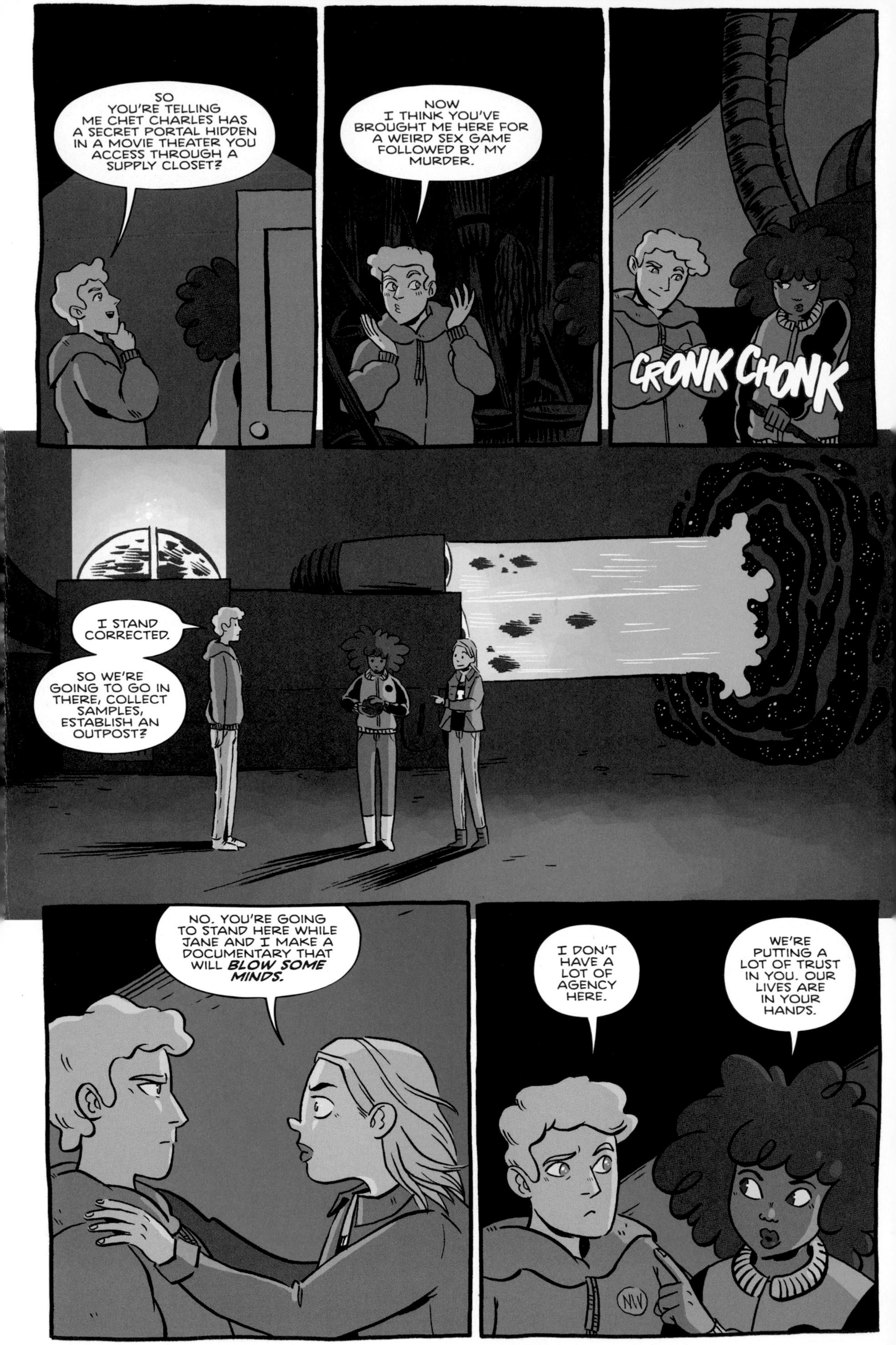
SO YOU'RE TELLING ME CHET CHARLES HAS A SECRET PORTAL HIDDEN IN A MOVIE THEATER YOU ACCESS THROUGH A SUPPLY CLOSET?
NOW I THINK YOU'VE BROUGHT ME HERE FOR A WEIRD SEX GAME FOLLOWED BY MY MURDER.
CRONK CHONK
I STAND CORRECTED.
SO WE'RE GOING TO GO IN THERE, COLLECT SAMPLES, ESTABLISH AN OUTPOST?
NO. YOU'RE GOING TO STAND HERE WHILE JANE AND I MAKE A DOCUMENTARY THAT WILL BLOW SOME MINDS.
I DON'T HAVE A LOT OF AGENCY HERE.
WE'RE PUTTING A LOT OF TRUST IN YOU. OUR LIVES ARE IN YOUR HANDS.

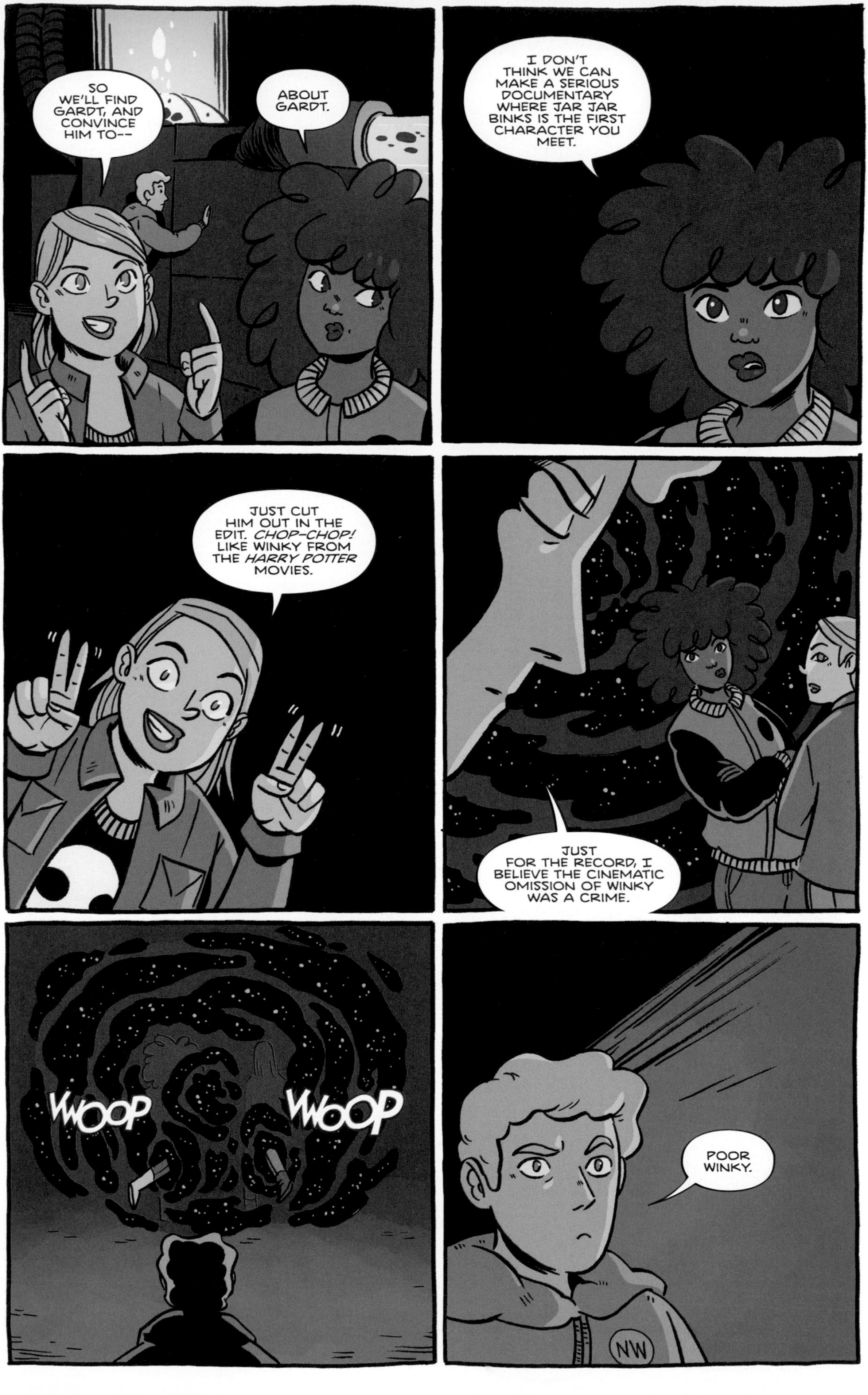
SO WE'LL FIND GARDT, AND CONVINCE HIM TO--
ABOUT GARDT.
I DON'T THINK WE CAN MAKE A SERIOUS DOCUMENTARY WHERE JAR JAR BINKS IS THE FIRST CHARACTER YOU MEET.
JUST CUT HIM OUT IN THE EDIT. *CHOP-CHOP!* LIKE WINKY FROM THE *HARRY POTTER* MOVIES.
JUST FOR THE RECORD, I BELIEVE THE CINEMATIC OMISSION OF WINKY WAS A CRIME.
VWOOP
VWOOP
POOR WINKY.
NW

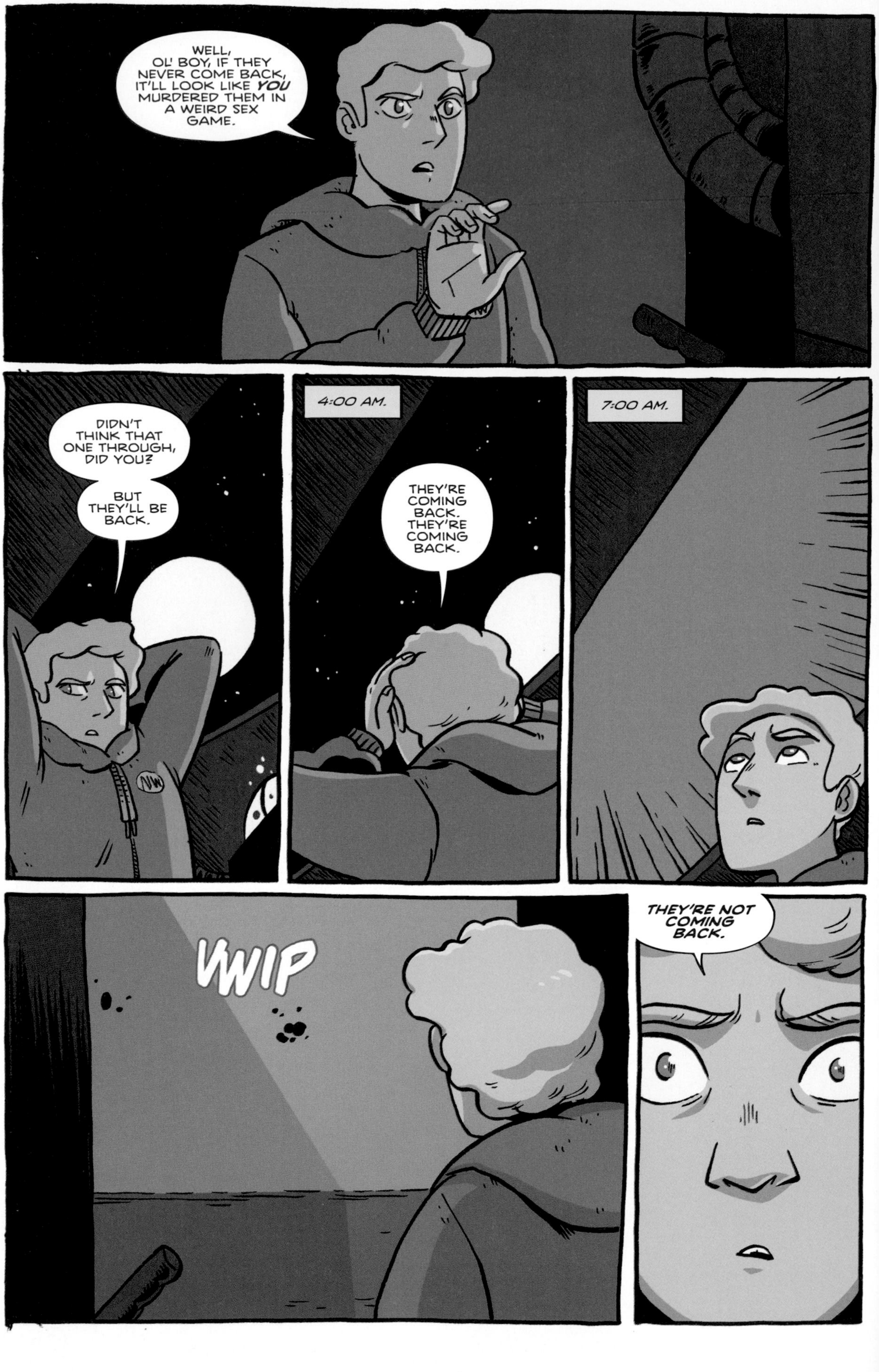
WELL, OL' BOY, IF THEY NEVER COME BACK, IT'LL LOOK LIKE *YOU* MURDERED THEM IN A WEIRD SEX GAME.
DIDN'T THINK THAT ONE THROUGH, DID YOU?
BUT THEY'LL BE BACK.
4:00 AM.
THEY'RE COMING BACK. THEY'RE COMING BACK.
7:00 AM.
VWIP
THEY'RE NOT COMING BACK.

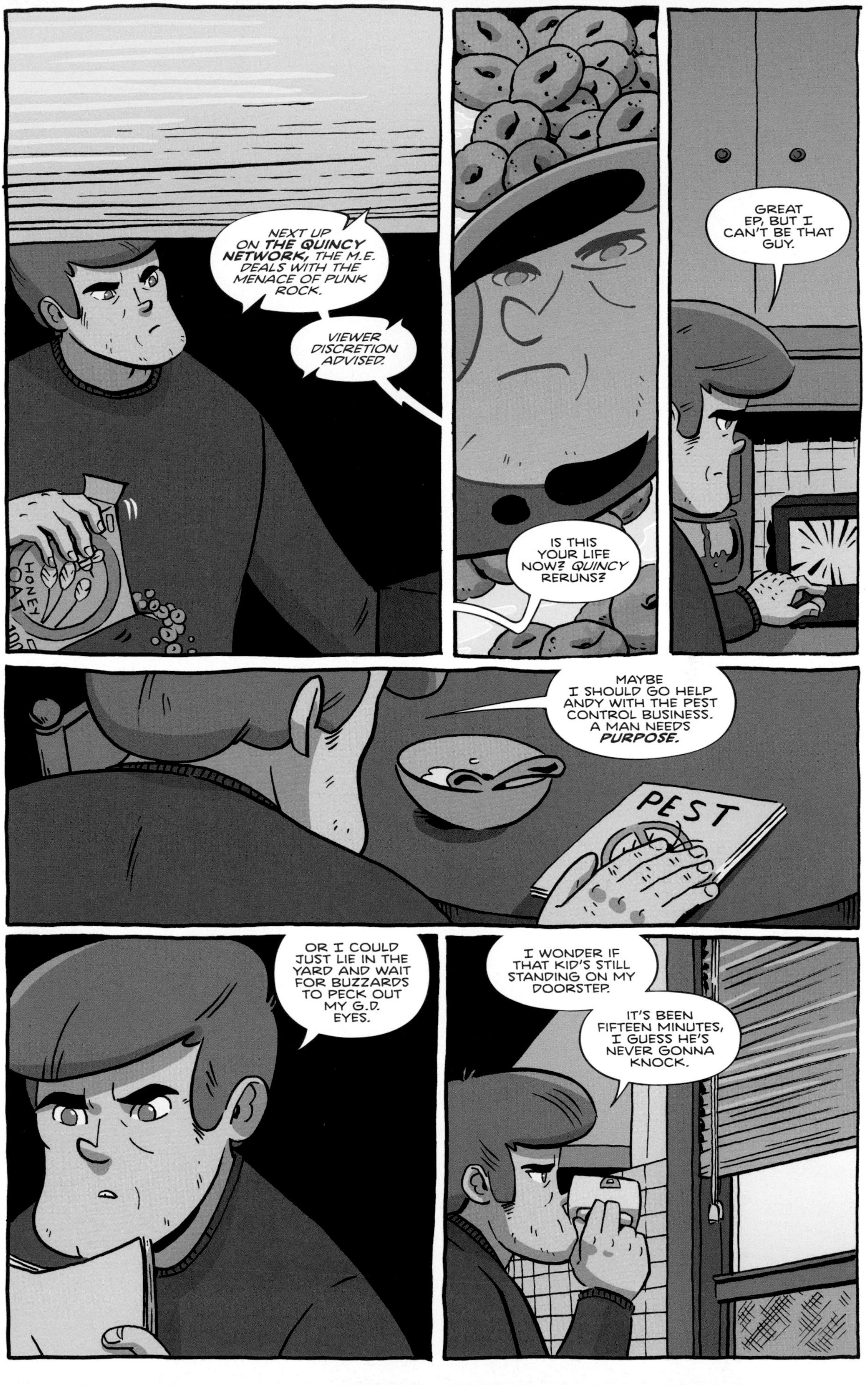
NEXT UP ON THE QUINCY NETWORK, THE M.E. DEALS WITH THE MENACE OF PUNK ROCK.
VIEWER DISCRETION ADVISED.
HONEY OAT
IS THIS YOUR LIFE NOW? QUINCY RERUNS?
GREAT EP, BUT I CAN'T BE THAT GUY.
MAYBE I SHOULD GO HELP ANDY WITH THE PEST CONTROL BUSINESS. A MAN NEEDS PURPOSE.
PEST
OR I COULD JUST LIE IN THE YARD AND WAIT FOR BUZZARDS TO PECK OUT MY G.D. EYES.
I WONDER IF THAT KID'S STILL STANDING ON MY DOORSTEP.
IT'S BEEN FIFTEEN MINUTES, I GUESS HE'S NEVER GONNA KNOCK.

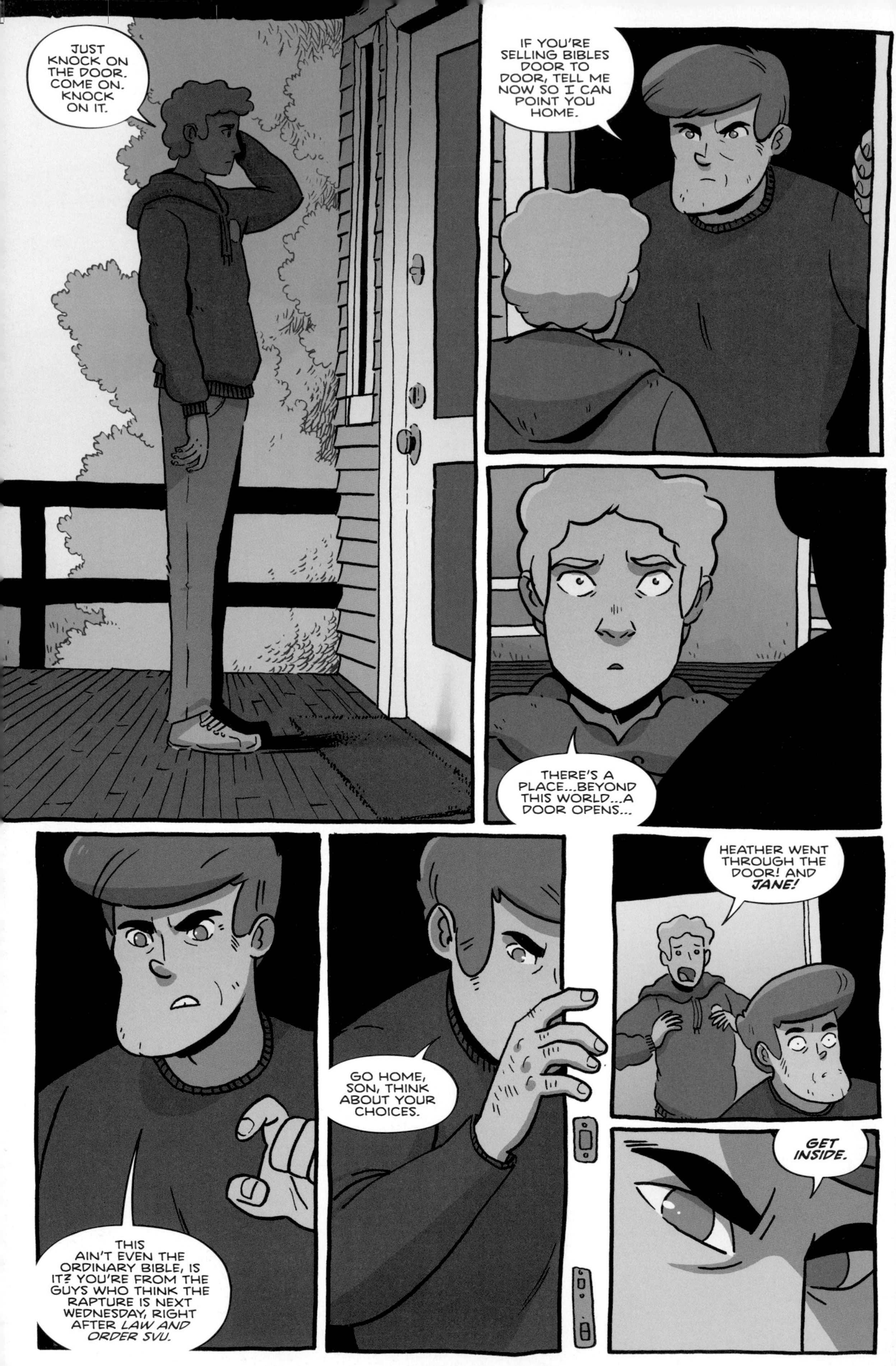
JUST KNOCK ON THE DOOR. COME ON. KNOCK ON IT.
IF YOU'RE SELLING BIBLES DOOR TO DOOR, TELL ME NOW SO I CAN POINT YOU HOME.
THERE'S A PLACE...BEYOND THIS WORLD...A DOOR OPENS...
THIS AIN'T EVEN THE ORDINARY BIBLE, IS IT? YOU'RE FROM THE GUYS WHO THINK THE RAPTURE IS NEXT WEDNESDAY, RIGHT AFTER *LAW AND ORDER SVU*.
GO HOME, SON, THINK ABOUT YOUR CHOICES.
HEATHER WENT THROUGH THE DOOR! AND *JANE!*
GET INSIDE.

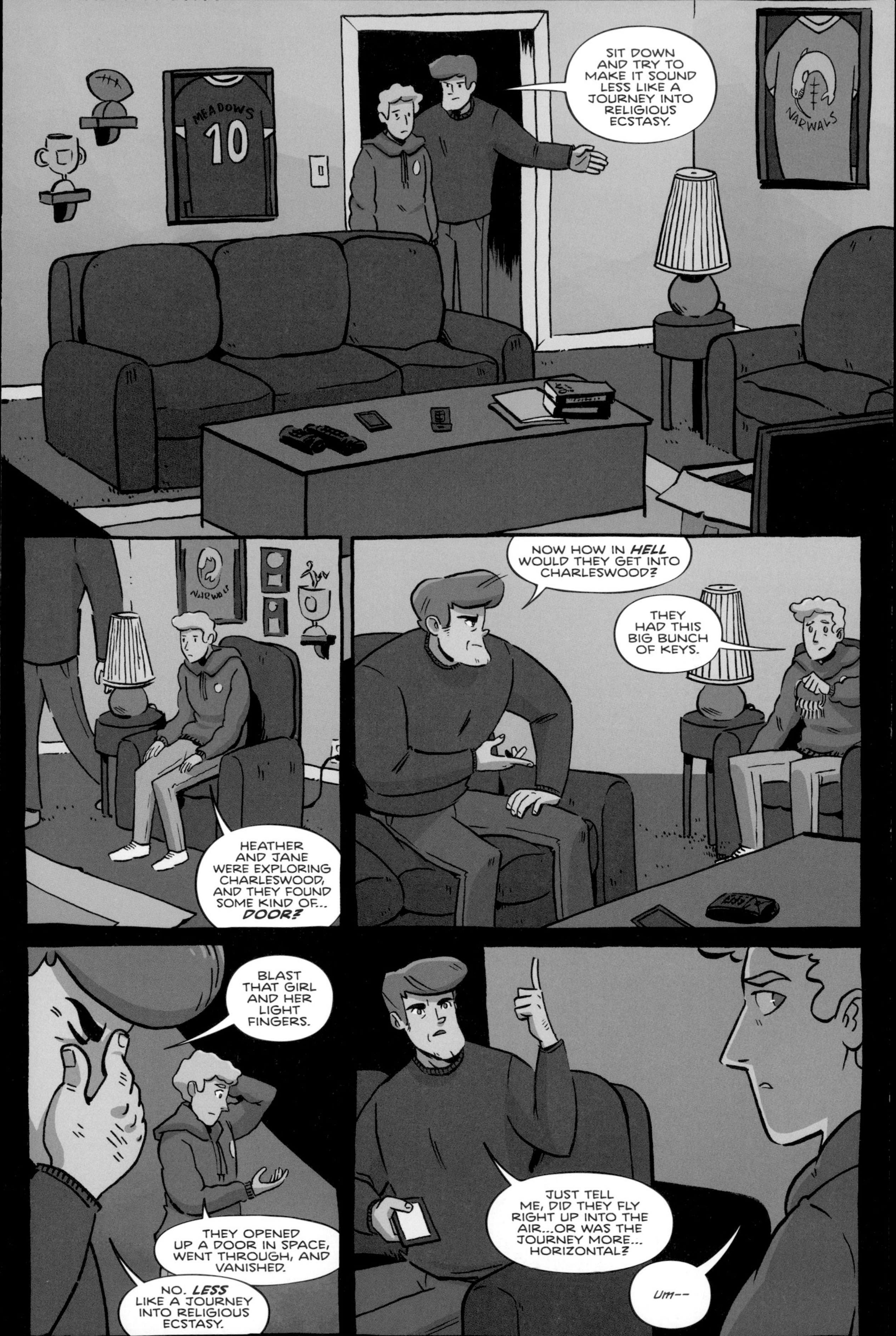
SIT DOWN AND TRY TO MAKE IT SOUND LESS LIKE A JOURNEY INTO RELIGIOUS ECSTASY.
MEADOWS 10
NARWALS
HEATHER AND JANE WERE EXPLORING CHARLESWOOD, AND THEY FOUND SOME KIND OF... DOOR?
NOW HOW IN HELL WOULD THEY GET INTO CHARLESWOOD?
THEY HAD THIS BIG BUNCH OF KEYS.
BLAST THAT GIRL AND HER LIGHT FINGERS.
THEY OPENED UP A DOOR IN SPACE, WENT THROUGH, AND VANISHED.
NO. LESS LIKE A JOURNEY INTO RELIGIOUS ECSTASY.
JUST TELL ME, DID THEY FLY RIGHT UP INTO THE AIR...OR WAS THE JOURNEY MORE... HORIZONTAL?
Um--

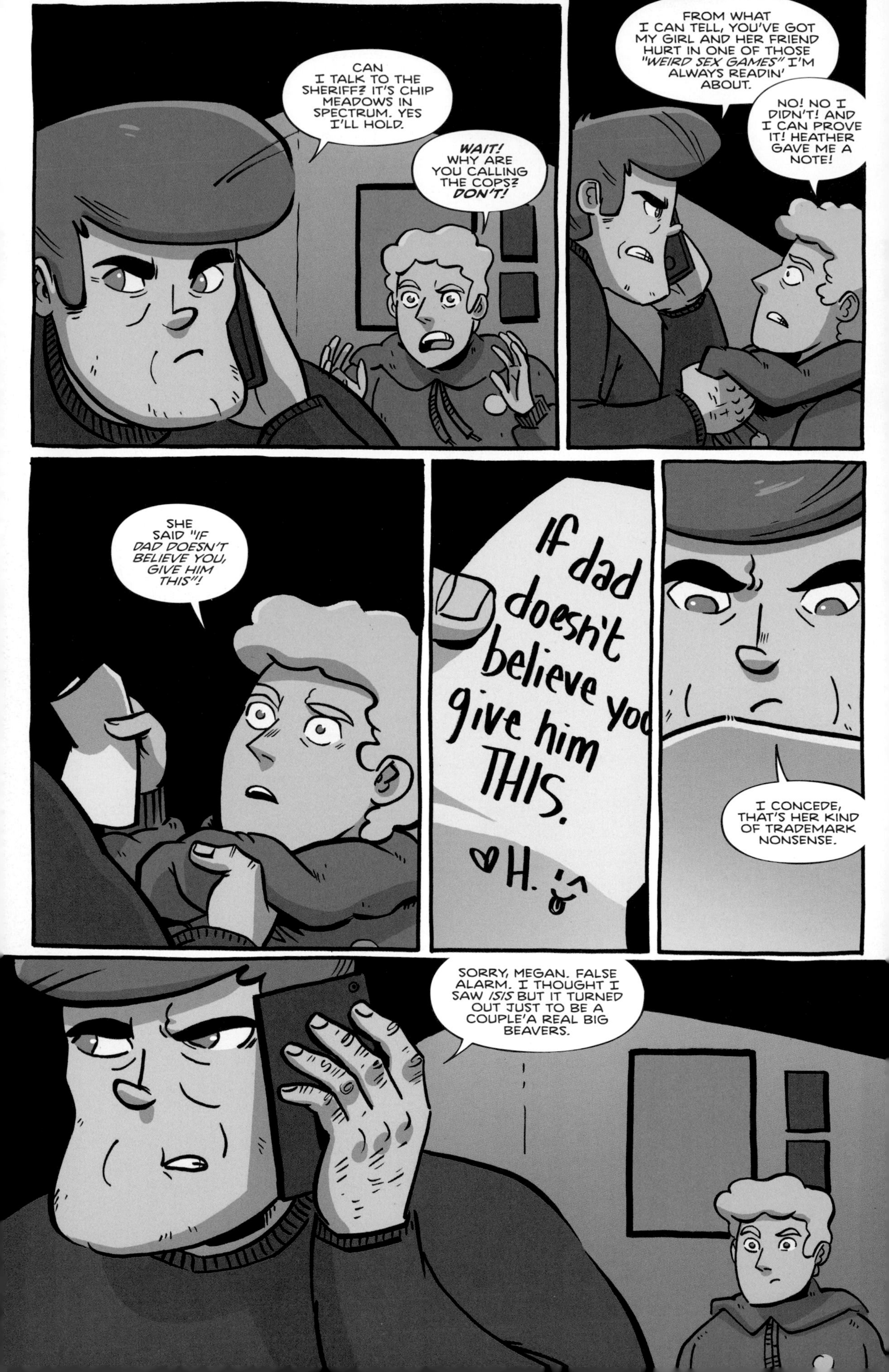
CAN I TALK TO THE SHERIFF? IT'S CHIP MEADOWS IN SPECTRUM. YES I'LL HOLD.
WAIT! WHY ARE YOU CALLING THE COPS? DON'T!
FROM WHAT I CAN TELL, YOU'VE GOT MY GIRL AND HER FRIEND HURT IN ONE OF THOSE "WEIRD SEX GAMES" I'M ALWAYS READIN' ABOUT.
NO! NO I DIDN'T! AND I CAN PROVE IT! HEATHER GAVE ME A NOTE!
SHE SAID "IF DAD DOESN'T BELIEVE YOU, GIVE HIM THIS"!
If dad doesn't believe you give him THIS.
H.
I CONCEDE, THAT'S HER KIND OF TRADEMARK NONSENSE.
SORRY, MEGAN. FALSE ALARM. I THOUGHT I SAW ISIS BUT IT TURNED OUT JUST TO BE A COUPLE'A REAL BIG BEAVERS.

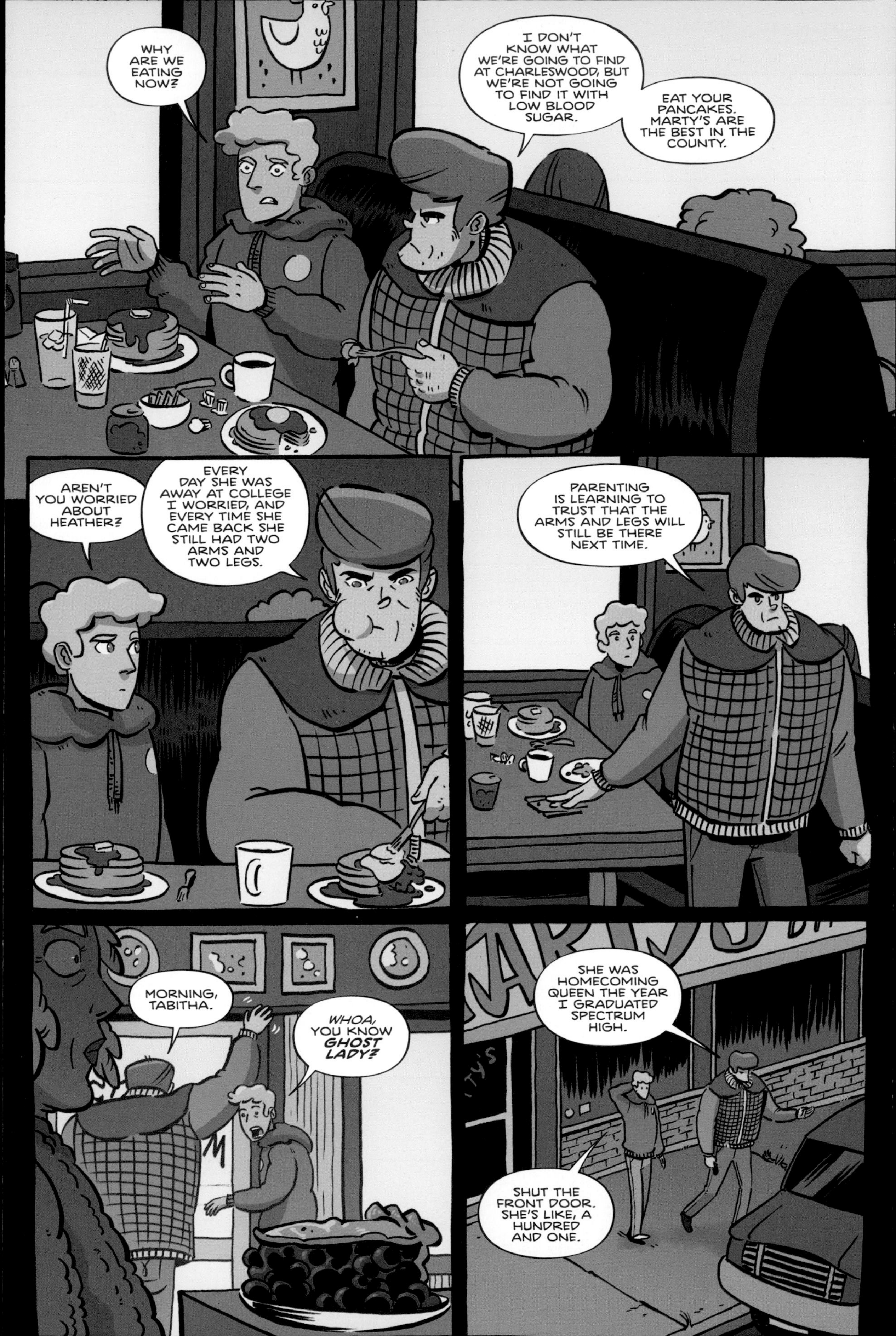
WHY ARE WE EATING NOW?
I DON'T KNOW WHAT WE'RE GOING TO FIND AT CHARLESWOOD, BUT WE'RE NOT GOING TO FIND IT WITH LOW BLOOD SUGAR.
EAT YOUR PANCAKES. MARTY'S ARE THE BEST IN THE COUNTY.
AREN'T YOU WORRIED ABOUT HEATHER?
EVERY DAY SHE WAS AWAY AT COLLEGE I WORRIED, AND EVERY TIME SHE CAME BACK SHE STILL HAD TWO ARMS AND TWO LEGS.
PARENTING IS LEARNING TO TRUST THAT THE ARMS AND LEGS WILL STILL BE THERE NEXT TIME.
MORNING, TABITHA.
WHOA, YOU KNOW ***GHOST LADY?***
SHE WAS HOMECOMING QUEEN THE YEAR I GRADUATED SPECTRUM HIGH.
SHUT THE FRONT DOOR. SHE'S LIKE, A HUNDRED AND ONE.

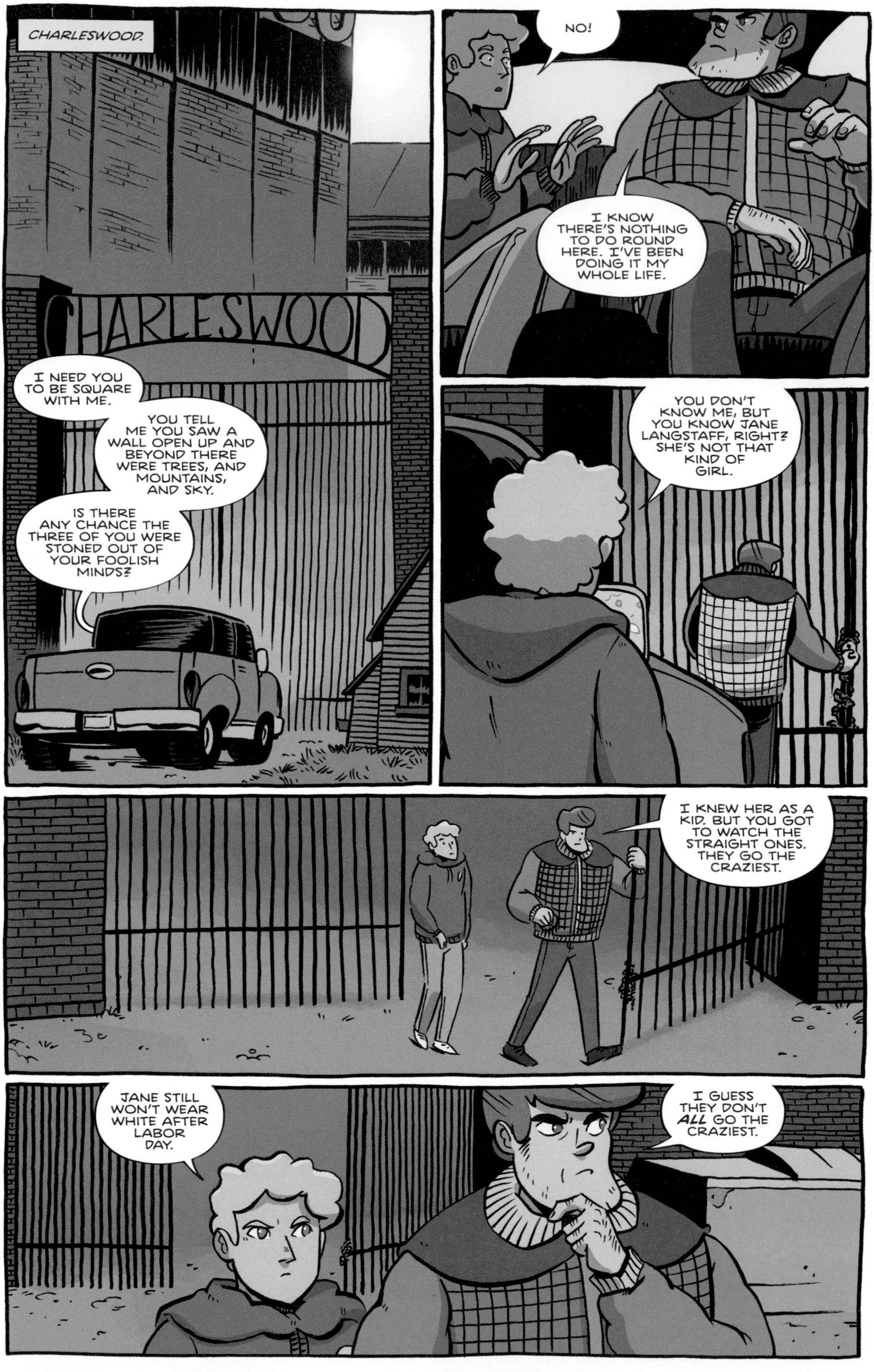
CHARLESWOOD.
CHARLESWOOD
NO!
I KNOW THERE'S NOTHING TO DO ROUND HERE. I'VE BEEN DOING IT MY WHOLE LIFE.
I NEED YOU TO BE SQUARE WITH ME.
YOU TELL ME YOU SAW A WALL OPEN UP AND BEYOND THERE WERE TREES, AND MOUNTAINS, AND SKY.
IS THERE ANY CHANCE THE THREE OF YOU WERE STONED OUT OF YOUR FOOLISH MINDS?
YOU DON'T KNOW ME, BUT YOU KNOW JANE LANGSTAFF, RIGHT? SHE'S NOT THAT KIND OF GIRL.
I KNEW HER AS A KID. BUT YOU GOT TO WATCH THE STRAIGHT ONES. THEY GO THE CRAZIEST.
JANE STILL WON'T WEAR WHITE AFTER LABOR DAY.
I GUESS THEY DON'T ALL GO THE CRAZIEST.

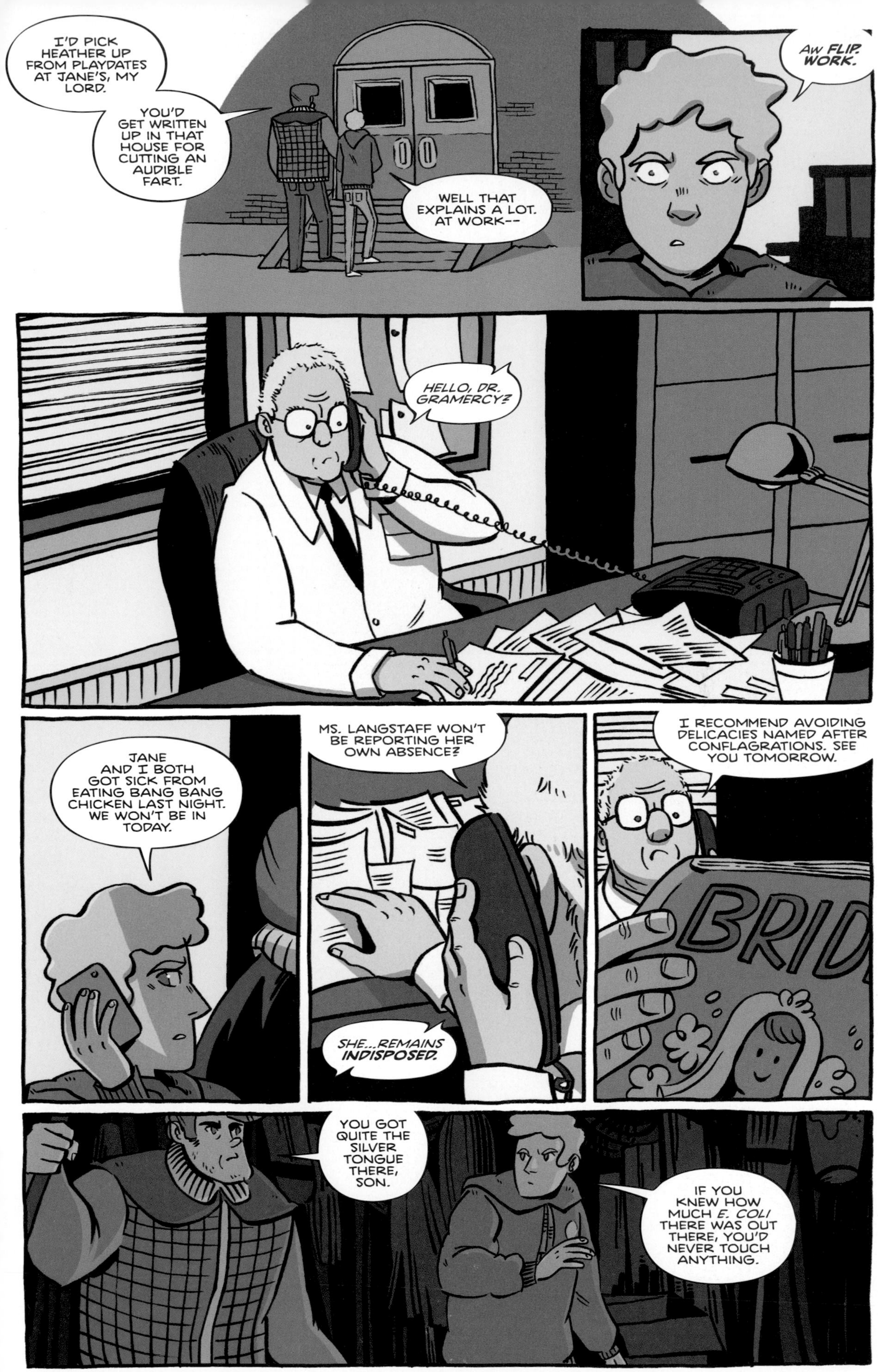
I'D PICK HEATHER UP FROM PLAYDATES AT JANE'S, MY LORD.
YOU'D GET WRITTEN UP IN THAT HOUSE FOR CUTTING AN AUDIBLE FART.
WELL THAT EXPLAINS A LOT. AT WORK--
Aw FLIP. WORK.
HELLO, DR. GRAMERCY?
JANE AND I BOTH GOT SICK FROM EATING BANG BANG CHICKEN LAST NIGHT. WE WON'T BE IN TODAY.
MS. LANGSTAFF WON'T BE REPORTING HER OWN ABSENCE?
SHE...REMAINS INDISPOSED.
I RECOMMEND AVOIDING DELICACIES NAMED AFTER CONFLAGRATIONS. SEE YOU TOMORROW.
BRID
YOU GOT QUITE THE SILVER TONGUE THERE, SON.
IF YOU KNEW HOW MUCH E. COLI THERE WAS OUT THERE, YOU'D NEVER TOUCH ANYTHING.

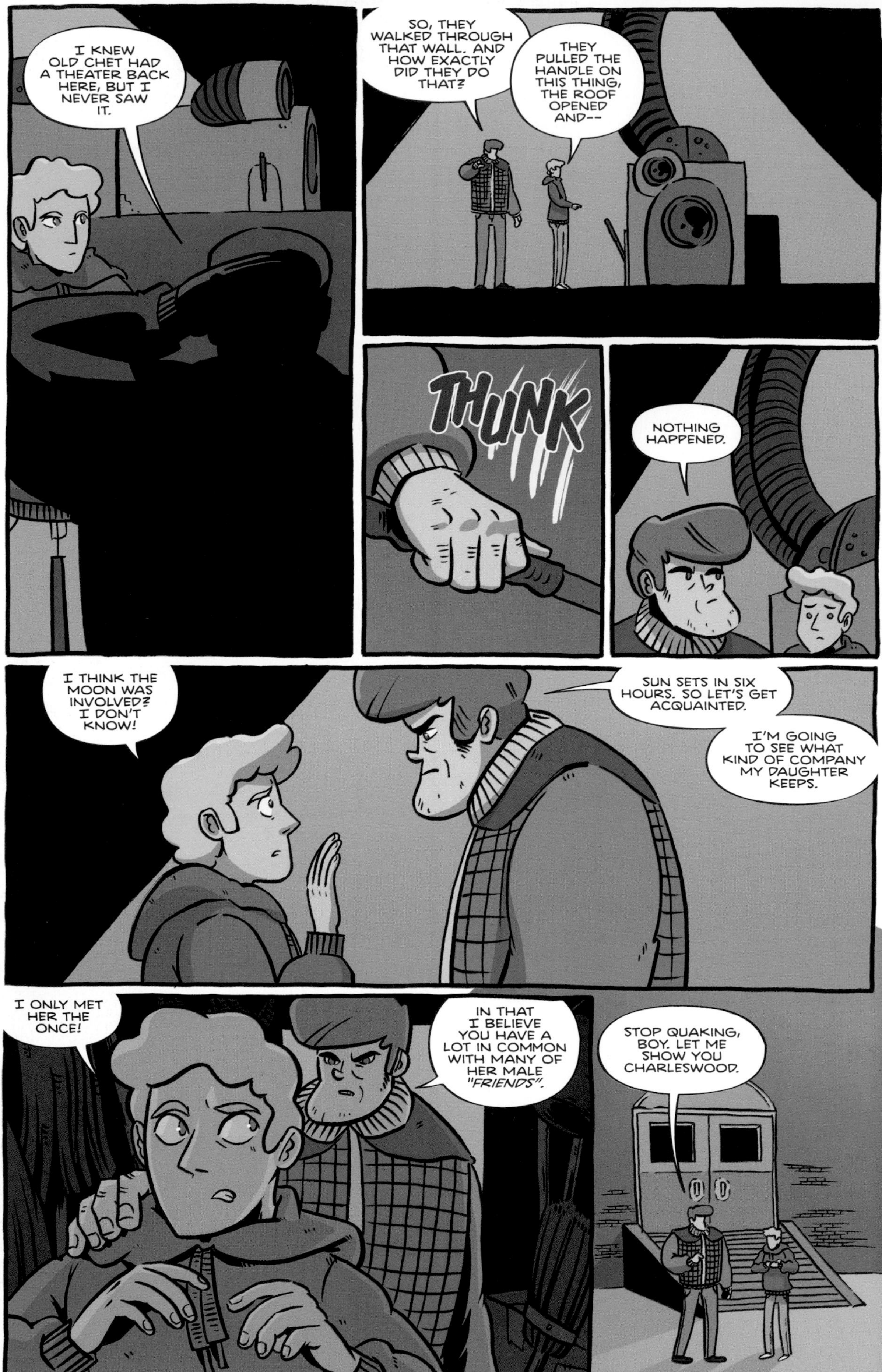
I KNEW OLD CHET HAD A THEATER BACK HERE, BUT I NEVER SAW IT.
SO, THEY WALKED THROUGH THAT WALL. AND HOW EXACTLY DID THEY DO THAT?
THEY PULLED THE HANDLE ON THIS THING, THE ROOF OPENED AND--
THUNK
NOTHING HAPPENED.
I THINK THE MOON WAS INVOLVED? I DON'T KNOW!
SUN SETS IN SIX HOURS. SO LET'S GET ACQUAINTED.
I'M GOING TO SEE WHAT KIND OF COMPANY MY DAUGHTER KEEPS.
I ONLY MET HER THE ONCE!
IN THAT I BELIEVE YOU HAVE A LOT IN COMMON WITH MANY OF HER MALE *"FRIENDS"*.
STOP QUAKING, BOY. LET ME SHOW YOU CHARLESWOOD.

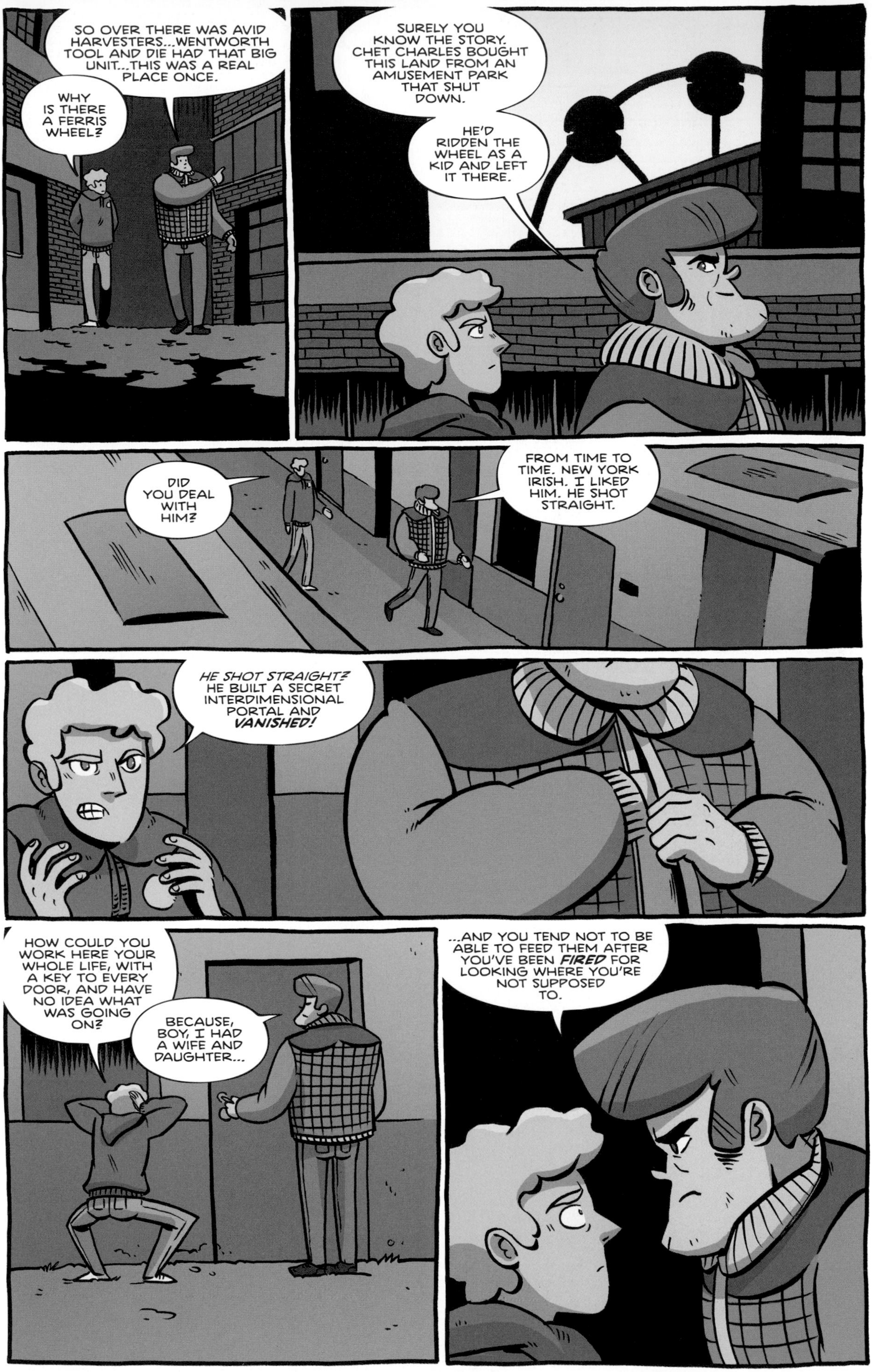
SO OVER THERE WAS AVID HARVESTERS...WENTWORTH TOOL AND DIE HAD THAT BIG UNIT...THIS WAS A REAL PLACE ONCE.
WHY IS THERE A FERRIS WHEEL?
SURELY YOU KNOW THE STORY. CHET CHARLES BOUGHT THIS LAND FROM AN AMUSEMENT PARK THAT SHUT DOWN.
HE'D RIDDEN THE WHEEL AS A KID AND LEFT IT THERE.
DID YOU DEAL WITH HIM?
FROM TIME TO TIME. NEW YORK IRISH. I LIKED HIM. HE SHOT STRAIGHT.
HE SHOT STRAIGHT? HE BUILT A SECRET INTERDIMENSIONAL PORTAL AND ***VANISHED!***
HOW COULD YOU WORK HERE YOUR WHOLE LIFE, WITH A KEY TO EVERY DOOR, AND HAVE NO IDEA WHAT WAS GOING ON?
BECAUSE, BOY, I HAD A WIFE AND DAUGHTER...
...AND YOU TEND NOT TO BE ABLE TO FEED THEM AFTER YOU'VE BEEN ***FIRED*** FOR LOOKING WHERE YOU'RE NOT SUPPOSED TO.

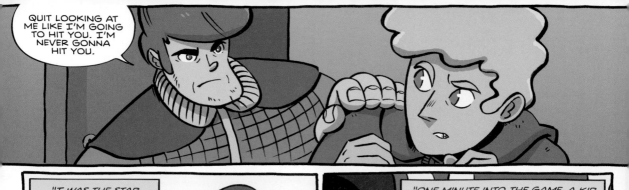

QUIT LOOKING AT ME LIKE I'M GOING TO HIT YOU. I'M NEVER GONNA HIT YOU.

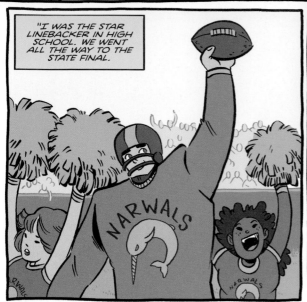

"I WAS THE STAR LINEBACKER IN HIGH SCHOOL. WE WENT ALL THE WAY TO THE STATE FINAL.

"ONE MINUTE INTO THE GAME, A KID KICKED MY KNEE SO HARD THAT MY KNEECAP ENDED UP ON THE BACK OF MY LEG."

SORRY, BRO.

THAT KICK TOOK AWAY COLLEGE, THE NFL, EVERYTHING.

PERFORMANCE ENHANCING DRUGS, BRAIN DAMAGE.

Heh. WELL, THAT TOO.

BUT I LIVED MY LIFE CAREFUL SINCE THEN.

I MARRIED MY GIRL, SETTLED DOWN, WORKED HARD, DIDN'T ROCK THE DAMN BOAT.

DRESSED EXCLUSIVELY IN EARTH TONES.

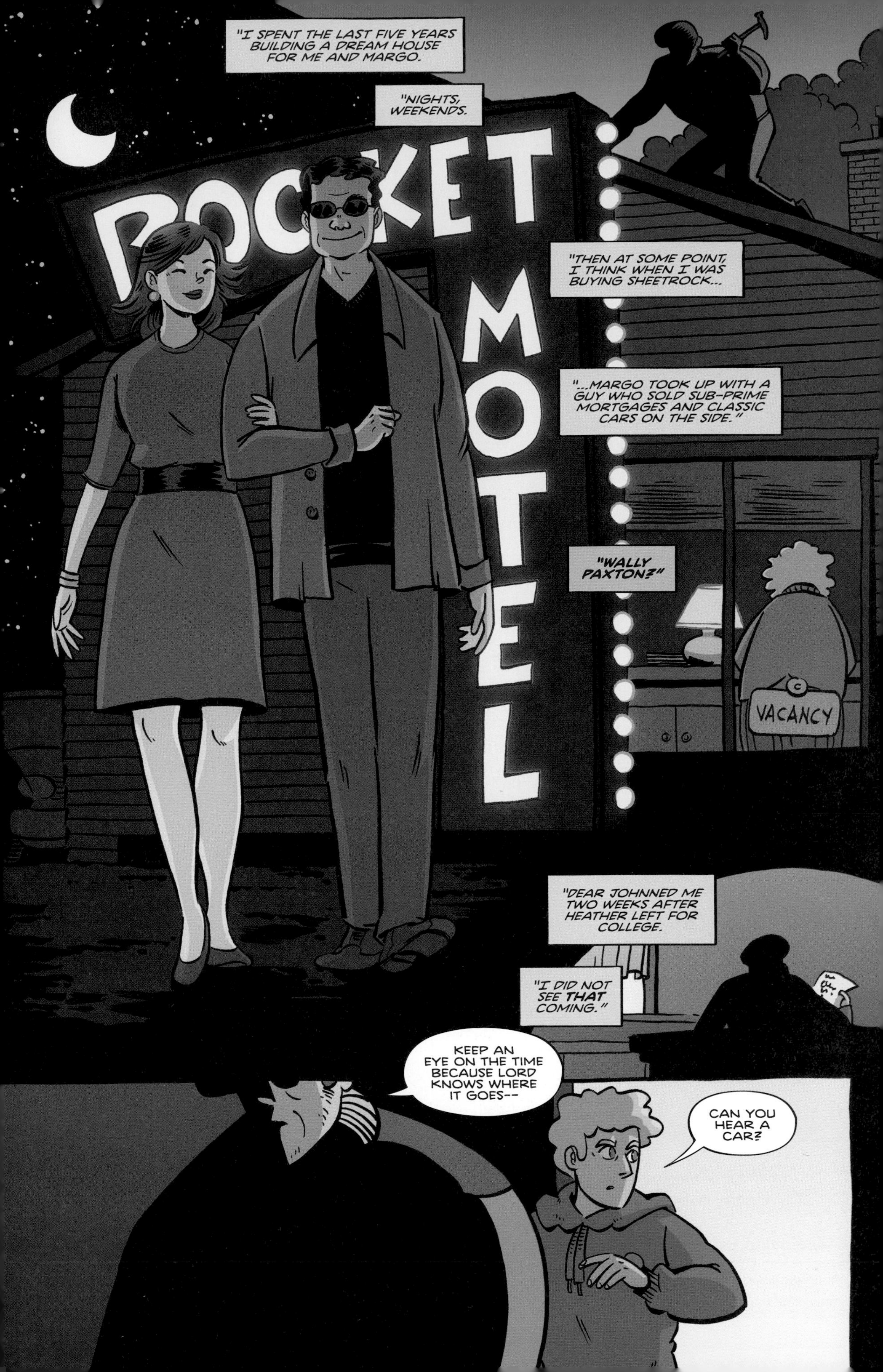
"I SPENT THE LAST FIVE YEARS BUILDING A DREAM HOUSE FOR ME AND MARGO.
"NIGHTS, WEEKENDS.
ROCKET MOTEL
"THEN AT SOME POINT, I THINK WHEN I WAS BUYING SHEETROCK...
"...MARGO TOOK UP WITH A GUY WHO SOLD SUB-PRIME MORTGAGES AND CLASSIC CARS ON THE SIDE."
"WALLY PAXTON?"
VACANCY
"DEAR JOHNNED ME TWO WEEKS AFTER HEATHER LEFT FOR COLLEGE.
"I DID NOT SEE THAT COMING."
KEEP AN EYE ON THE TIME BECAUSE LORD KNOWS WHERE IT GOES--
CAN YOU HEAR A CAR?

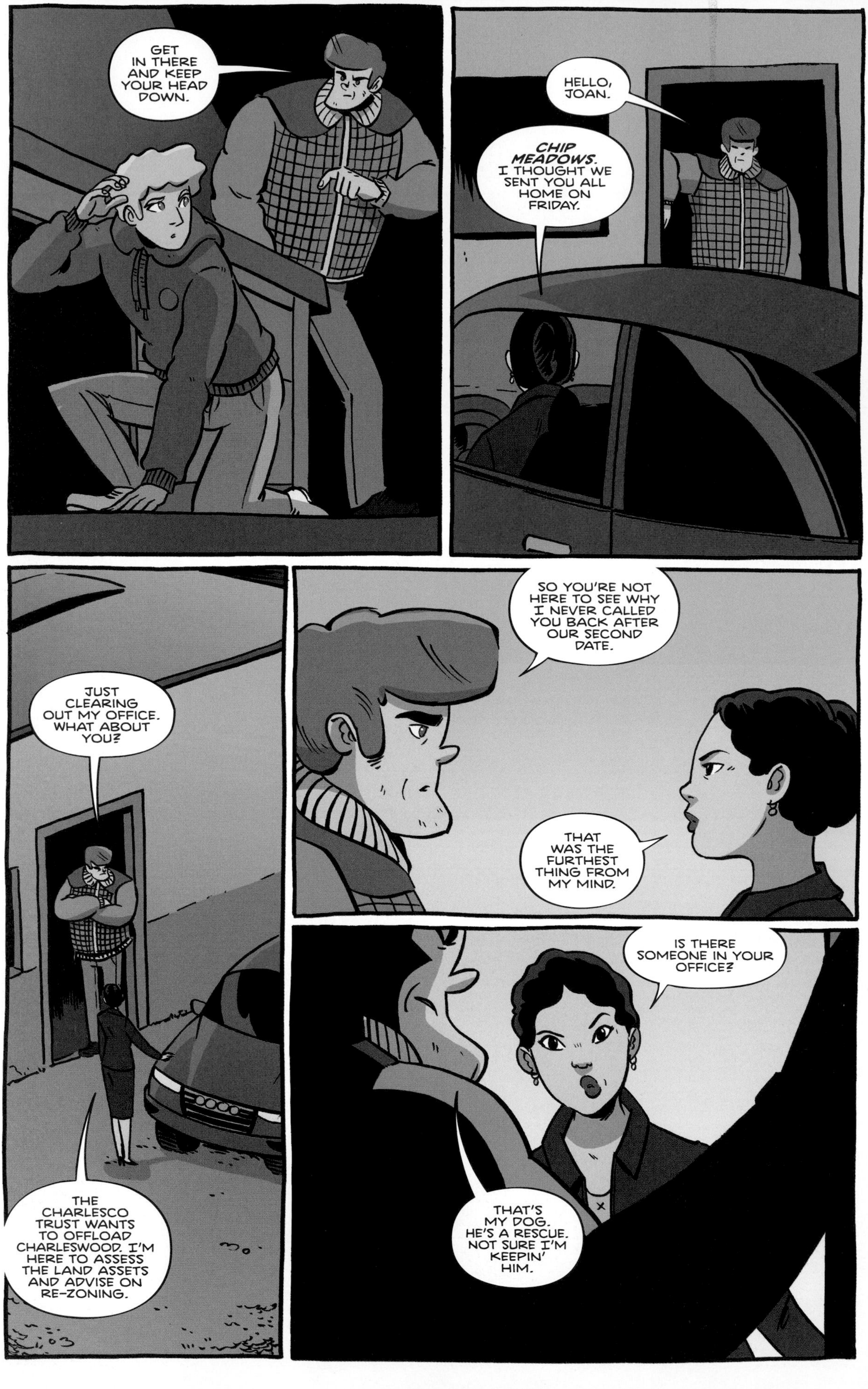
GET IN THERE AND KEEP YOUR HEAD DOWN.
HELLO, JOAN.
CHIP MEADOWS. I THOUGHT WE SENT YOU ALL HOME ON FRIDAY.
JUST CLEARING OUT MY OFFICE. WHAT ABOUT YOU?
THE CHARLESCO TRUST WANTS TO OFFLOAD CHARLESWOOD. I'M HERE TO ASSESS THE LAND ASSETS AND ADVISE ON RE-ZONING.
SO YOU'RE NOT HERE TO SEE WHY I NEVER CALLED YOU BACK AFTER OUR SECOND DATE.
THAT WAS THE FURTHEST THING FROM MY MIND.
IS THERE SOMEONE IN YOUR OFFICE?
THAT'S MY DOG. HE'S A RESCUE. NOT SURE I'M KEEPIN' HIM.

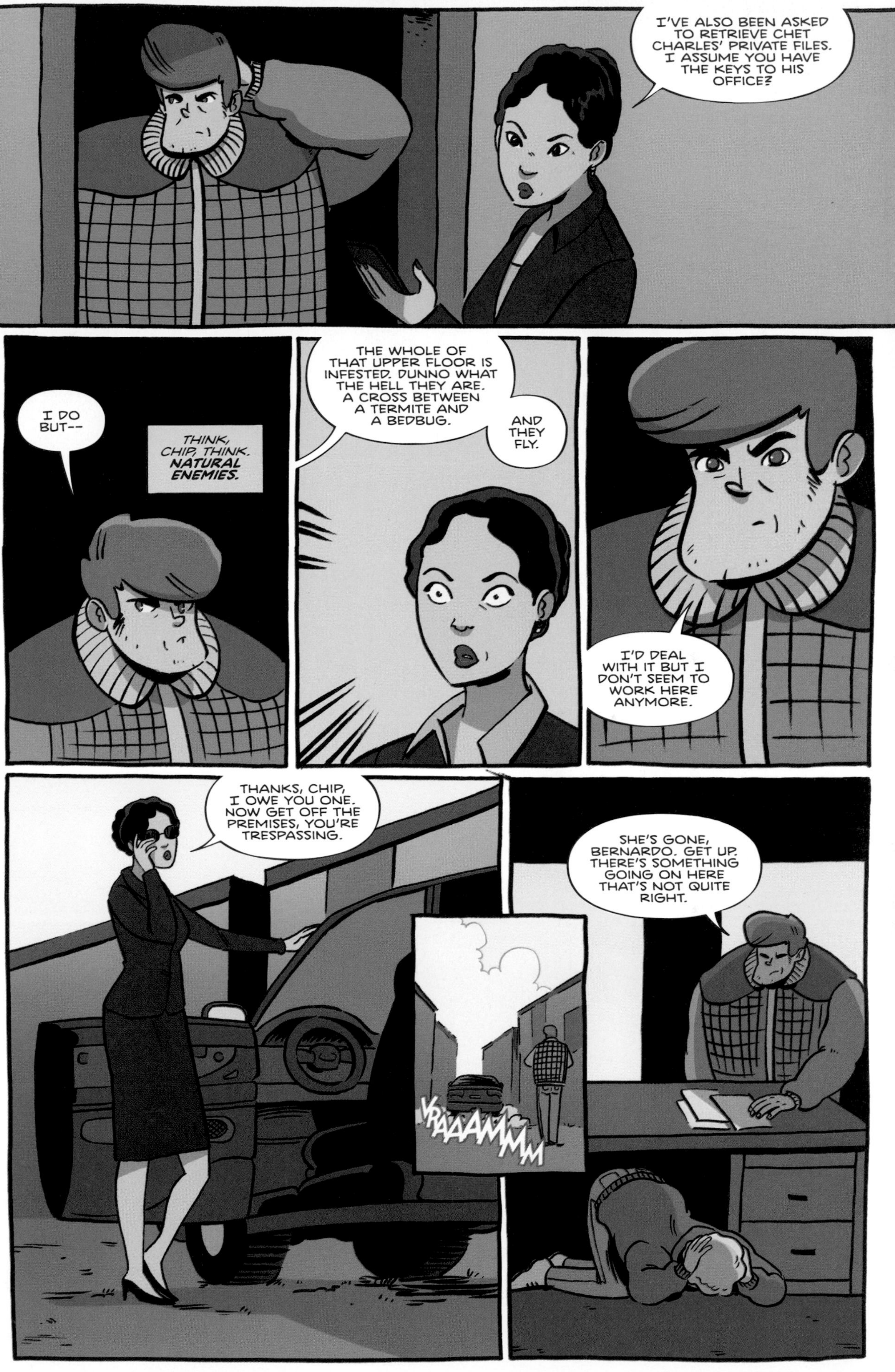
I'VE ALSO BEEN ASKED TO RETRIEVE CHET CHARLES' PRIVATE FILES. I ASSUME YOU HAVE THE KEYS TO HIS OFFICE?
I DO BUT--
THINK, CHIP, THINK. NATURAL ENEMIES.
THE WHOLE OF THAT UPPER FLOOR IS INFESTED. DUNNO WHAT THE HELL THEY ARE. A CROSS BETWEEN A TERMITE AND A BEDBUG.
AND THEY FLY.
I'D DEAL WITH IT BUT I DON'T SEEM TO WORK HERE ANYMORE.
THANKS, CHIP, I OWE YOU ONE. NOW GET OFF THE PREMISES, YOU'RE TRESPASSING.
VRAAAMMM
SHE'S GONE, BERNARDO. GET UP. THERE'S SOMETHING GOING ON HERE THAT'S NOT QUITE RIGHT.

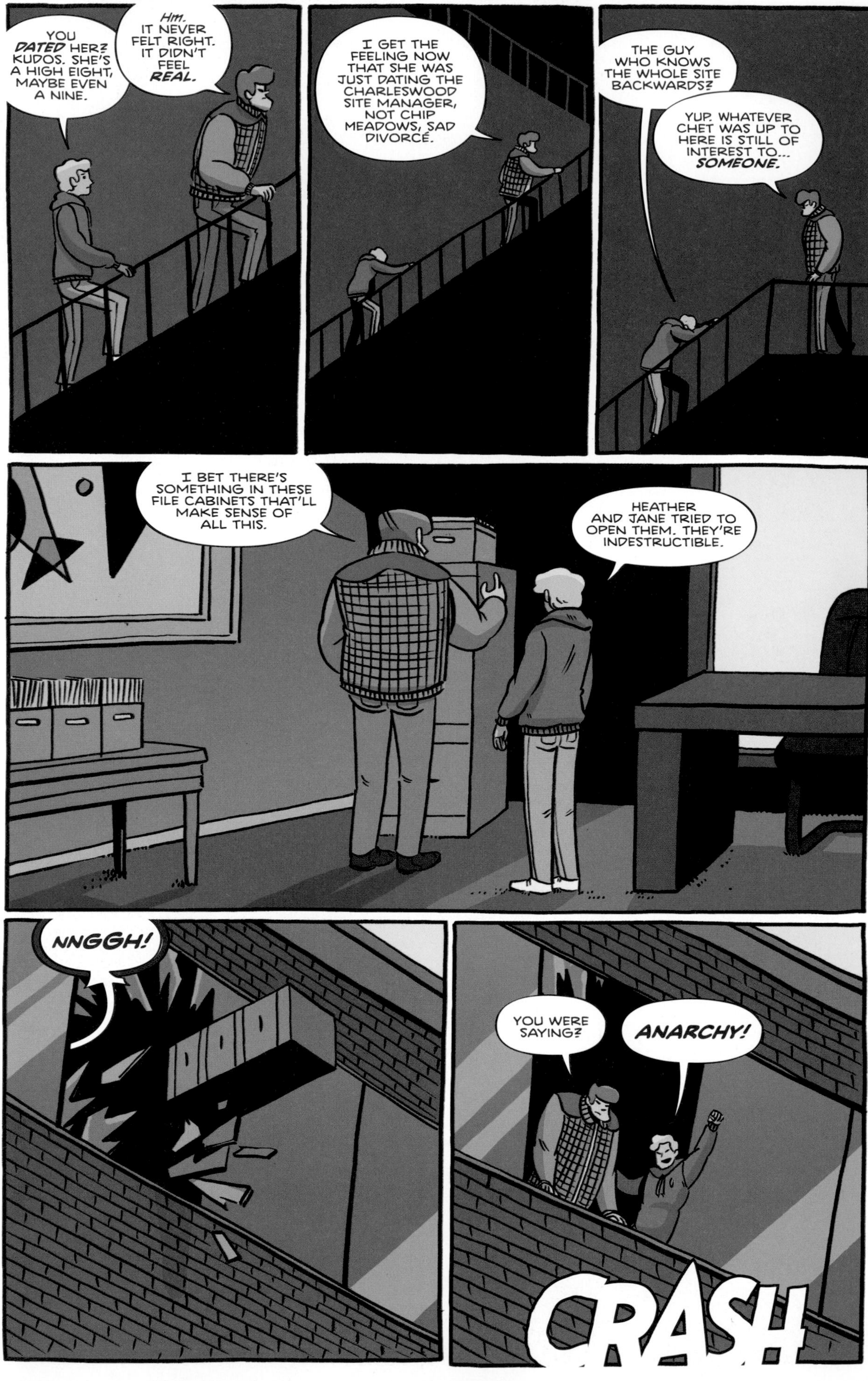

YOU *DATED* HER? KUDOS. SHE'S A HIGH EIGHT, MAYBE EVEN A NINE.
HM. IT NEVER FELT RIGHT. IT DIDN'T FEEL ***REAL.***
I GET THE FEELING NOW THAT SHE WAS JUST DATING THE CHARLESWOOD SITE MANAGER, NOT CHIP MEADOWS, SAD DIVORCÉ.
THE GUY WHO KNOWS THE WHOLE SITE BACKWARDS?
YUP. WHATEVER CHET WAS UP TO HERE IS STILL OF INTEREST TO... ***SOMEONE.***
I BET THERE'S SOMETHING IN THESE FILE CABINETS THAT'LL MAKE SENSE OF ALL THIS.
HEATHER AND JANE TRIED TO OPEN THEM. THEY'RE INDESTRUCTIBLE.
NNGGH!
YOU WERE SAYING?
ANARCHY!
CRASH

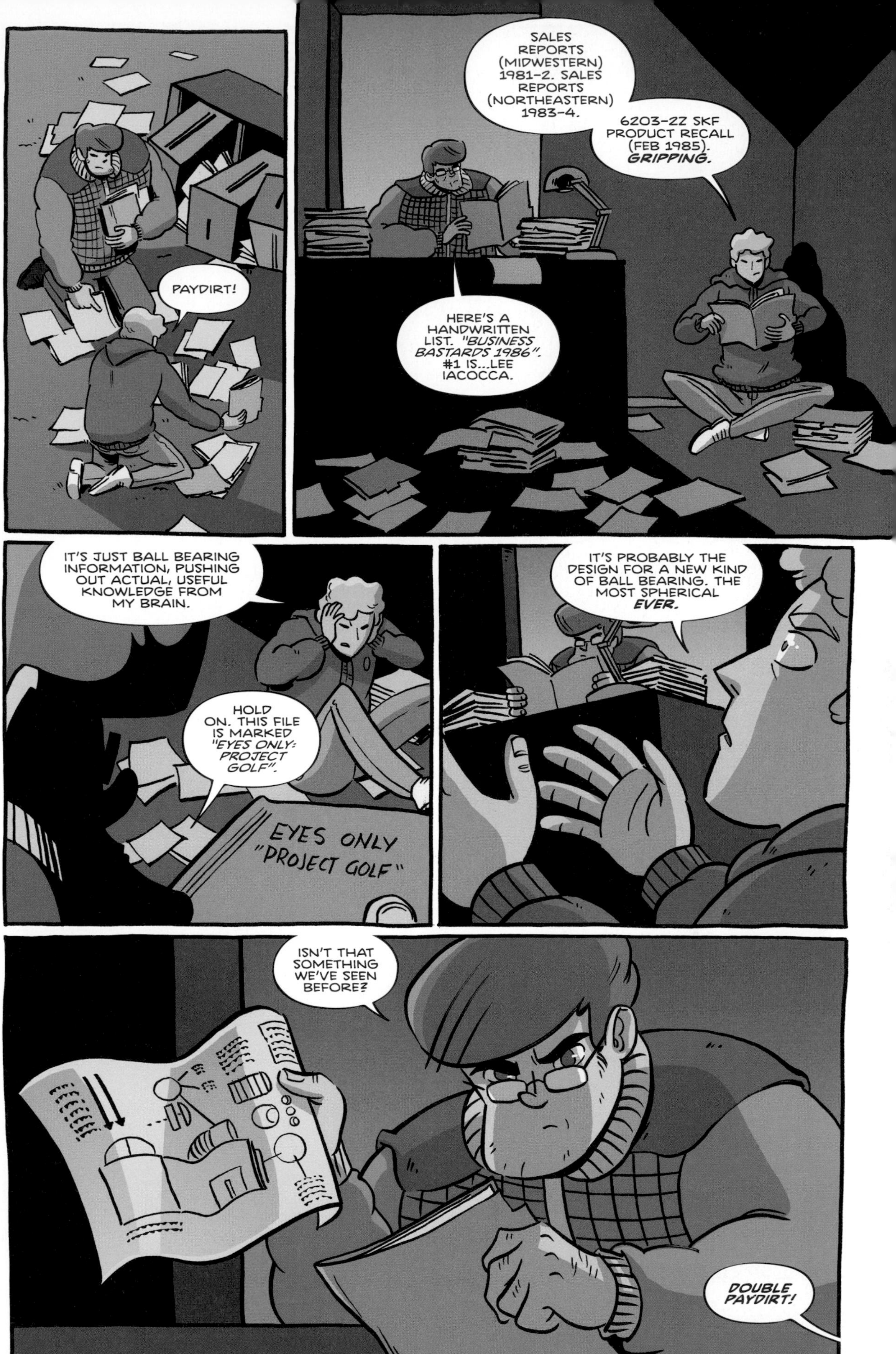
PAYDIRT!
SALES REPORTS (MIDWESTERN) 1981-2. SALES REPORTS (NORTHEASTERN) 1983-4.
6203-2Z SKF PRODUCT RECALL (FEB 1985). GRIPPING.
HERE'S A HANDWRITTEN LIST. "BUSINESS BASTARDS 1986". #1 IS...LEE IACOCCA.
IT'S JUST BALL BEARING INFORMATION, PUSHING OUT ACTUAL, USEFUL KNOWLEDGE FROM MY BRAIN.
HOLD ON. THIS FILE IS MARKED "EYES ONLY: PROJECT GOLF".
EYES ONLY "PROJECT GOLF"
IT'S PROBABLY THE DESIGN FOR A NEW KIND OF BALL BEARING. THE MOST SPHERICAL EVER.
ISN'T THAT SOMETHING WE'VE SEEN BEFORE?
DOUBLE PAYDIRT!

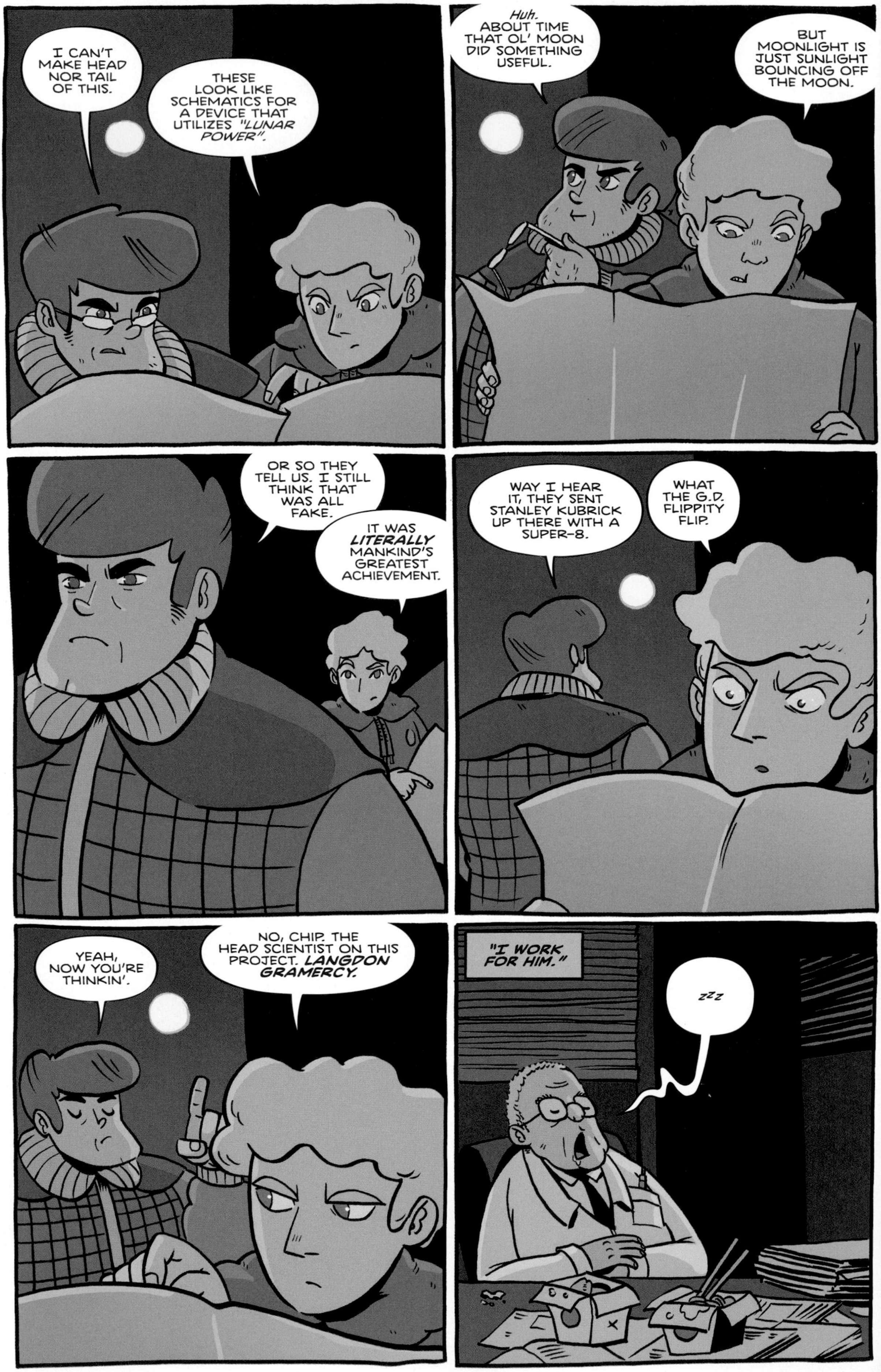
I CAN'T MAKE HEAD NOR TAIL OF THIS.
THESE LOOK LIKE SCHEMATICS FOR A DEVICE THAT UTILIZES *"LUNAR POWER"*.
Huh. ABOUT TIME THAT OL' MOON DID SOMETHING USEFUL.
BUT MOONLIGHT IS JUST SUNLIGHT BOUNCING OFF THE MOON.
OR SO THEY TELL US. I STILL THINK THAT WAS ALL FAKE.
IT WAS ***LITERALLY*** MANKIND'S GREATEST ACHIEVEMENT.
WAY I HEAR IT, THEY SENT STANLEY KUBRICK UP THERE WITH A SUPER-8.
WHAT THE G.D. FLIPPITY FLIP.
YEAH, NOW YOU'RE THINKIN'.
NO, CHIP. THE HEAD SCIENTIST ON THIS PROJECT. ***LANGDON GRAMERCY.***
"I WORK FOR HIM."
zzz

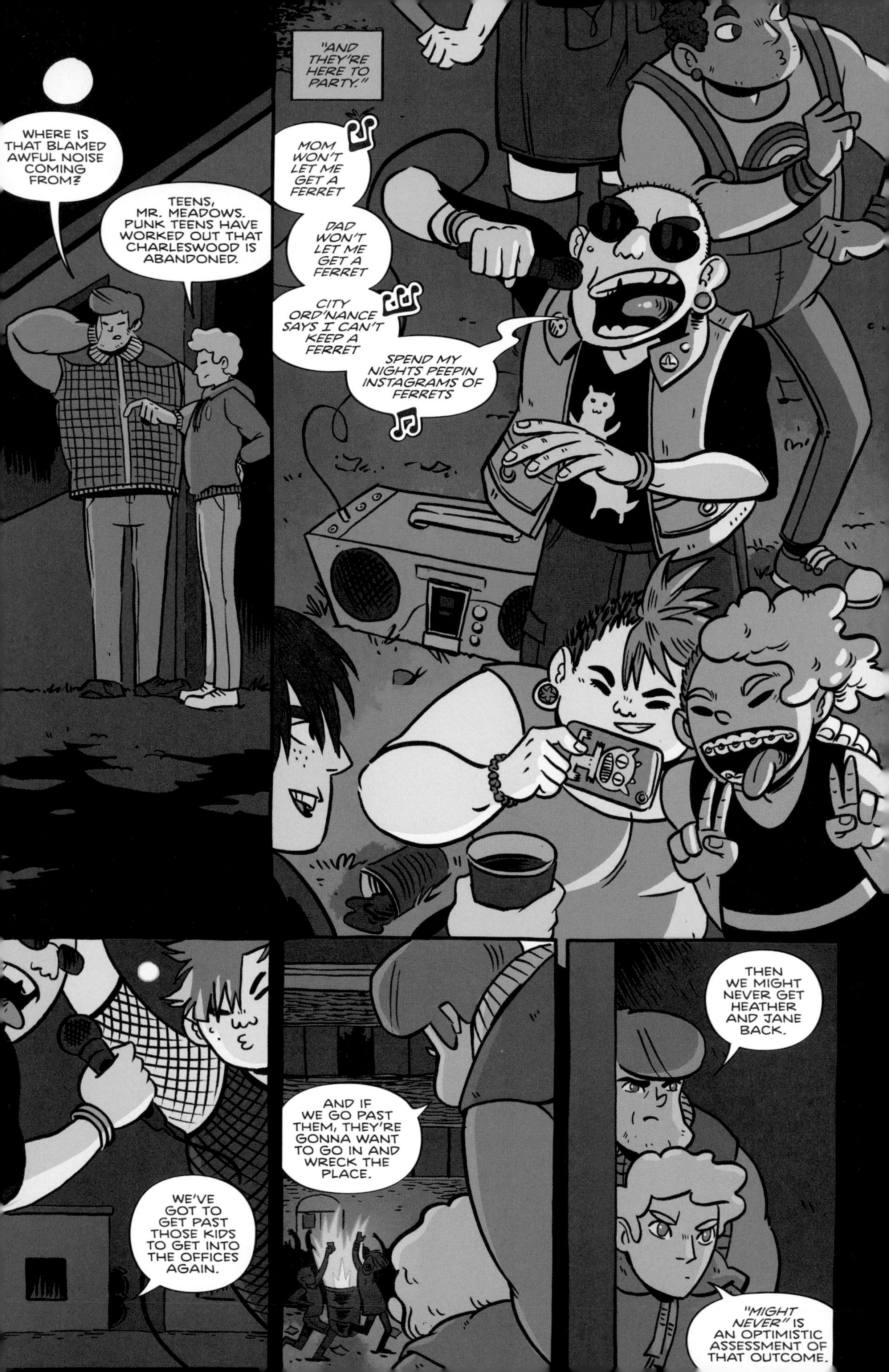
WHERE IS THAT BLAMED AWFUL NOISE COMING FROM?
TEENS, MR. MEADOWS. PUNK TEENS HAVE WORKED OUT THAT CHARLESWOOD IS ABANDONED.
"AND THEY'RE HERE TO PARTY."
MOM WON'T LET ME GET A FERRET
DAD WON'T LET ME GET A FERRET
CITY ORD'NANCE SAYS I CAN'T KEEP A FERRET
SPEND MY NIGHTS PEEPIN INSTAGRAMS OF FERRETS
WE'VE GOT TO GET PAST THOSE KIDS TO GET INTO THE OFFICES AGAIN.
AND IF WE GO PAST THEM, THEY'RE GONNA WANT TO GO IN AND WRECK THE PLACE.
THEN WE MIGHT NEVER GET HEATHER AND JANE BACK.
"MIGHT NEVER" IS AN OPTIMISTIC ASSESSMENT OF THAT OUTCOME.

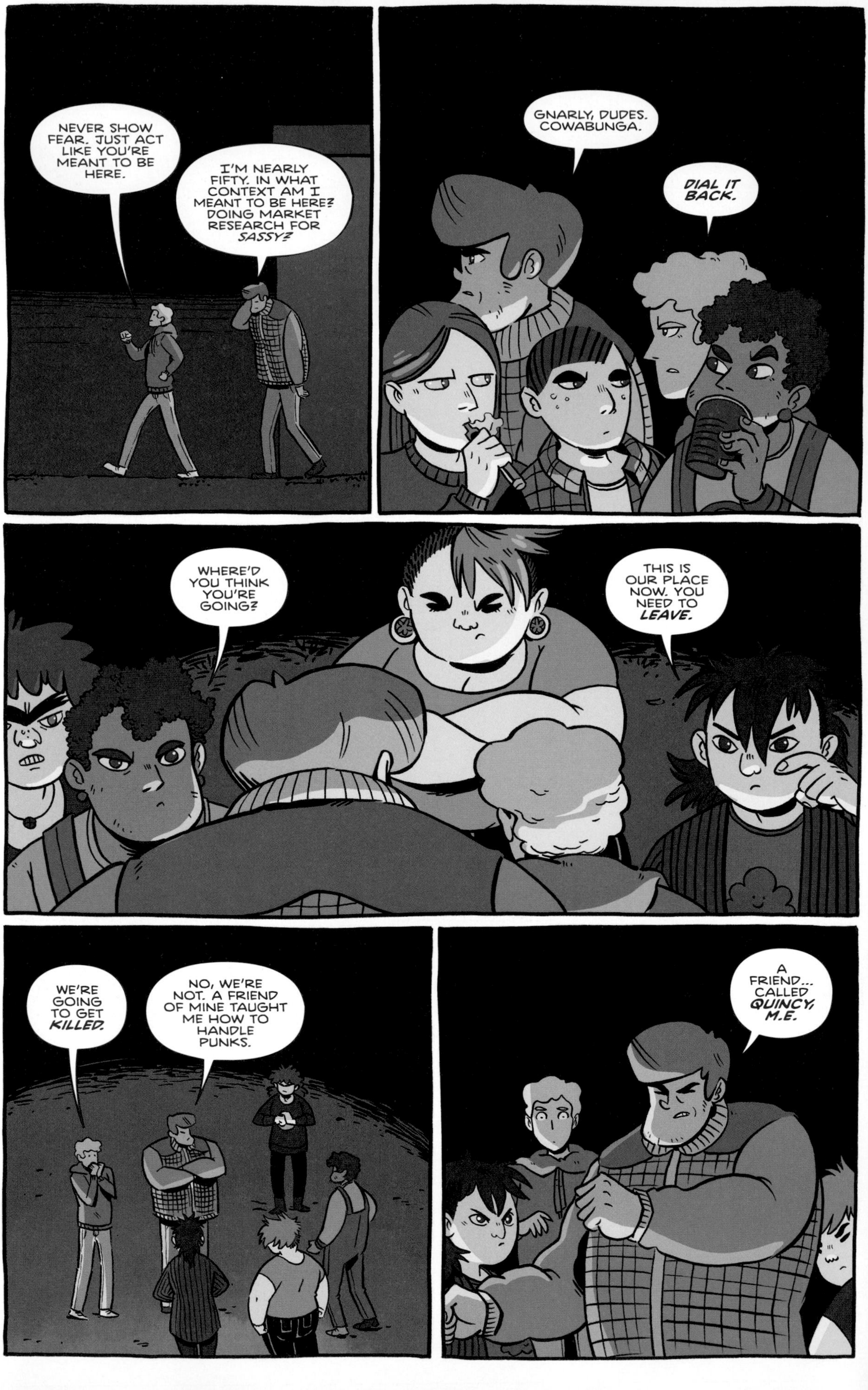
NEVER SHOW FEAR. JUST ACT LIKE YOU'RE MEANT TO BE HERE.
I'M NEARLY FIFTY. IN WHAT CONTEXT AM I MEANT TO BE HERE? DOING MARKET RESEARCH FOR SASSY?
GNARLY, DUDES. COWABUNGA.
DIAL IT BACK.
WHERE'D YOU THINK YOU'RE GOING?
THIS IS OUR PLACE NOW. YOU NEED TO LEAVE.
WE'RE GOING TO GET KILLED.
NO, WE'RE NOT. A FRIEND OF MINE TAUGHT ME HOW TO HANDLE PUNKS.
A FRIEND... CALLED QUINCY, M.E.

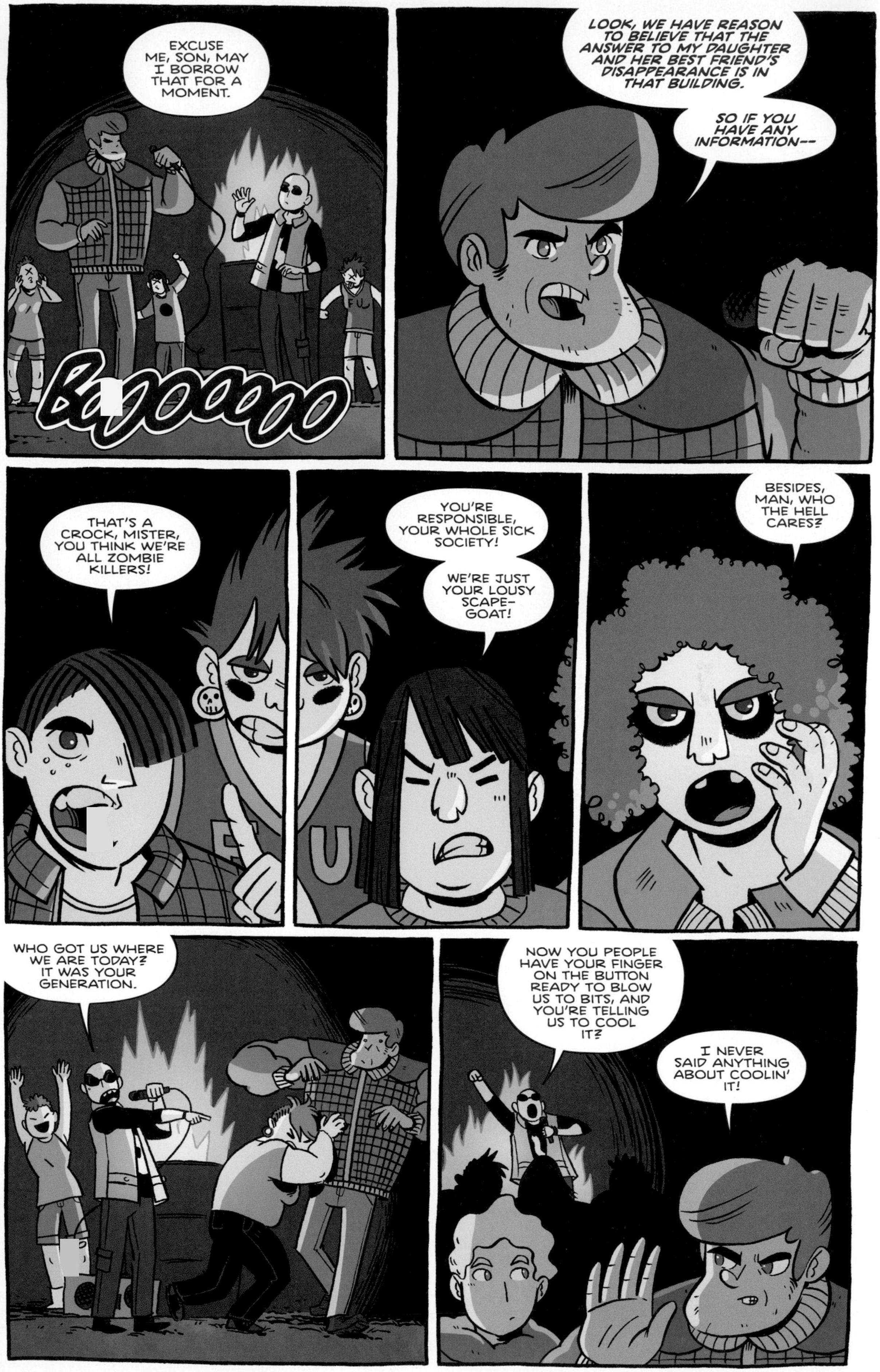
EXCUSE ME, SON, MAY I BORROW THAT FOR A MOMENT.
LOOK, WE HAVE REASON TO BELIEVE THAT THE ANSWER TO MY DAUGHTER AND HER BEST FRIEND'S DISAPPEARANCE IS IN THAT BUILDING.
SO IF YOU HAVE ANY INFORMATION--
THAT'S A CROCK, MISTER, YOU THINK WE'RE ALL ZOMBIE KILLERS!
YOU'RE RESPONSIBLE, YOUR WHOLE SICK SOCIETY!
WE'RE JUST YOUR LOUSY SCAPE-GOAT!
BESIDES, MAN, WHO THE HELL CARES?
WHO GOT US WHERE WE ARE TODAY? IT WAS YOUR GENERATION.
NOW YOU PEOPLE HAVE YOUR FINGER ON THE BUTTON READY TO BLOW US TO BITS, AND YOU'RE TELLING US TO COOL IT?
I NEVER SAID ANYTHING ABOUT COOLIN' IT!

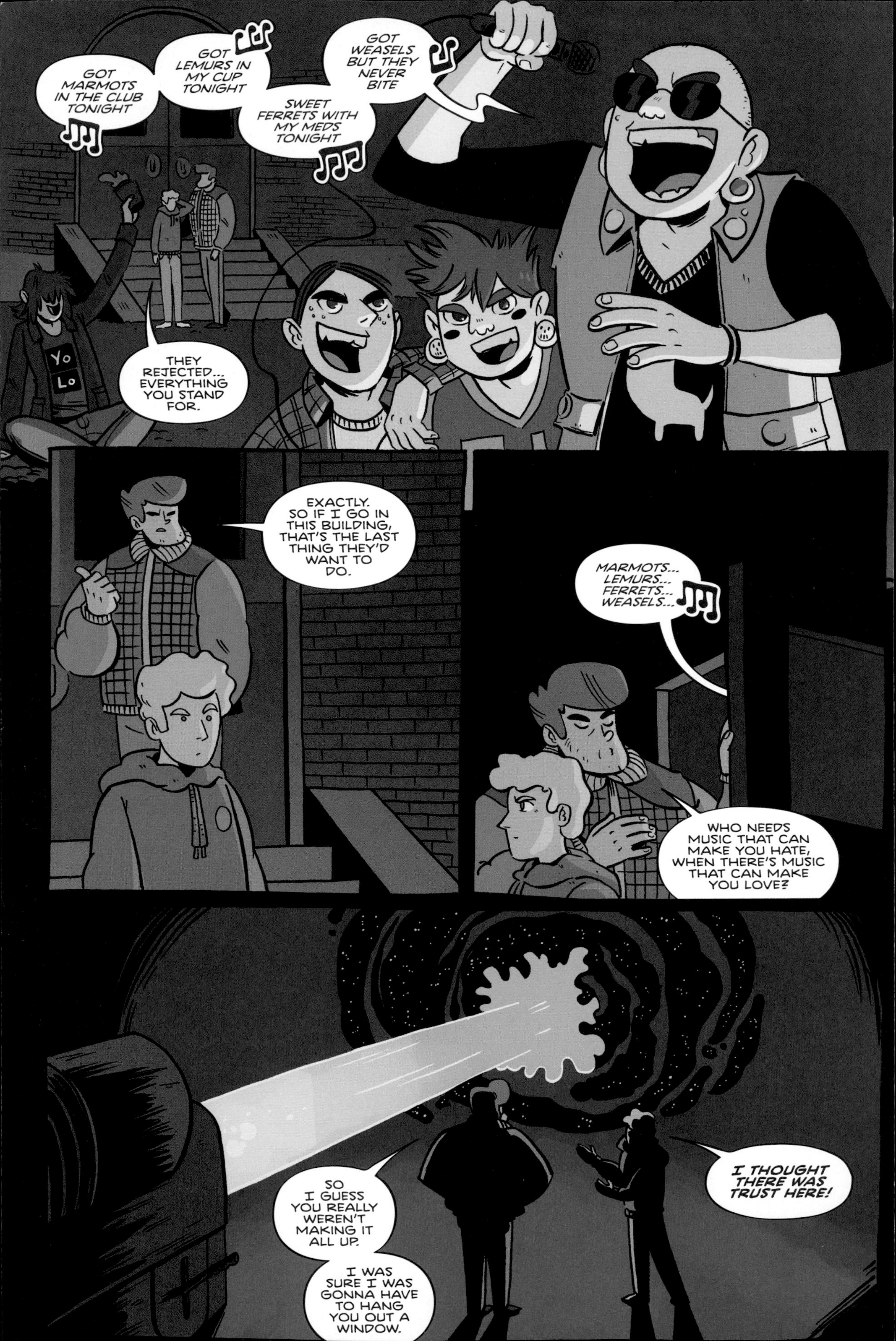

GOT MARMOTS IN THE CLUB TONIGHT
GOT LEMURS IN MY CUP TONIGHT
SWEET FERRETS WITH MY MEDS TONIGHT
GOT WEASELS BUT THEY NEVER BITE
Yo Lo
THEY REJECTED... EVERYTHING YOU STAND FOR.
EXACTLY. SO IF I GO IN THIS BUILDING, THAT'S THE LAST THING THEY'D WANT TO DO.
MARMOTS... LEMURS... FERRETS... WEASELS...
WHO NEEDS MUSIC THAT CAN MAKE YOU HATE, WHEN THERE'S MUSIC THAT CAN MAKE YOU LOVE?
I THOUGHT THERE WAS TRUST HERE!
SO I GUESS YOU REALLY WEREN'T MAKING IT ALL UP.
I WAS SURE I WAS GONNA HAVE TO HANG YOU OUT A WINDOW.

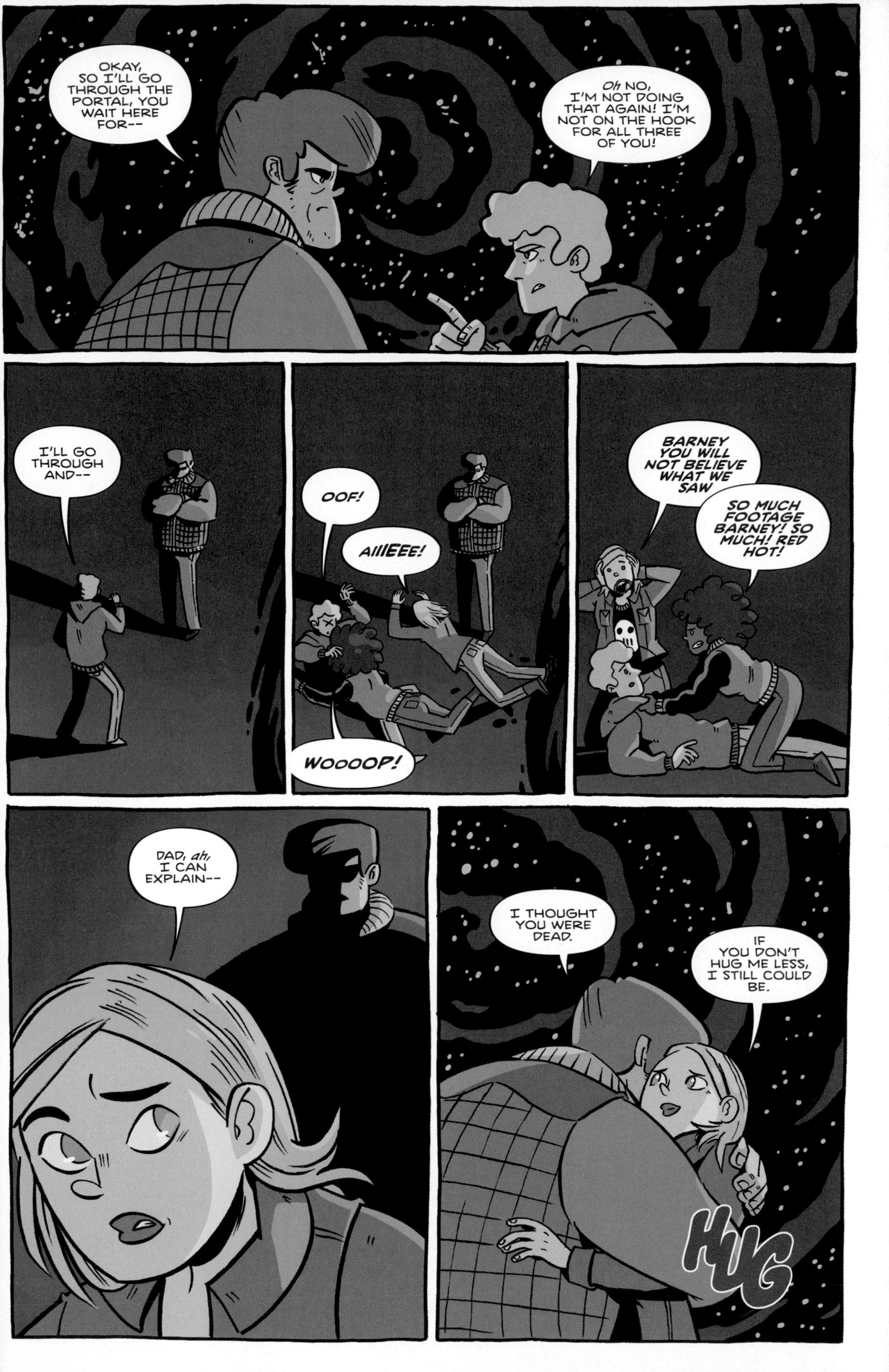
OKAY, SO I'LL GO THROUGH THE PORTAL, YOU WAIT HERE FOR--
Oh NO, I'M NOT DOING THAT AGAIN! I'M NOT ON THE HOOK FOR ALL THREE OF YOU!
I'LL GO THROUGH AND--
OOF!
AIIIEEE!
WOOOOP!
BARNEY YOU WILL NOT BELIEVE WHAT WE SAW
SO MUCH FOOTAGE BARNEY! SO MUCH! RED HOT!
DAD, *ah,* I CAN EXPLAIN--
I THOUGHT YOU WERE DEAD.
IF YOU DON'T HUG ME LESS, I STILL COULD BE.
HUG

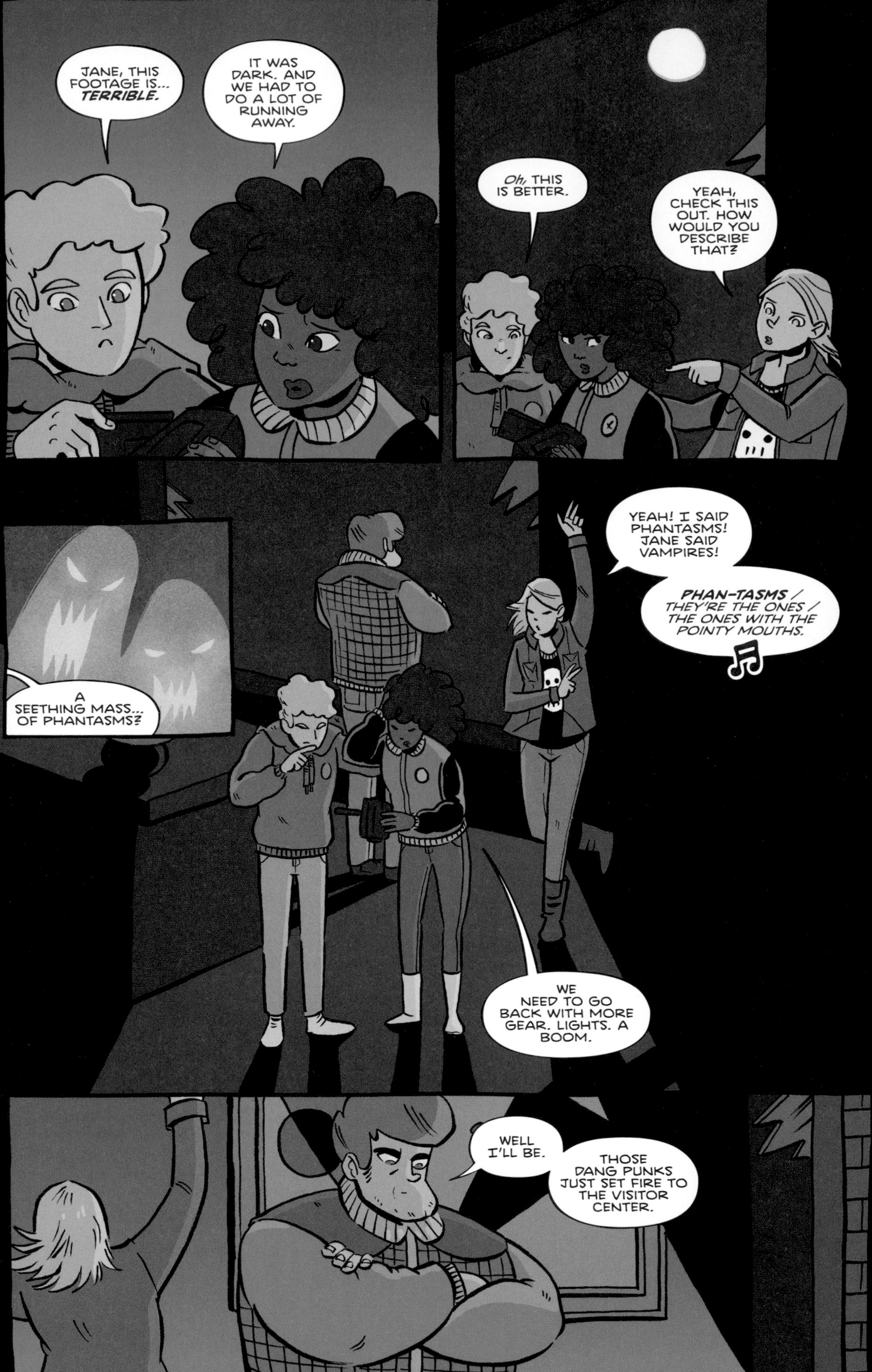
JANE, THIS FOOTAGE IS... *TERRIBLE.*
IT WAS DARK. AND WE HAD TO DO A LOT OF RUNNING AWAY.
Oh, THIS IS BETTER.
YEAH, CHECK THIS OUT. HOW WOULD YOU DESCRIBE THAT?
A SEETHING MASS... OF PHANTASMS?
YEAH! I SAID PHANTASMS! JANE SAID VAMPIRES!
PHAN-TASMS */ THEY'RE THE ONES / THE ONES WITH THE POINTY MOUTHS.*
WE NEED TO GO BACK WITH MORE GEAR. LIGHTS. A BOOM.
WELL I'LL BE.
THOSE DANG PUNKS JUST SET FIRE TO THE VISITOR CENTER.

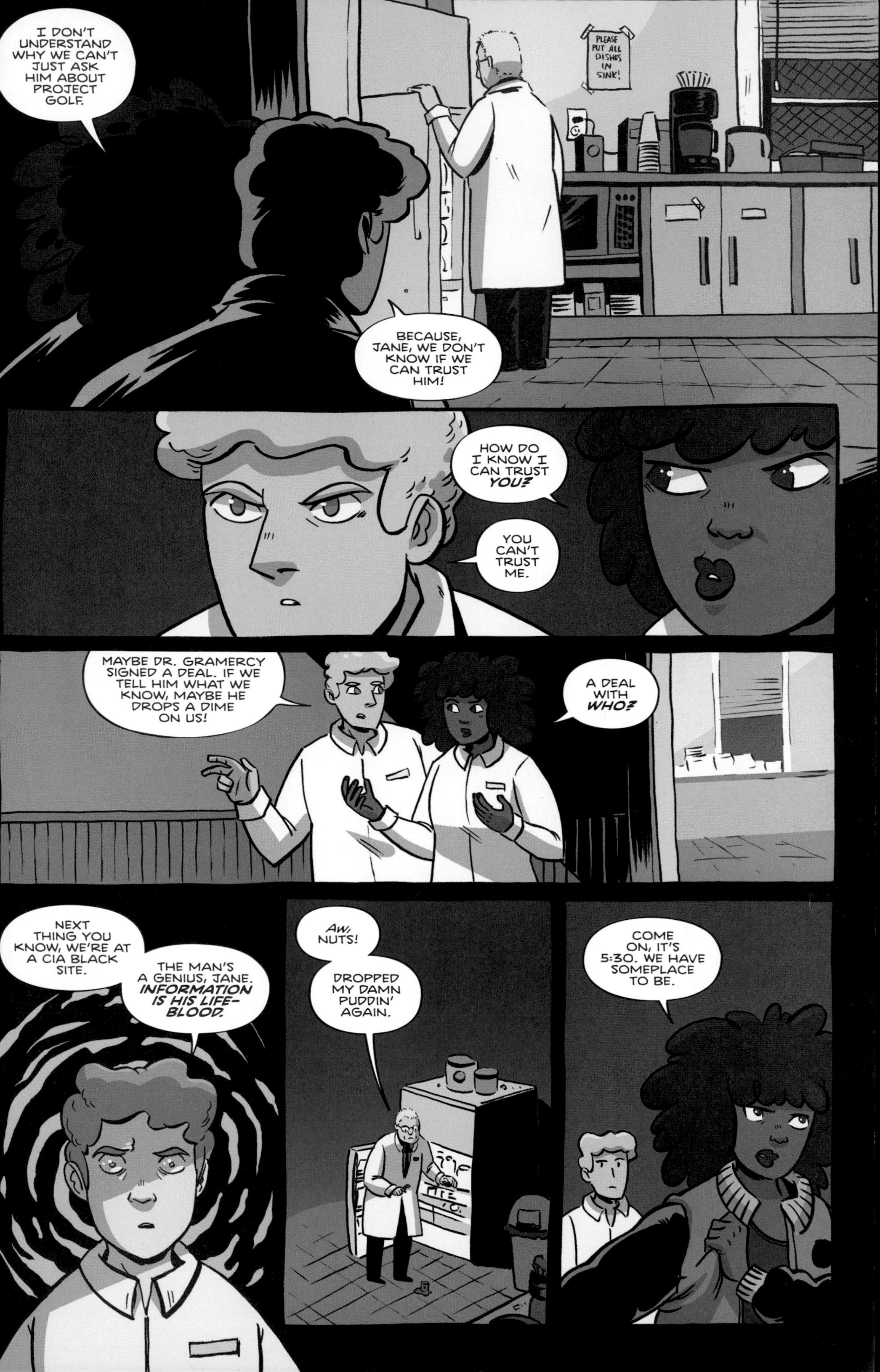
I DON'T UNDERSTAND WHY WE CAN'T JUST ASK HIM ABOUT PROJECT GOLF.
PLEASE PUT ALL DISHES IN SINK!
BECAUSE, JANE, WE DON'T KNOW IF WE CAN TRUST HIM!
HOW DO I KNOW I CAN TRUST *YOU?*
YOU CAN'T TRUST ME.
MAYBE DR. GRAMERCY SIGNED A DEAL. IF WE TELL HIM WHAT WE KNOW, MAYBE HE DROPS A DIME ON US!
A DEAL WITH *WHO?*
NEXT THING YOU KNOW, WE'RE AT A CIA BLACK SITE.
THE MAN'S A GENIUS, JANE. *INFORMATION IS HIS LIFE-BLOOD.*
AW, NUTS!
DROPPED MY DAMN PUDDIN' AGAIN.
COME ON, IT'S 5:30. WE HAVE SOMEPLACE TO BE.

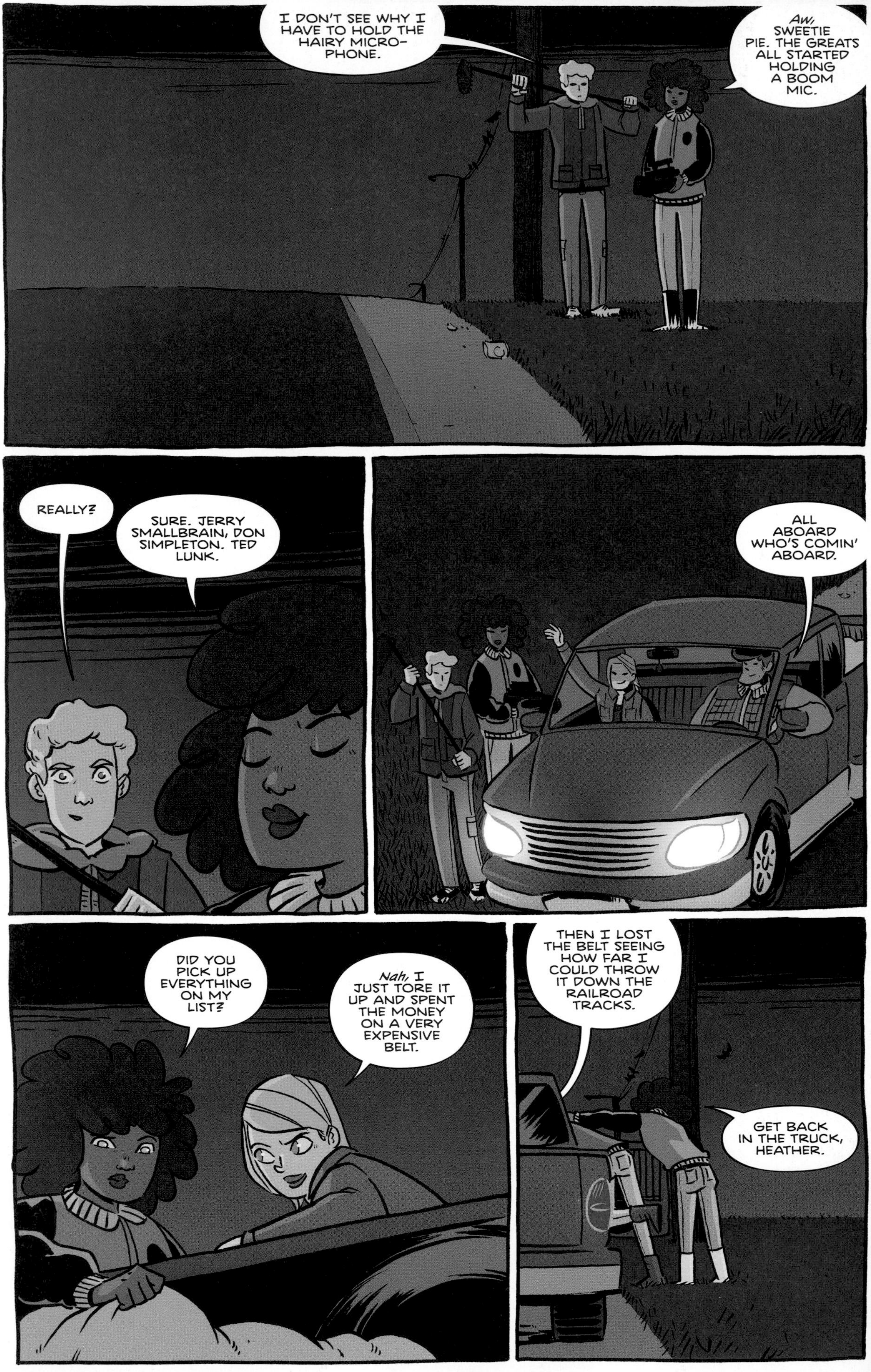
I DON'T SEE WHY I HAVE TO HOLD THE HAIRY MICRO-PHONE.
Aw, SWEETIE PIE. THE GREATS ALL STARTED HOLDING A BOOM MIC.
REALLY?
SURE. JERRY SMALLBRAIN, DON SIMPLETON. TED LUNK.
ALL ABOARD WHO'S COMIN' ABOARD.
DID YOU PICK UP EVERYTHING ON MY LIST?
Nah, I JUST TORE IT UP AND SPENT THE MONEY ON A VERY EXPENSIVE BELT.
THEN I LOST THE BELT SEEING HOW FAR I COULD THROW IT DOWN THE RAILROAD TRACKS.
GET BACK IN THE TRUCK, HEATHER.

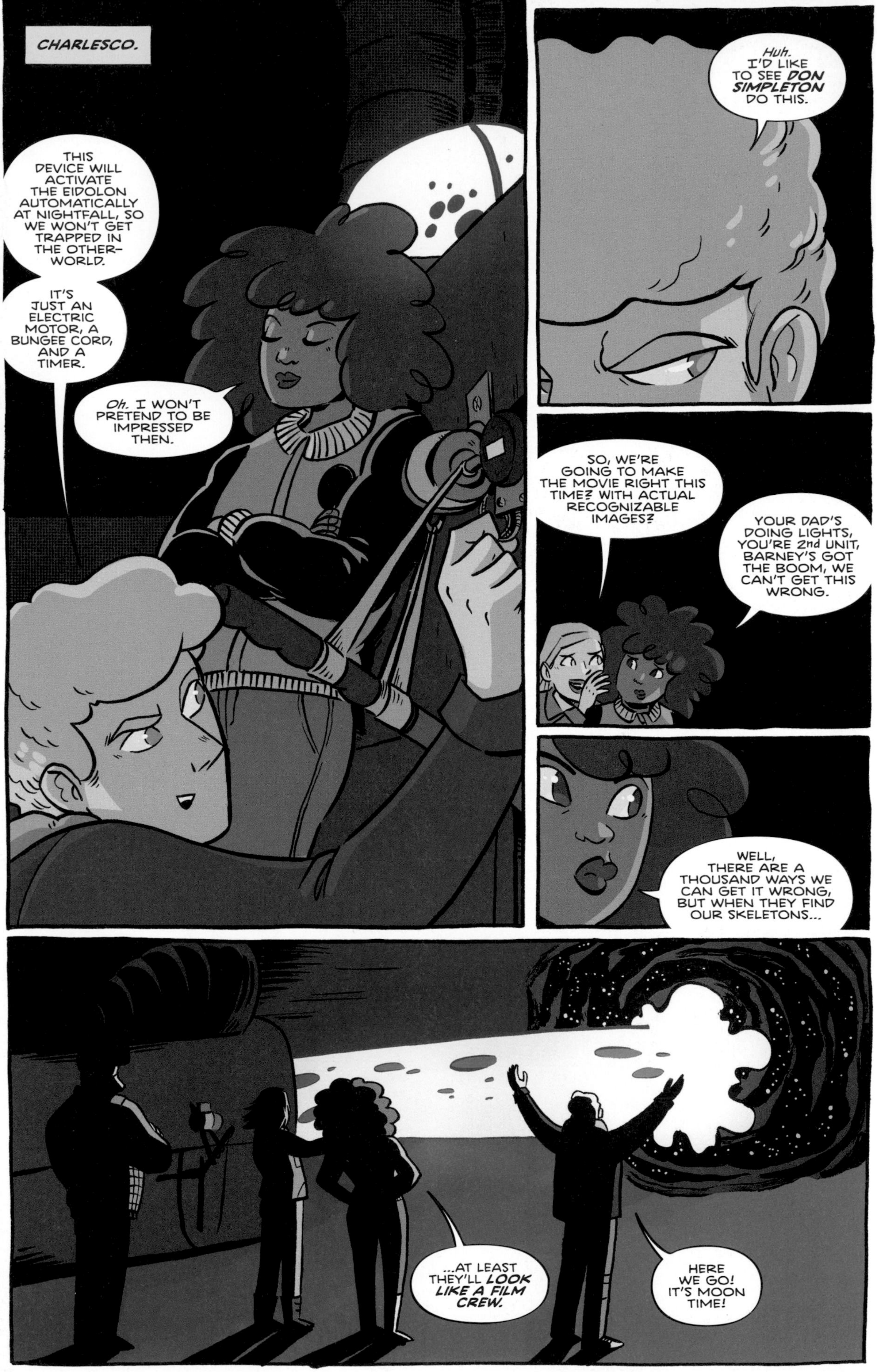
CHARLESCO.
THIS DEVICE WILL ACTIVATE THE EIDOLON AUTOMATICALLY AT NIGHTFALL, SO WE WON'T GET TRAPPED IN THE OTHER-WORLD.
IT'S JUST AN ELECTRIC MOTOR, A BUNGEE CORD, AND A TIMER.
Oh. I WON'T PRETEND TO BE IMPRESSED THEN.
Huh. I'D LIKE TO SEE ***DON SIMPLETON*** DO THIS.
SO, WE'RE GOING TO MAKE THE MOVIE RIGHT THIS TIME? WITH ACTUAL RECOGNIZABLE IMAGES?
YOUR DAD'S DOING LIGHTS, YOU'RE 2nd UNIT, BARNEY'S GOT THE BOOM, WE CAN'T GET THIS WRONG.
WELL, THERE ARE A THOUSAND WAYS WE CAN GET IT WRONG, BUT WHEN THEY FIND OUR SKELETONS...
...AT LEAST THEY'LL ***LOOK LIKE A FILM CREW.***
HERE WE GO! IT'S MOON TIME!

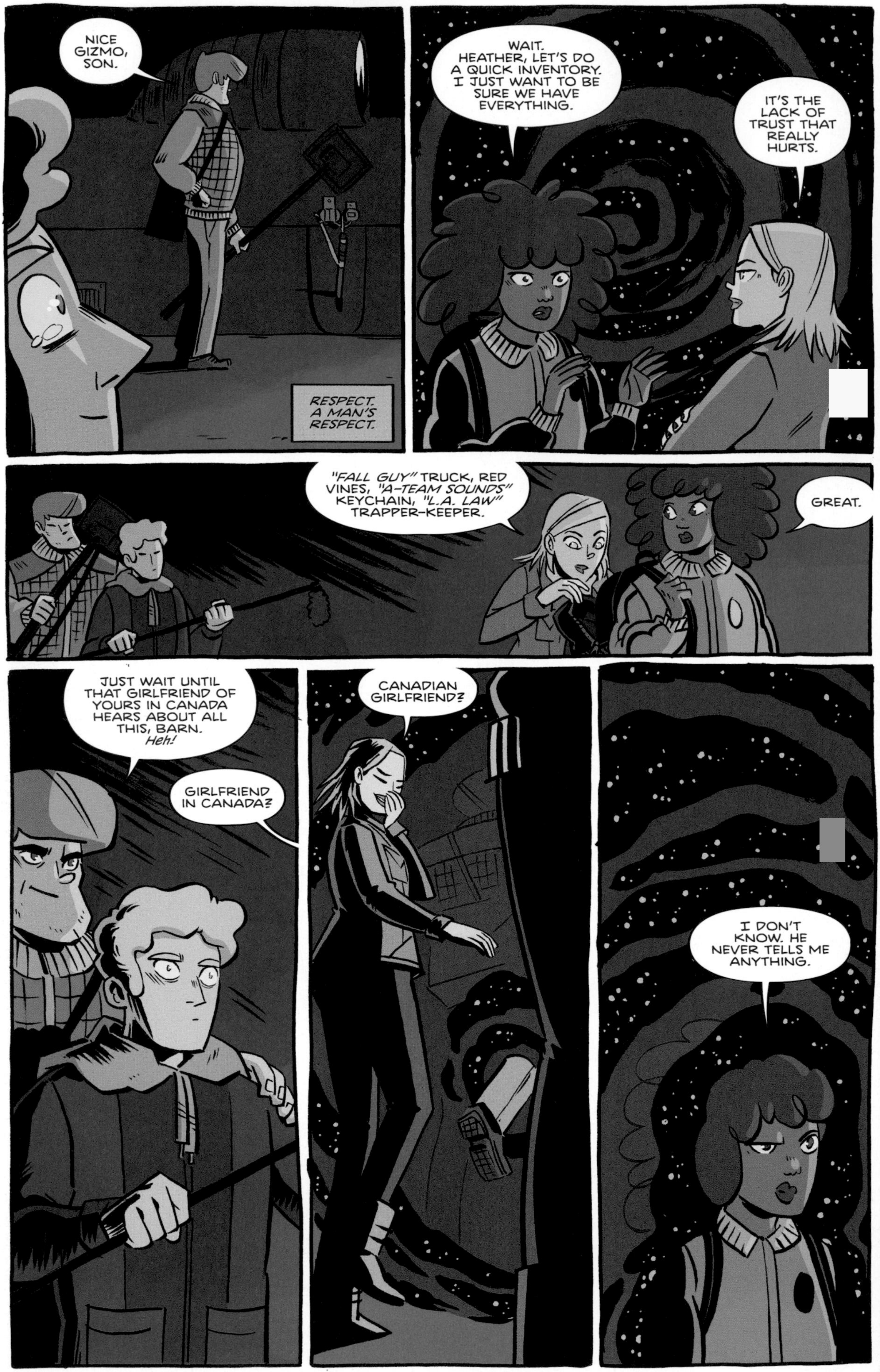
NICE GIZMO, SON.
RESPECT. A MAN'S RESPECT.
WAIT. HEATHER, LET'S DO A QUICK INVENTORY. I JUST WANT TO BE SURE WE HAVE EVERYTHING.
IT'S THE LACK OF TRUST THAT REALLY HURTS.
"FALL GUY" TRUCK, RED VINES, "A-TEAM SOUNDS" KEYCHAIN, "L.A. LAW" TRAPPER-KEEPER.
GREAT.
JUST WAIT UNTIL THAT GIRLFRIEND OF YOURS IN CANADA HEARS ABOUT ALL THIS, BARN. Heh!
GIRLFRIEND IN CANADA?
CANADIAN GIRLFRIEND?
I DON'T KNOW. HE NEVER TELLS ME ANYTHING.

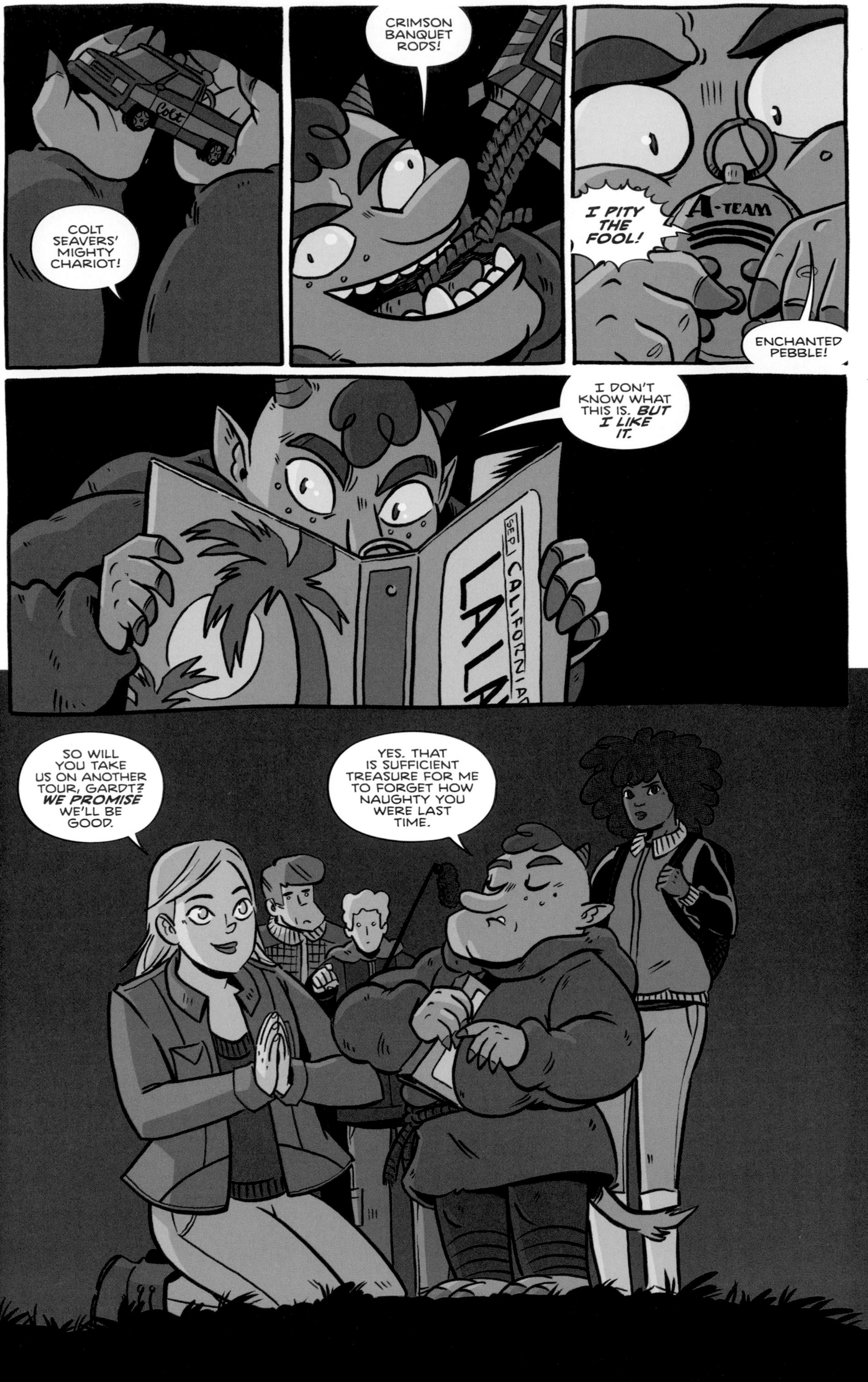
COLT SEAVERS' MIGHTY CHARIOT!
Colt
CRIMSON BANQUET RODS!
I PITY THE FOOL!
A-TEAM
ENCHANTED PEBBLE!
I DON'T KNOW WHAT THIS IS. BUT I LIKE IT.
SEP CALIFORNIA
LA LA
SO WILL YOU TAKE US ON ANOTHER TOUR, GARDT? WE PROMISE WE'LL BE GOOD.
YES. THAT IS SUFFICIENT TREASURE FOR ME TO FORGET HOW NAUGHTY YOU WERE LAST TIME.

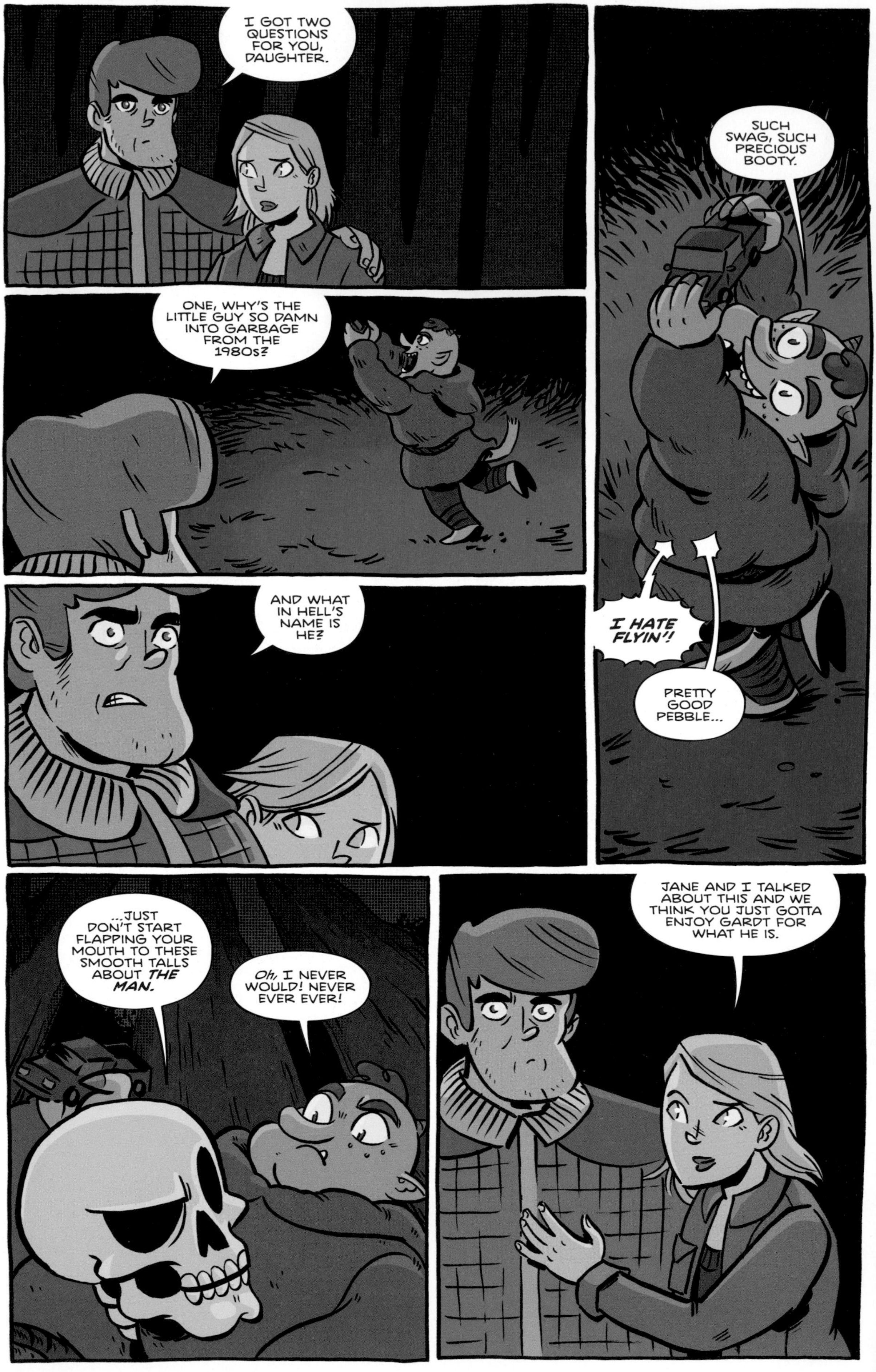
I GOT TWO QUESTIONS FOR YOU, DAUGHTER.
ONE, WHY'S THE LITTLE GUY SO DAMN INTO GARBAGE FROM THE 1980s?
AND WHAT IN HELL'S NAME IS HE?
SUCH SWAG, SUCH PRECIOUS BOOTY.
I HATE FLYIN'!
PRETTY GOOD PEBBLE...
...JUST DON'T START FLAPPING YOUR MOUTH TO THESE SMOOTH TALLS ABOUT THE MAN.
Oh, I NEVER WOULD! NEVER EVER EVER!
JANE AND I TALKED ABOUT THIS AND WE THINK YOU JUST GOTTA ENJOY GARDT FOR WHAT HE IS.

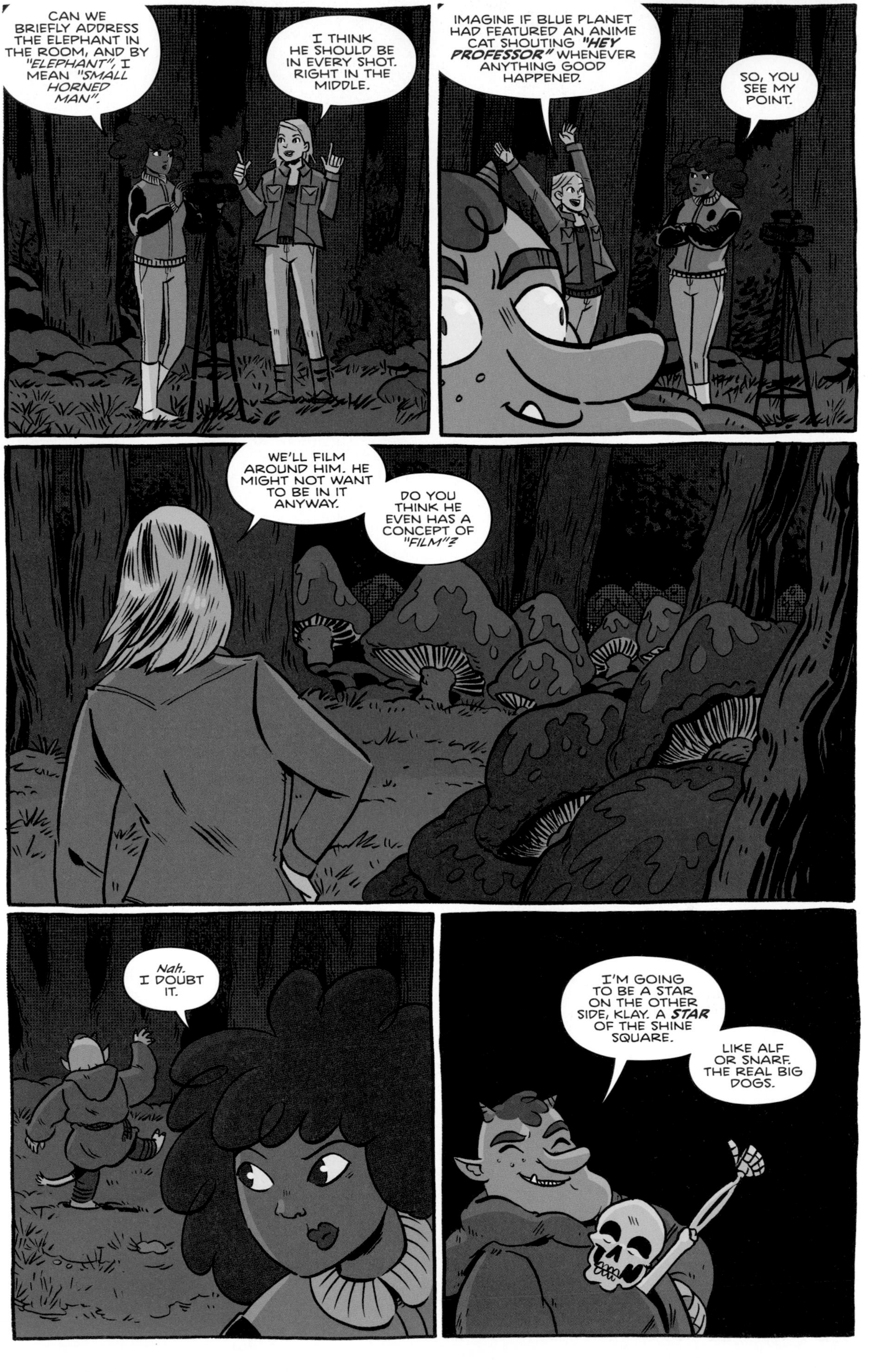
CAN WE BRIEFLY ADDRESS THE ELEPHANT IN THE ROOM, AND BY *"ELEPHANT"*, I MEAN *"SMALL HORNED MAN"*.
I THINK HE SHOULD BE IN EVERY SHOT. RIGHT IN THE MIDDLE.
IMAGINE IF BLUE PLANET HAD FEATURED AN ANIME CAT SHOUTING ***"HEY PROFESSOR"*** WHENEVER ANYTHING GOOD HAPPENED.
SO, YOU SEE MY POINT.
WE'LL FILM AROUND HIM. HE MIGHT NOT WANT TO BE IN IT ANYWAY.
DO YOU THINK HE EVEN HAS A CONCEPT OF *"FILM"*?
Nah. I DOUBT IT.
I'M GOING TO BE A STAR ON THE OTHER SIDE, KLAY. A ***STAR*** OF THE SHINE SQUARE.
LIKE ALF OR SNARF. THE REAL BIG DOGS.

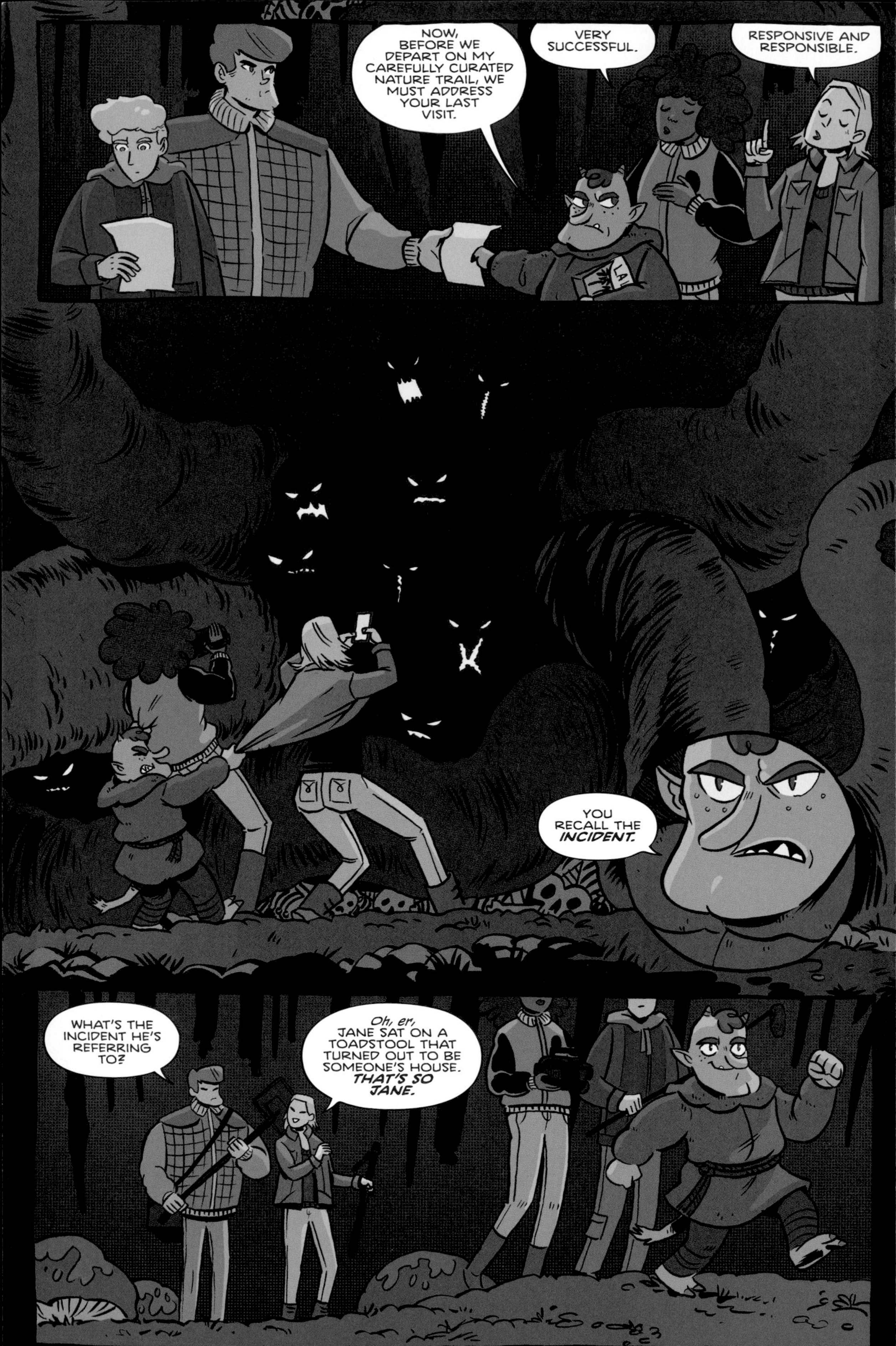
NOW, BEFORE WE DEPART ON MY CAREFULLY CURATED NATURE TRAIL, WE MUST ADDRESS YOUR LAST VISIT.
VERY SUCCESSFUL.
RESPONSIVE AND RESPONSIBLE.
YOU RECALL THE *INCIDENT.*
WHAT'S THE INCIDENT HE'S REFERRING TO?
Oh, er, JANE SAT ON A TOADSTOOL THAT TURNED OUT TO BE SOMEONE'S HOUSE. ***THAT'S SO JANE.***

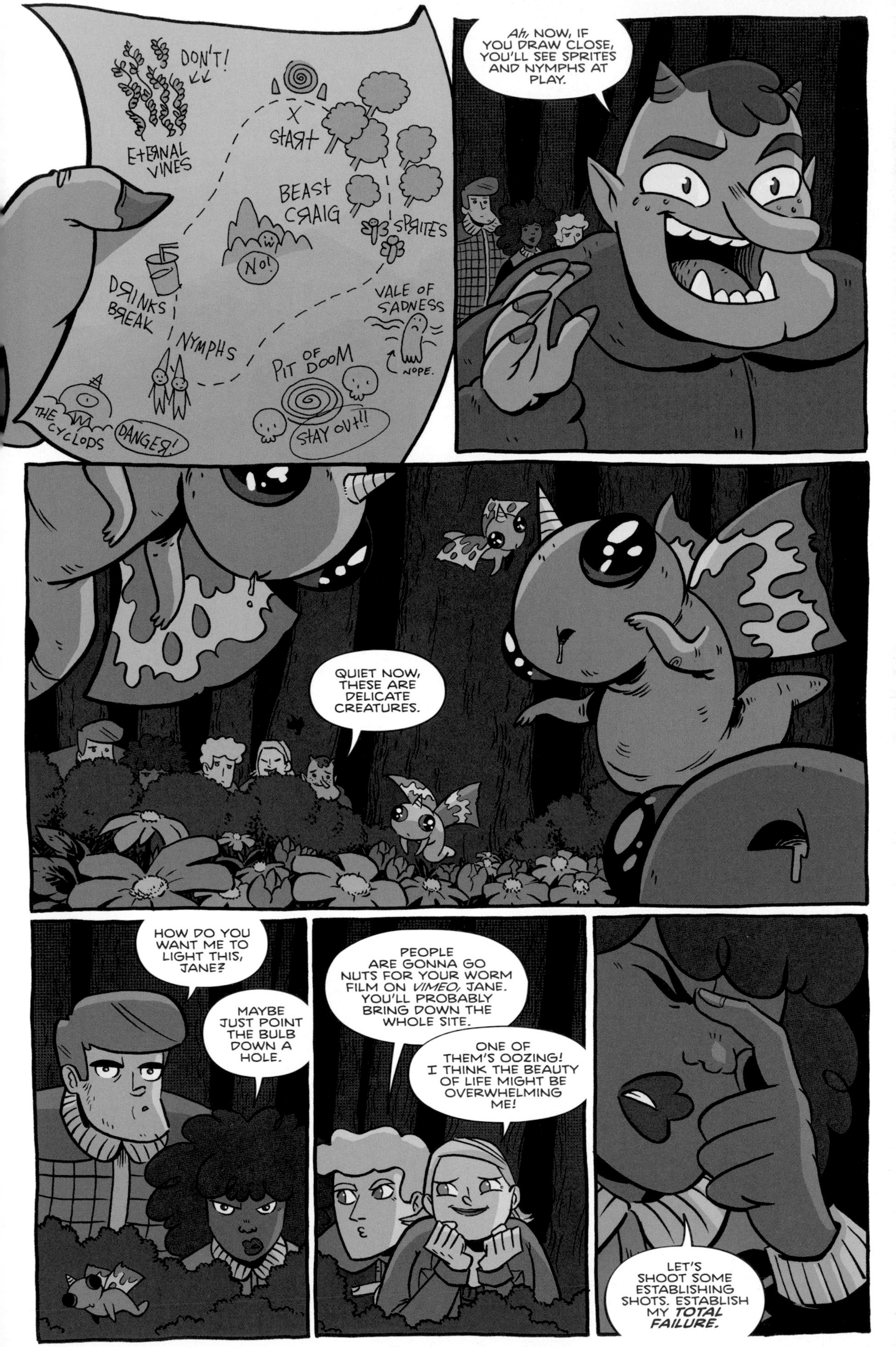
DON'T!
ETERNAL VINES
START
BEAST CRAIG
SPRITES
NO!
DRINKS BREAK
VALE OF SADNESS
NOPE.
NYMPHS
PIT OF DOOM
THE CYCLOPS
DANGER!
STAY OUT!!
Ah, NOW, IF YOU DRAW CLOSE, YOU'LL SEE SPRITES AND NYMPHS AT PLAY.
QUIET NOW, THESE ARE DELICATE CREATURES.
HOW DO YOU WANT ME TO LIGHT THIS, JANE?
MAYBE JUST POINT THE BULB DOWN A HOLE.
PEOPLE ARE GONNA GO NUTS FOR YOUR WORM FILM ON VIMEO, JANE. YOU'LL PROBABLY BRING DOWN THE WHOLE SITE.
ONE OF THEM'S OOZING! I THINK THE BEAUTY OF LIFE MIGHT BE OVERWHELMING ME!
LET'S SHOOT SOME ESTABLISHING SHOTS. ESTABLISH MY TOTAL FAILURE.

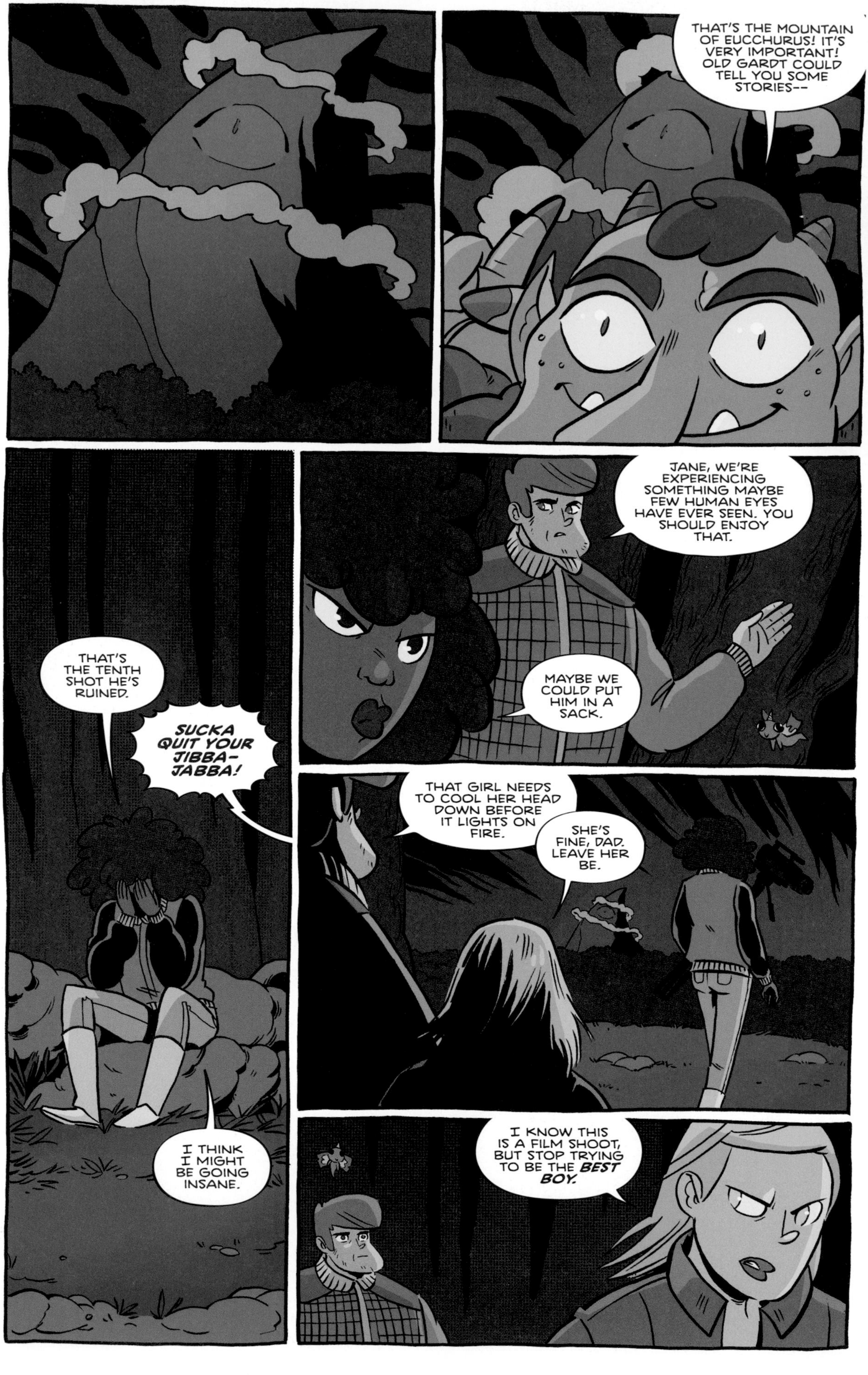
THAT'S THE MOUNTAIN OF EUCCHURUS! IT'S VERY IMPORTANT! OLD GARDT COULD TELL YOU SOME STORIES--
JANE, WE'RE EXPERIENCING SOMETHING MAYBE FEW HUMAN EYES HAVE EVER SEEN. YOU SHOULD ENJOY THAT.
MAYBE WE COULD PUT HIM IN A SACK.
THAT'S THE TENTH SHOT HE'S RUINED.
SUCKA QUIT YOUR JIBBA-JABBA!
I THINK I MIGHT BE GOING INSANE.
THAT GIRL NEEDS TO COOL HER HEAD DOWN BEFORE IT LIGHTS ON FIRE.
SHE'S FINE, DAD. LEAVE HER BE.
I KNOW THIS IS A FILM SHOOT, BUT STOP TRYING TO BE THE BEST BOY.

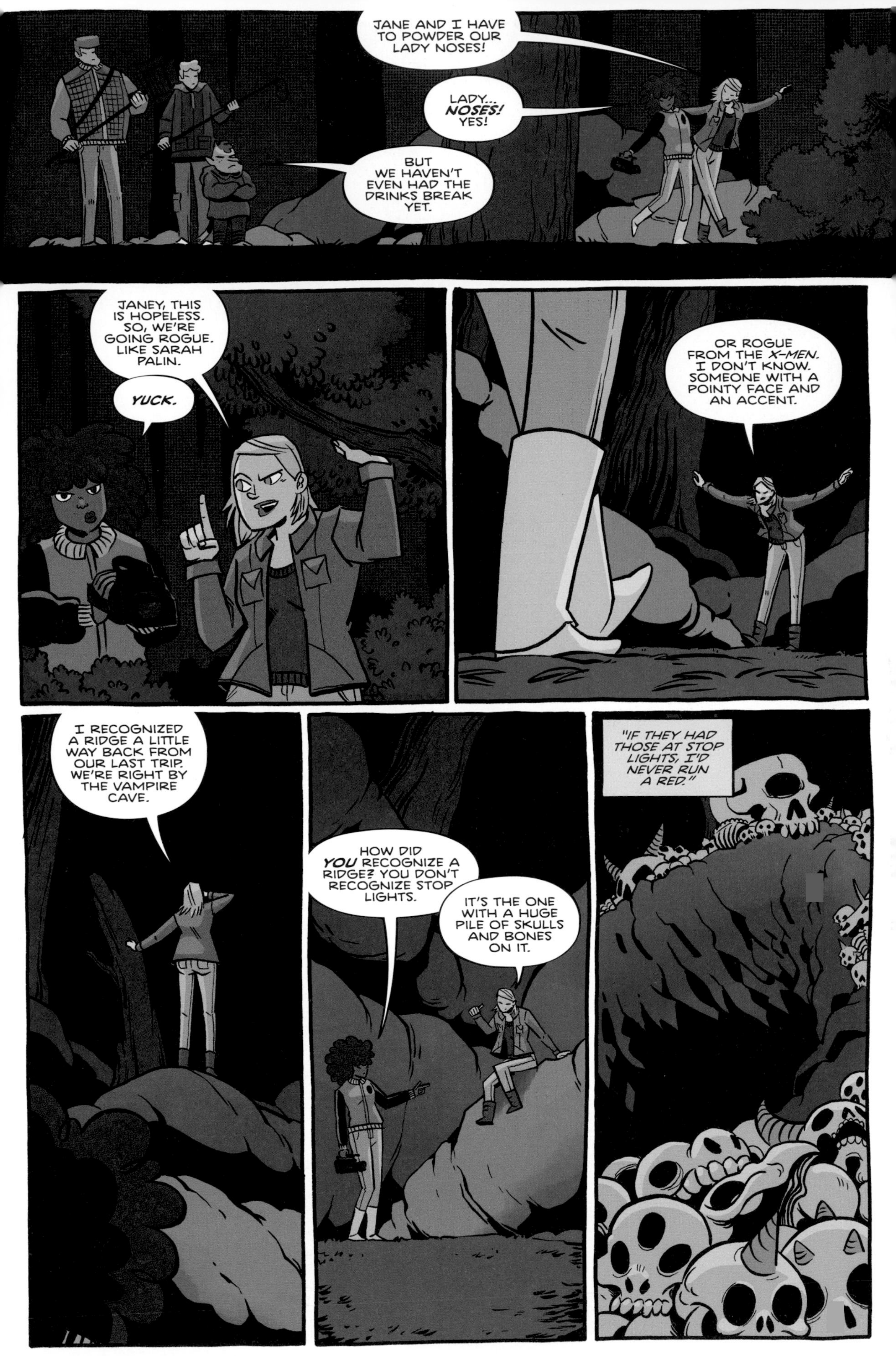
JANE AND I HAVE TO POWDER OUR LADY NOSES!
LADY... NOSES! YES!
BUT WE HAVEN'T EVEN HAD THE DRINKS BREAK YET.
JANEY, THIS IS HOPELESS. SO, WE'RE GOING ROGUE. LIKE SARAH PALIN.
YUCK.
OR ROGUE FROM THE X-MEN. I DON'T KNOW. SOMEONE WITH A POINTY FACE AND AN ACCENT.
I RECOGNIZED A RIDGE A LITTLE WAY BACK FROM OUR LAST TRIP. WE'RE RIGHT BY THE VAMPIRE CAVE.
HOW DID YOU RECOGNIZE A RIDGE? YOU DON'T RECOGNIZE STOP LIGHTS.
IT'S THE ONE WITH A HUGE PILE OF SKULLS AND BONES ON IT.
"IF THEY HAD THOSE AT STOP LIGHTS, I'D NEVER RUN A RED."

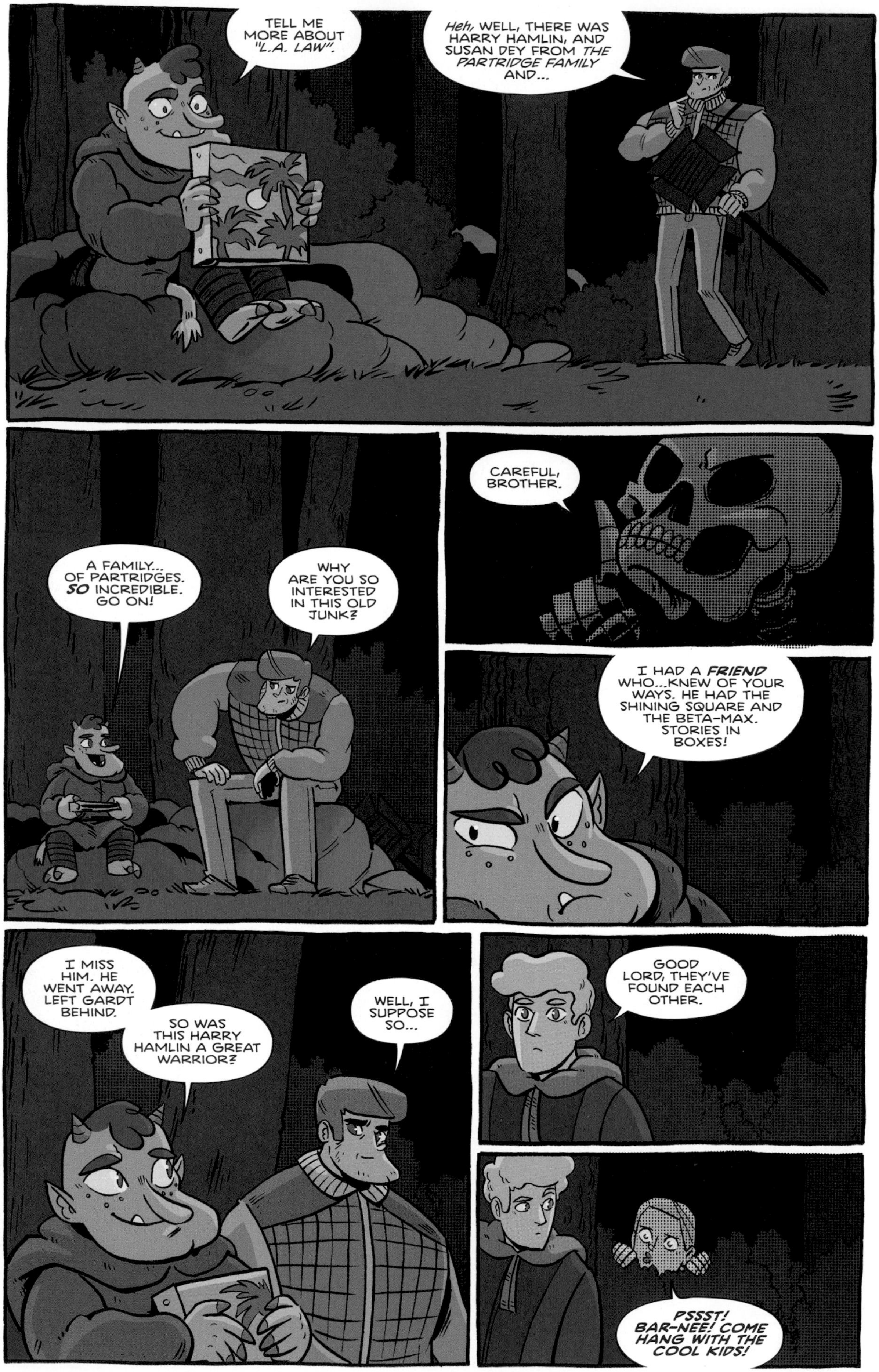

TELL ME MORE ABOUT "L.A. LAW".
Heh, WELL, THERE WAS HARRY HAMLIN, AND SUSAN DEY FROM THE PARTRIDGE FAMILY AND...
A FAMILY... OF PARTRIDGES. SO INCREDIBLE. GO ON!
WHY ARE YOU SO INTERESTED IN THIS OLD JUNK?
CAREFUL, BROTHER.
I HAD A FRIEND WHO...KNEW OF YOUR WAYS. HE HAD THE SHINING SQUARE AND THE BETA-MAX. STORIES IN BOXES!
I MISS HIM. HE WENT AWAY. LEFT GARDT BEHIND.
SO WAS THIS HARRY HAMLIN A GREAT WARRIOR?
WELL, I SUPPOSE SO...
GOOD LORD, THEY'VE FOUND EACH OTHER.
PSSST! BAR-NEE! COME HANG WITH THE COOL KIDS!

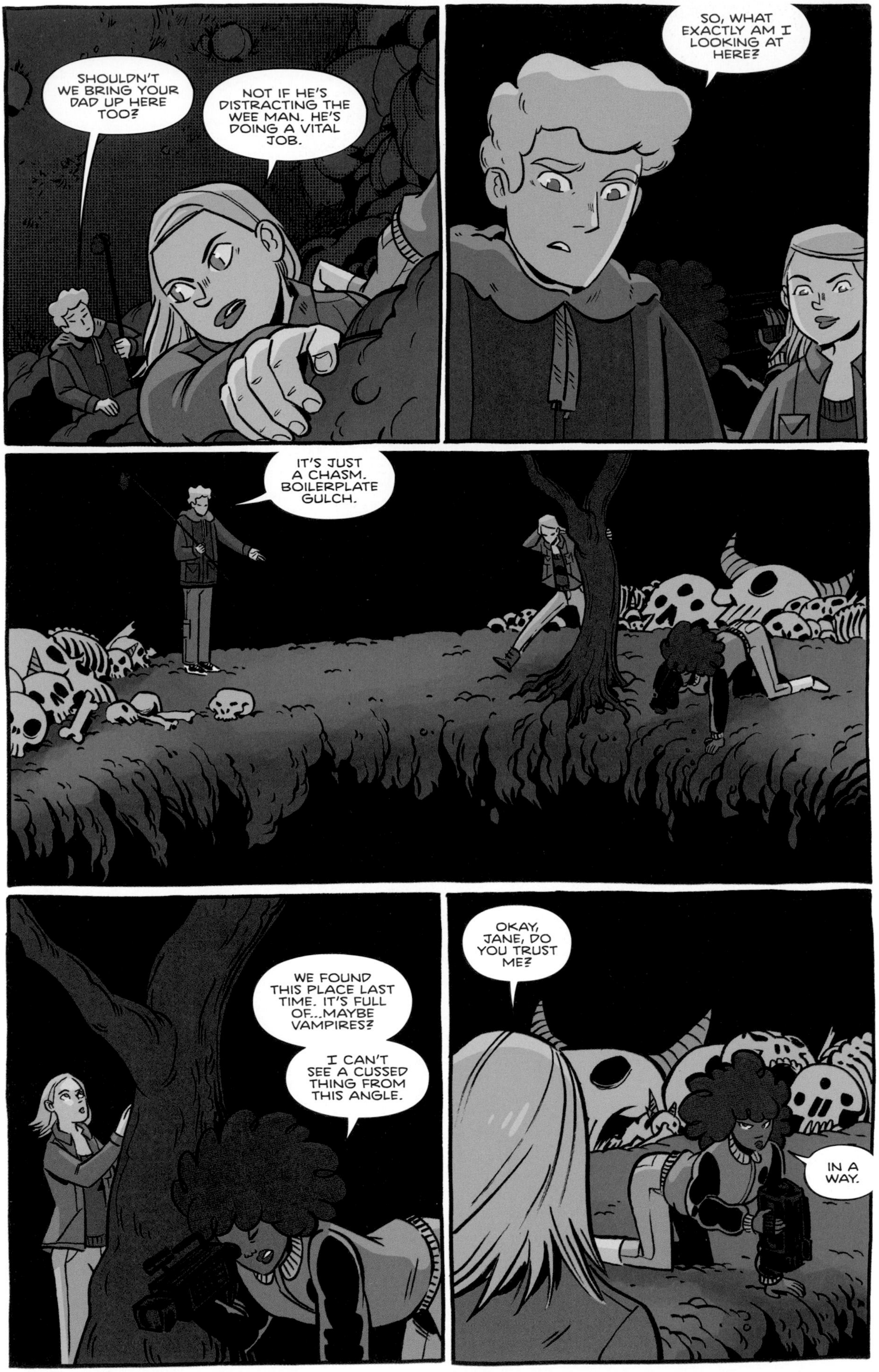
SHOULDN'T WE BRING YOUR DAD UP HERE TOO?
NOT IF HE'S DISTRACTING THE WEE MAN. HE'S DOING A VITAL JOB.
SO, WHAT EXACTLY AM I LOOKING AT HERE?
IT'S JUST A CHASM. BOILERPLATE GULCH.
WE FOUND THIS PLACE LAST TIME. IT'S FULL OF...MAYBE VAMPIRES?
I CAN'T SEE A CUSSED THING FROM THIS ANGLE.
OKAY, JANE, DO YOU TRUST ME?
IN A WAY.

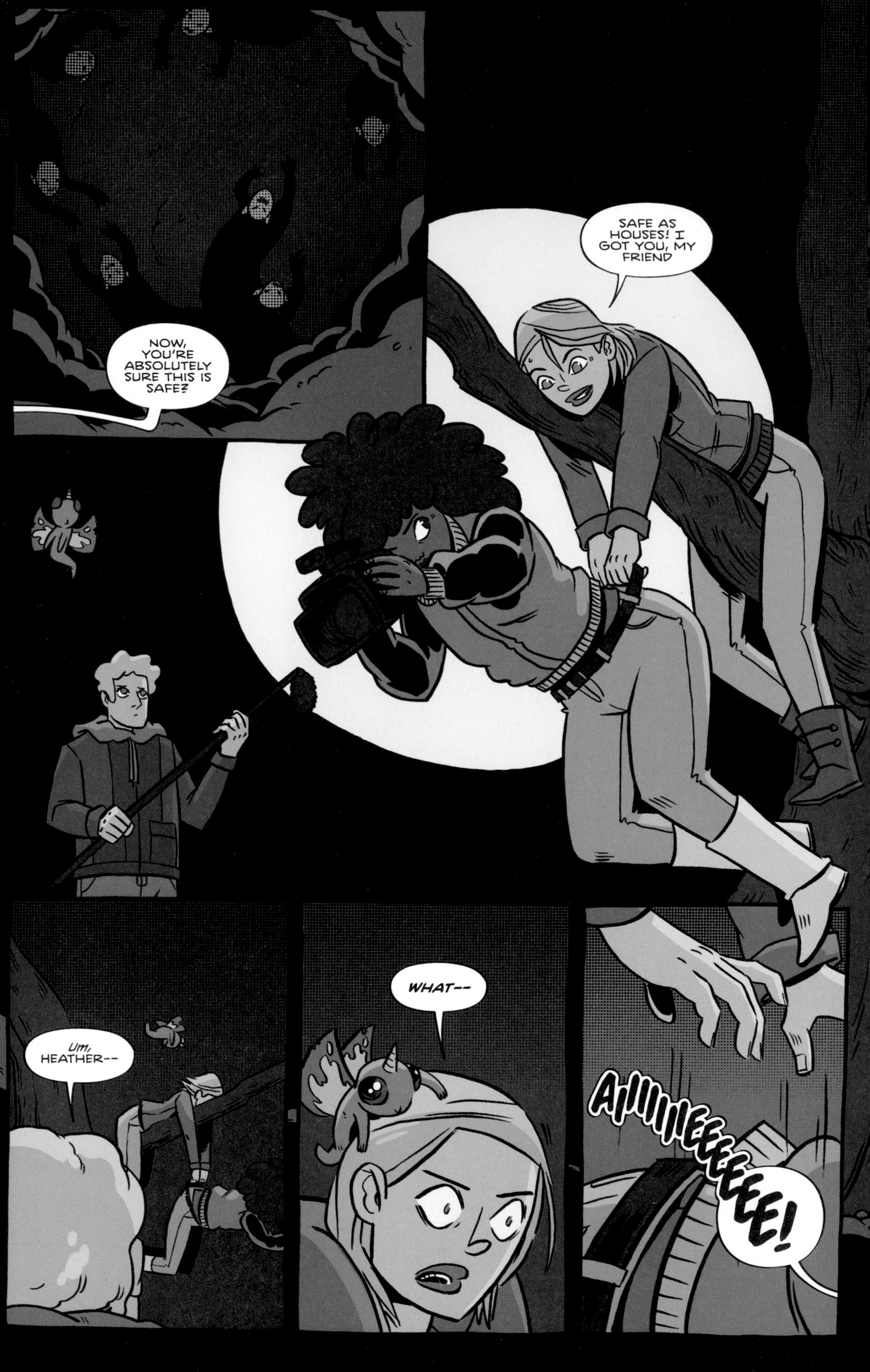
NOW, YOU'RE ABSOLUTELY SURE THIS IS SAFE?
SAFE AS HOUSES! I GOT YOU, MY FRIEND
UM, HEATHER--
WHAT--
AIIIIIEEEEEEEEE!

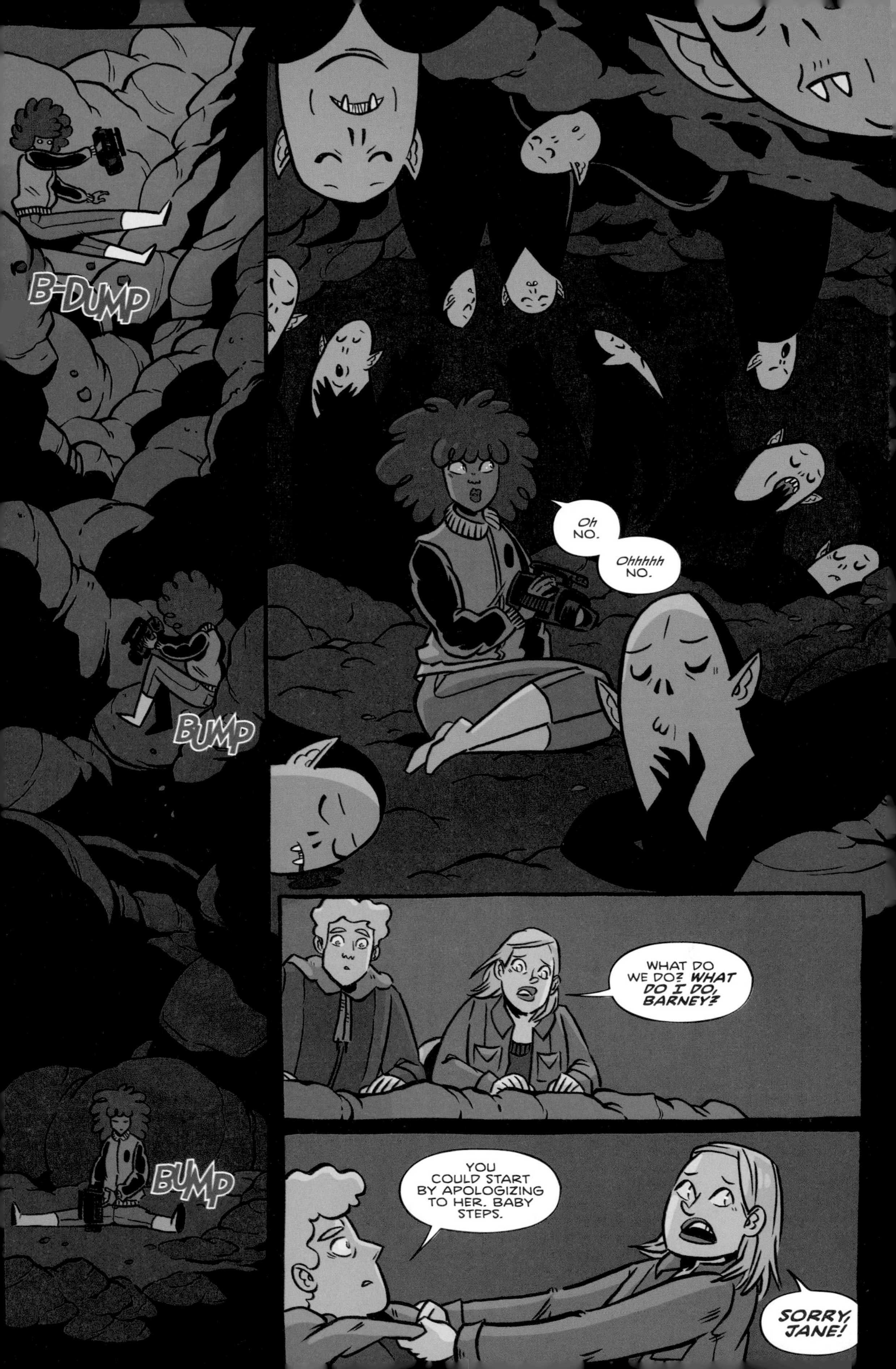
B-DUMP
BUMP
BUMP
Oh NO.
Ohhhhh NO.
WHAT DO WE DO? WHAT DO I DO, BARNEY?
YOU COULD START BY APOLOGIZING TO HER. BABY STEPS.
SORRY, JANE!

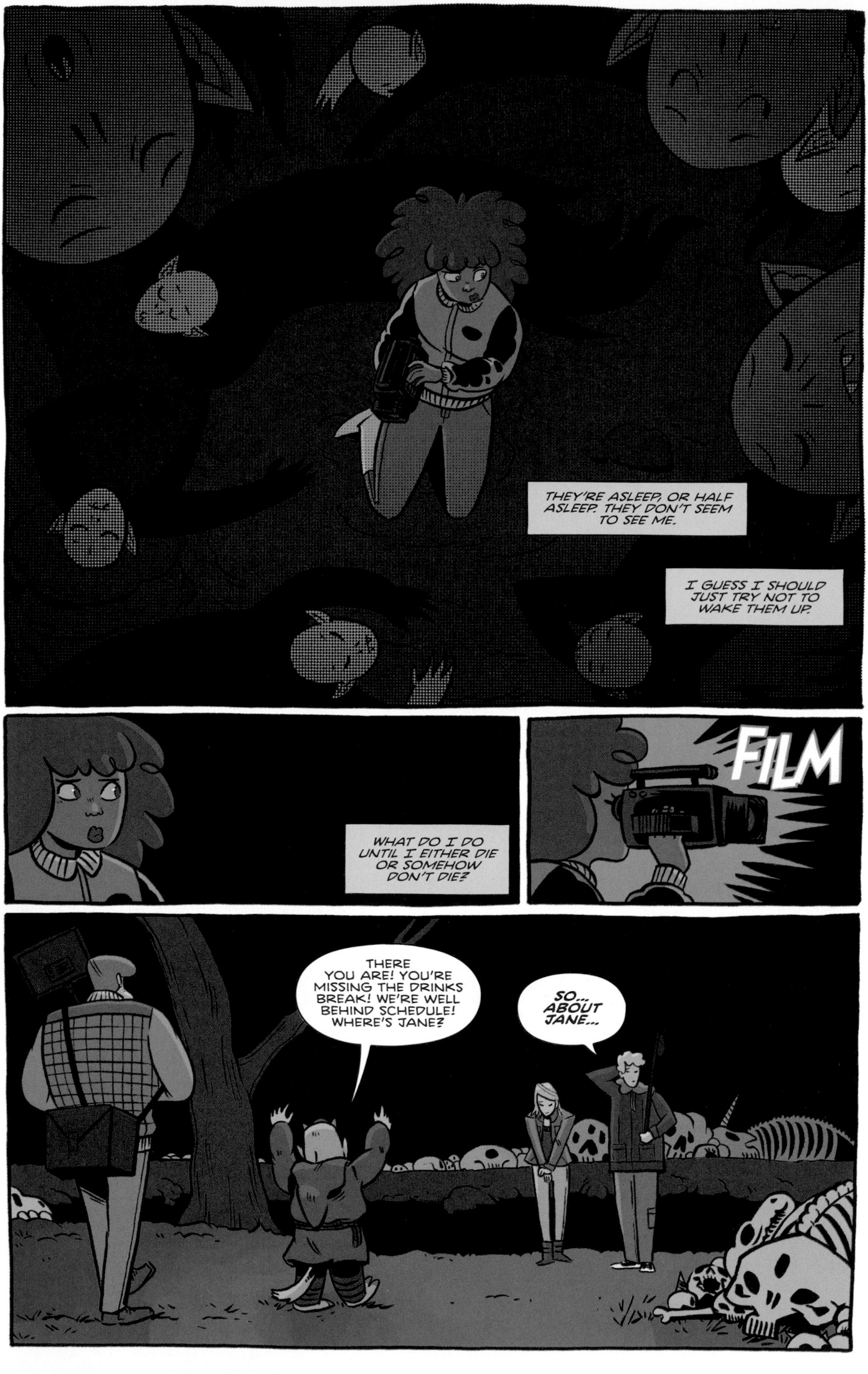

THEY'RE ASLEEP, OR HALF ASLEEP. THEY DON'T SEEM TO SEE ME.
I GUESS I SHOULD JUST TRY NOT TO WAKE THEM UP.
WHAT DO I DO UNTIL I EITHER DIE OR SOMEHOW DON'T DIE?
FILM
THERE YOU ARE! YOU'RE MISSING THE DRINKS BREAK! WE'RE WELL BEHIND SCHEDULE! WHERE'S JANE?
SO... ABOUT JANE...

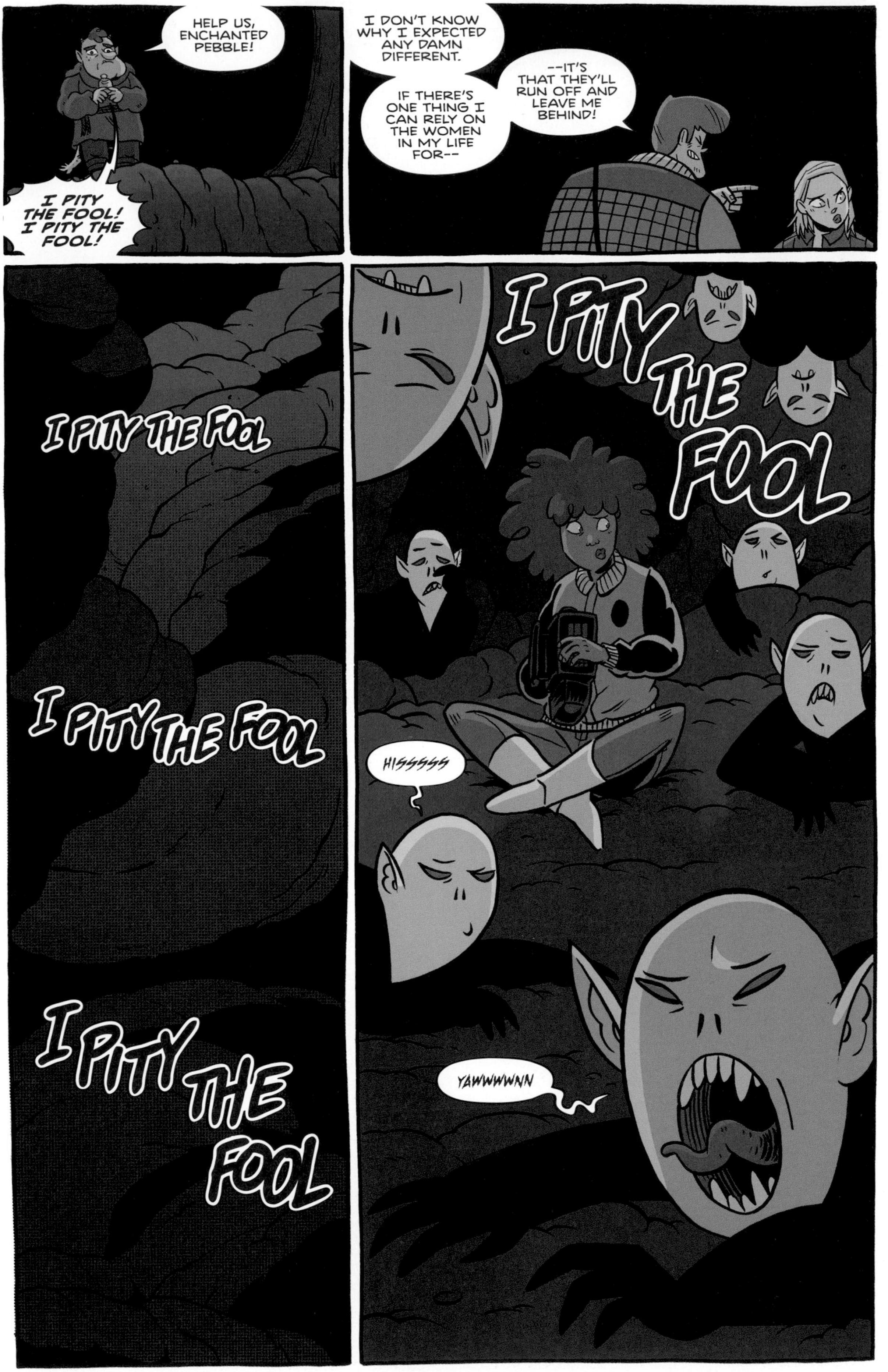

HELP US, ENCHANTED PEBBLE!
I PITY THE FOOL! I PITY THE FOOL!
I DON'T KNOW WHY I EXPECTED ANY DAMN DIFFERENT.
IF THERE'S ONE THING I CAN RELY ON THE WOMEN IN MY LIFE FOR--
--IT'S THAT THEY'LL RUN OFF AND LEAVE ME BEHIND!
I PITY THE FOOL
I PITY THE FOOL
I PITY THE FOOL
I PITY THE FOOL
HISSSSS
YAWWWWNN

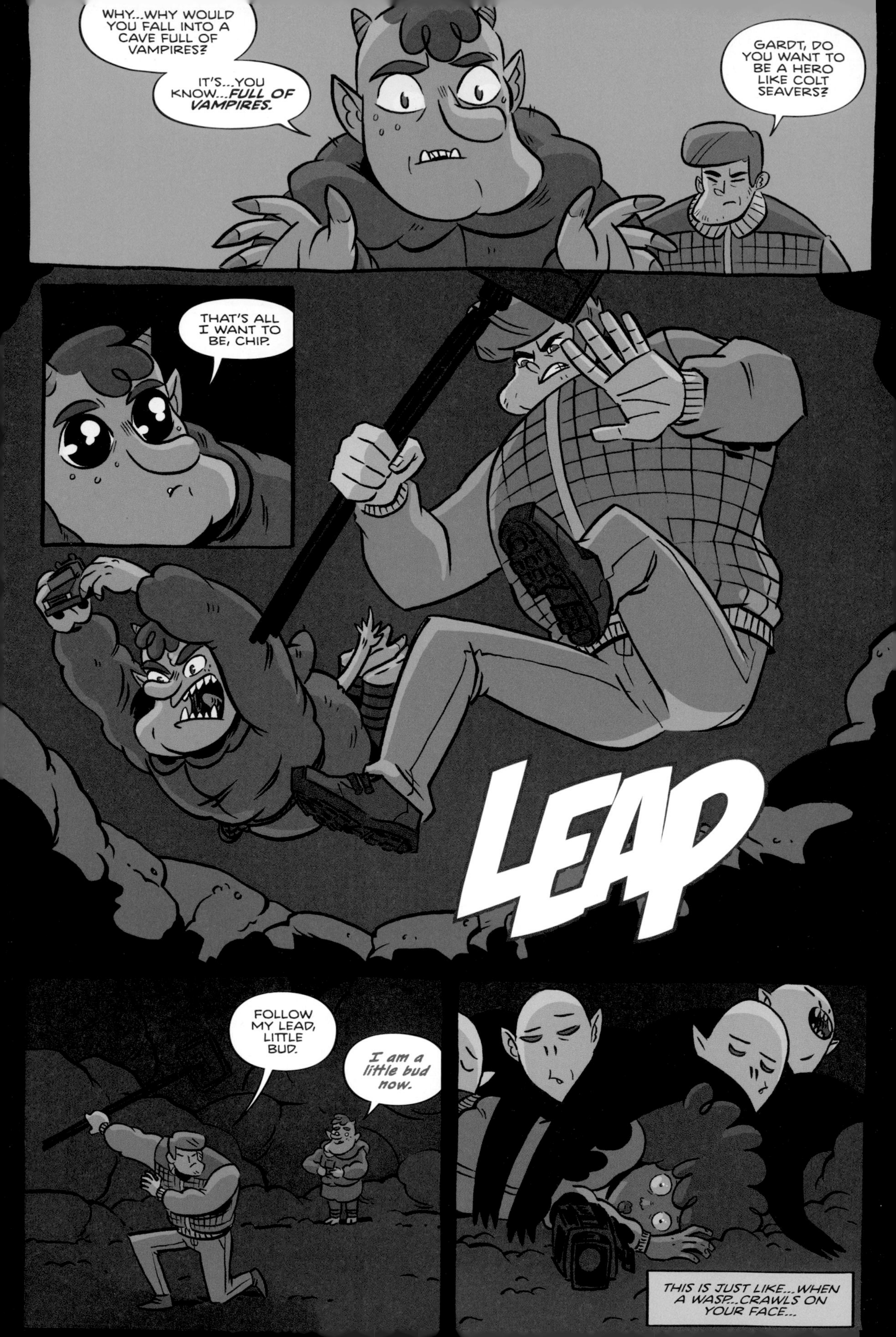
WHY...WHY WOULD YOU FALL INTO A CAVE FULL OF VAMPIRES?
IT'S...YOU KNOW...FULL OF VAMPIRES.
GARDT, DO YOU WANT TO BE A HERO LIKE COLT SEAVERS?
THAT'S ALL I WANT TO BE, CHIP.
LEAP
FOLLOW MY LEAD, LITTLE BUD.
I am a little bud now.
THIS IS JUST LIKE...WHEN A WASP...CRAWLS ON YOUR FACE...

THEY'RE BEHIND US, CHIP! AND THEY'RE EXTREMELY UNHAPPY ABOUT YOUR SHINE POLE!

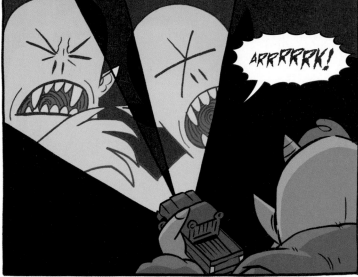

ARRRRRRK!

MOVE YOURSELF, JANE!

GARRRRDDDDDTTTT

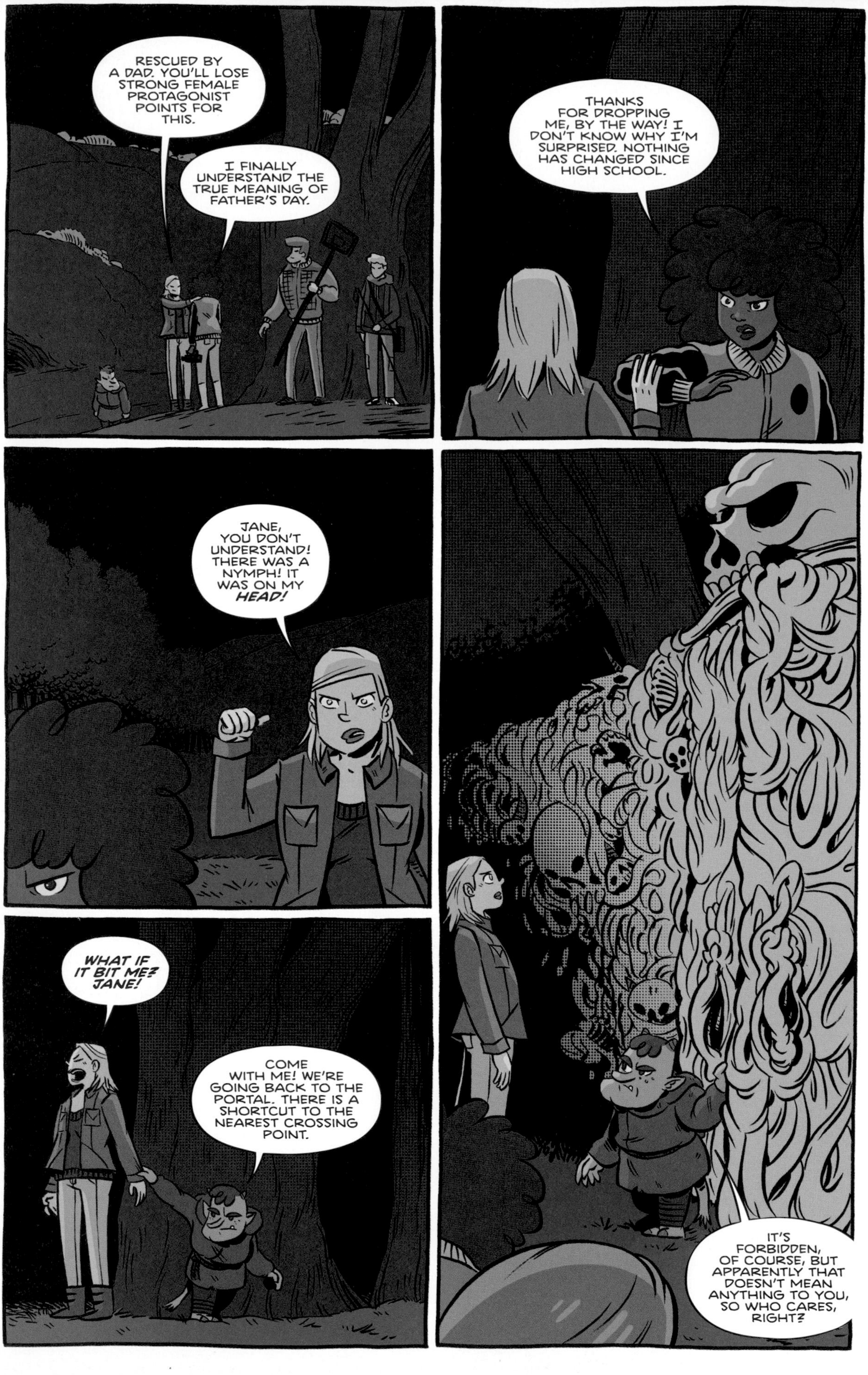
RESCUED BY A DAD. YOU'LL LOSE STRONG FEMALE PROTAGONIST POINTS FOR THIS.
I FINALLY UNDERSTAND THE TRUE MEANING OF FATHER'S DAY.
THANKS FOR DROPPING ME, BY THE WAY! I DON'T KNOW WHY I'M SURPRISED. NOTHING HAS CHANGED SINCE HIGH SCHOOL.
JANE, YOU DON'T UNDERSTAND! THERE WAS A NYMPH! IT WAS ON MY HEAD!
WHAT IF IT BIT ME? JANE!
COME WITH ME! WE'RE GOING BACK TO THE PORTAL. THERE IS A SHORTCUT TO THE NEAREST CROSSING POINT.
IT'S FORBIDDEN, OF COURSE, BUT APPARENTLY THAT DOESN'T MEAN ANYTHING TO YOU, SO WHO CARES, RIGHT?

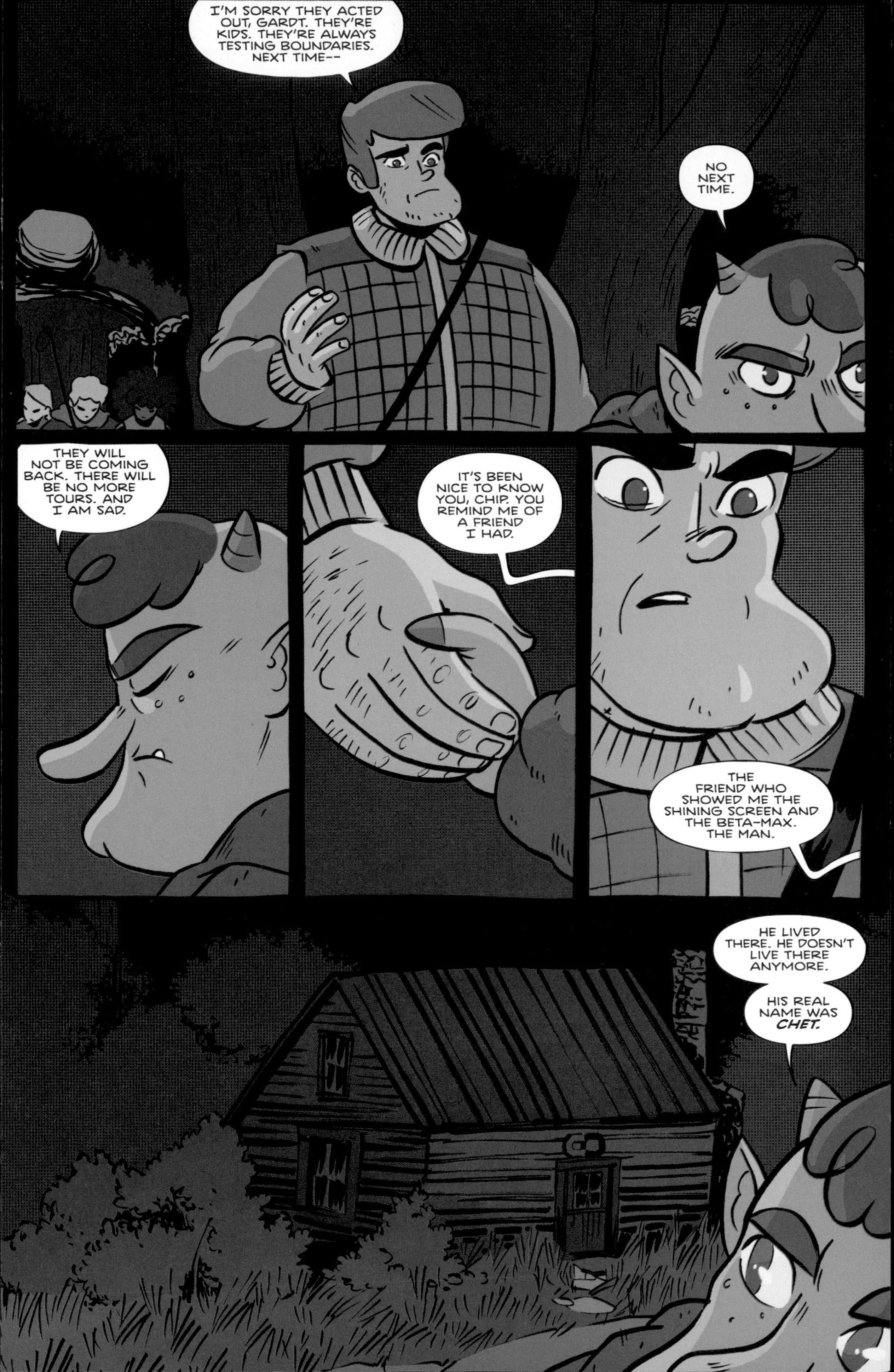
I'M SORRY THEY ACTED OUT, GARDT. THEY'RE KIDS. THEY'RE ALWAYS TESTING BOUNDARIES. NEXT TIME--
NO NEXT TIME.
THEY WILL NOT BE COMING BACK. THERE WILL BE NO MORE TOURS. AND I AM SAD.
IT'S BEEN NICE TO KNOW YOU, CHIP. YOU REMIND ME OF A FRIEND I HAD.
THE FRIEND WHO SHOWED ME THE SHINING SCREEN AND THE BETA-MAX. THE MAN.
HE LIVED THERE. HE DOESN'T LIVE THERE ANYMORE.
HIS REAL NAME WAS ***CHET.***

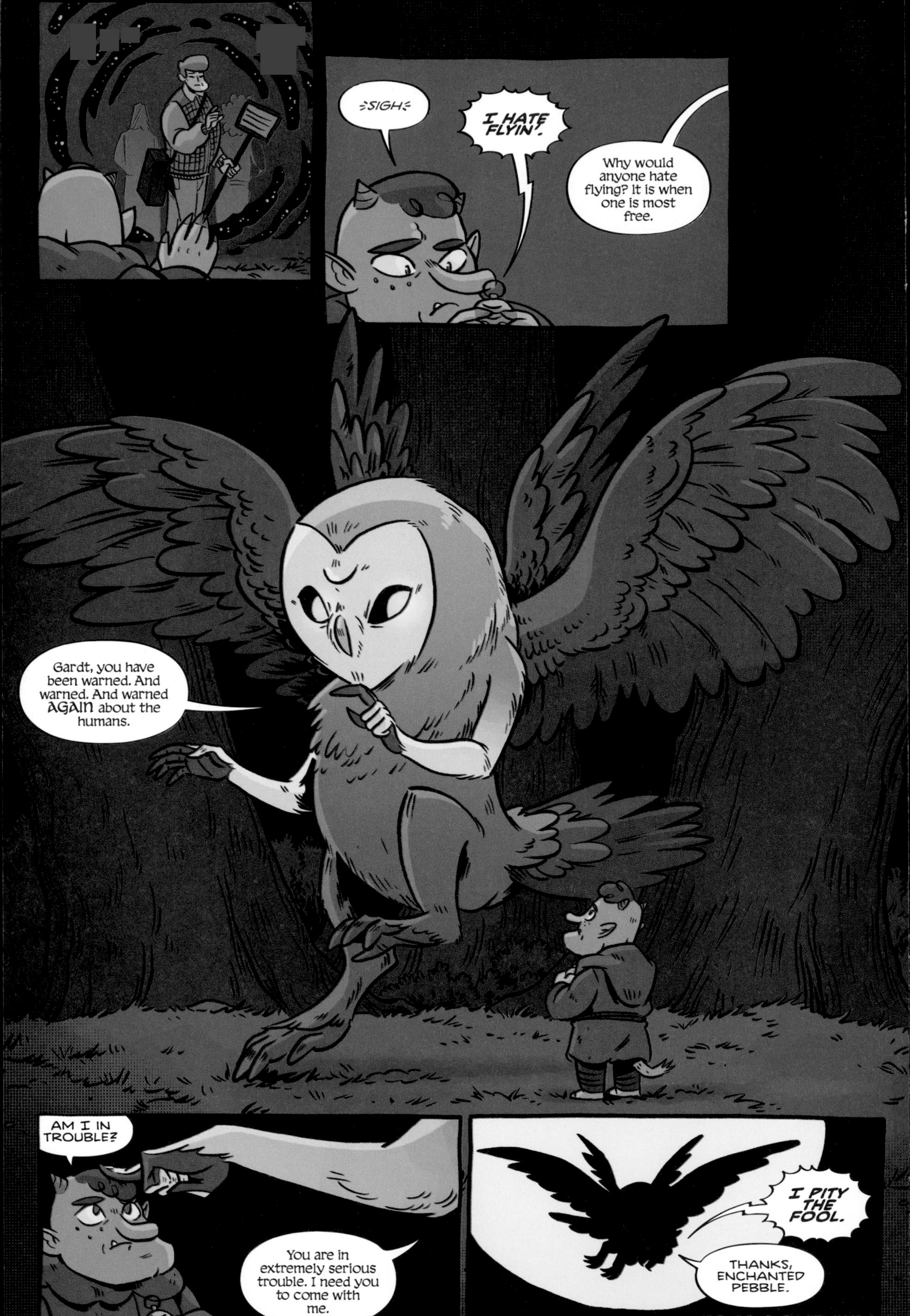
SIGH
I HATE FLYIN'.
Why would anyone hate flying? It is when one is most free.
Gardt, you have been warned. And warned. And warned AGAIN about the humans.
AM I IN TROUBLE?
You are in extremely serious trouble. I need you to come with me.
I PITY THE FOOL.
THANKS, ENCHANTED PEBBLE.

TO BE CONTINUED!

Cover
Gallery

Issue 1 Cover by
Christine Larsen

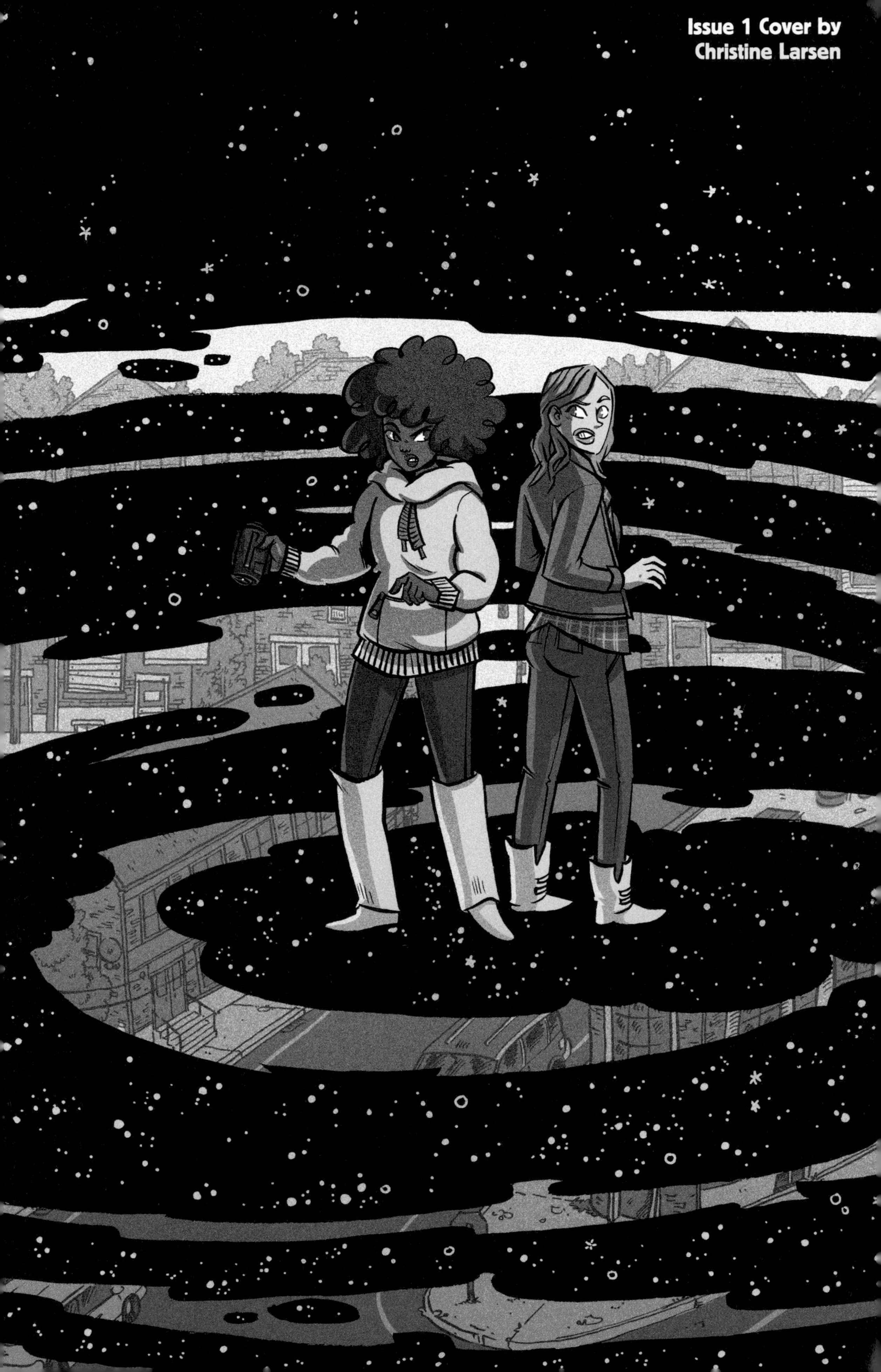

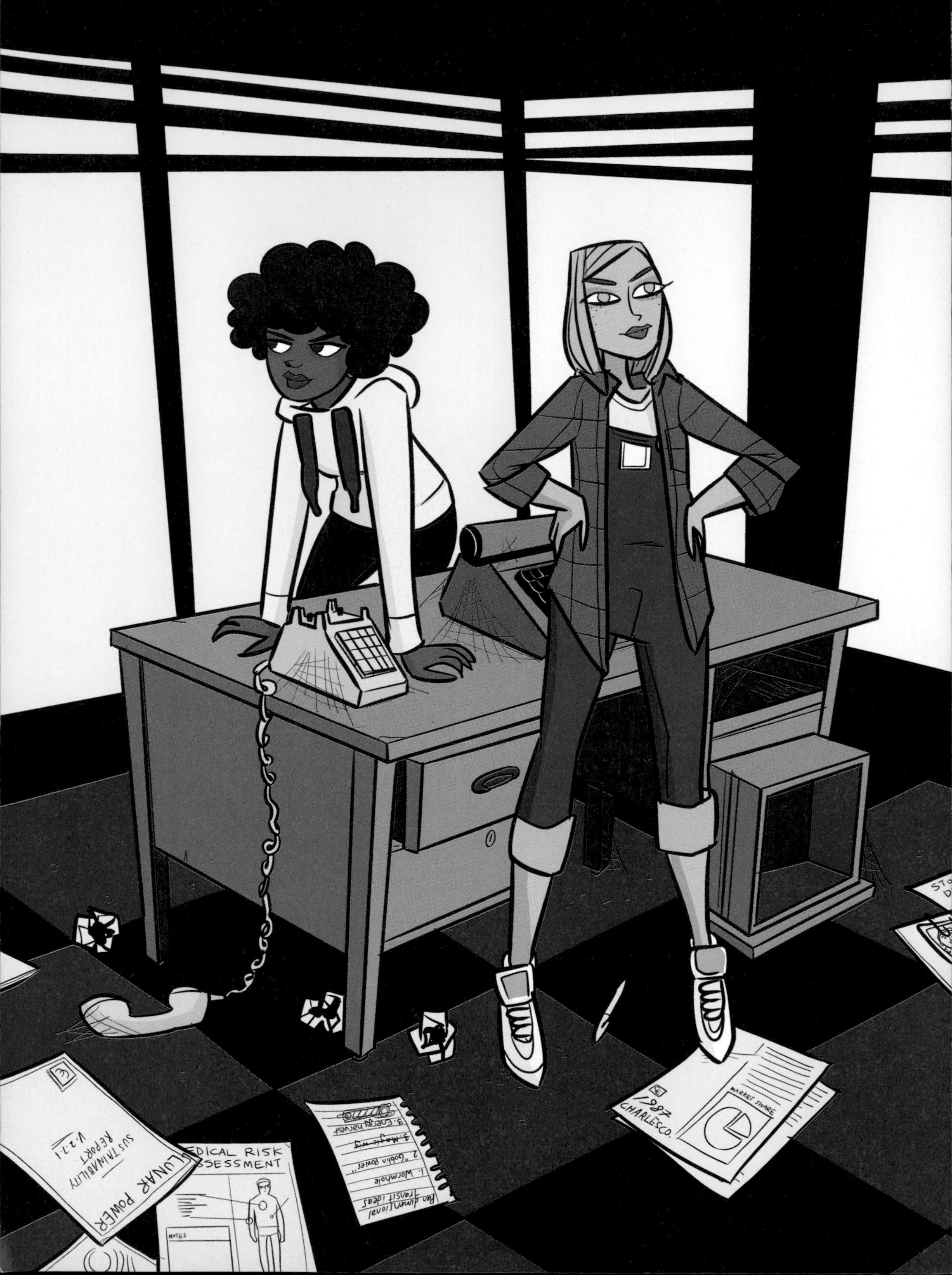
LUNAR POWER
SUSTAINABILITY REPORT
V.2.1
EDICAL RISK
SSESSMENT
NOTES
Pan dimensional transit ideas
1. Wormhole
2. "Goblin power"
3. Energy harvest
1987
CHARLESCO.
MARKET SHARE

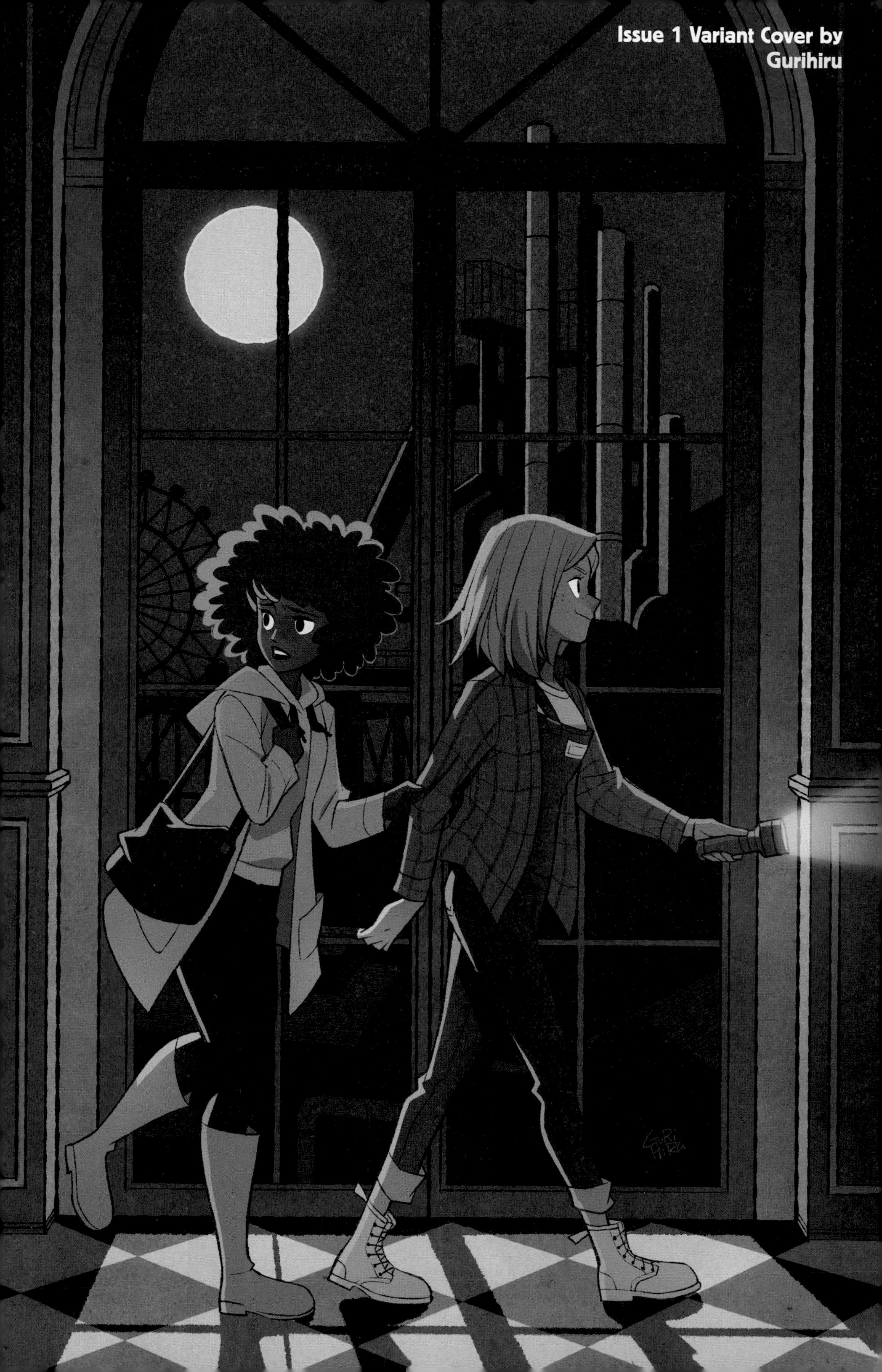

Issue 1 Variant Cover by Gurihiru

Issue 2 Cover by
Christine Larsen

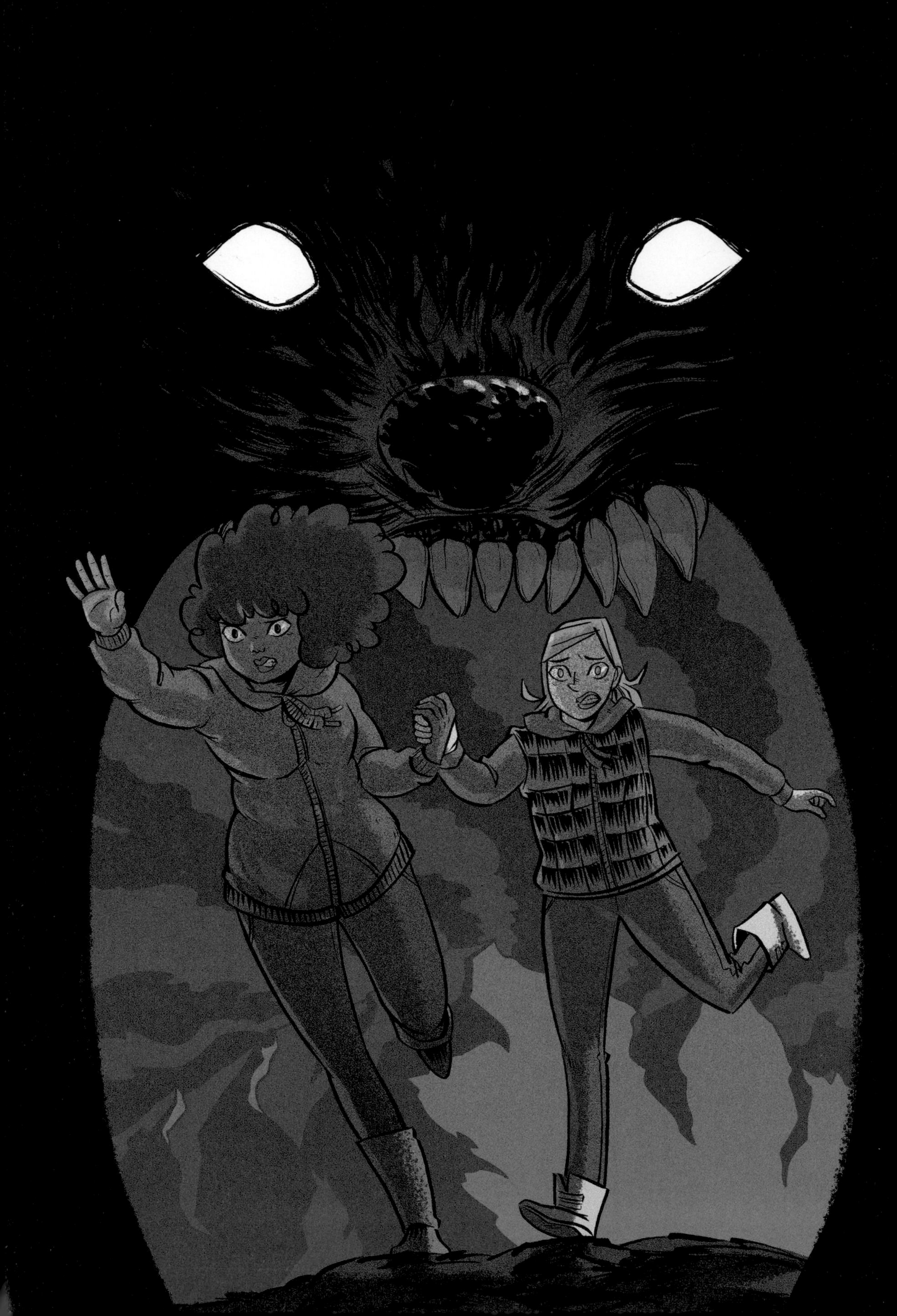

Issue 2 Subscription Cover by
John Allison

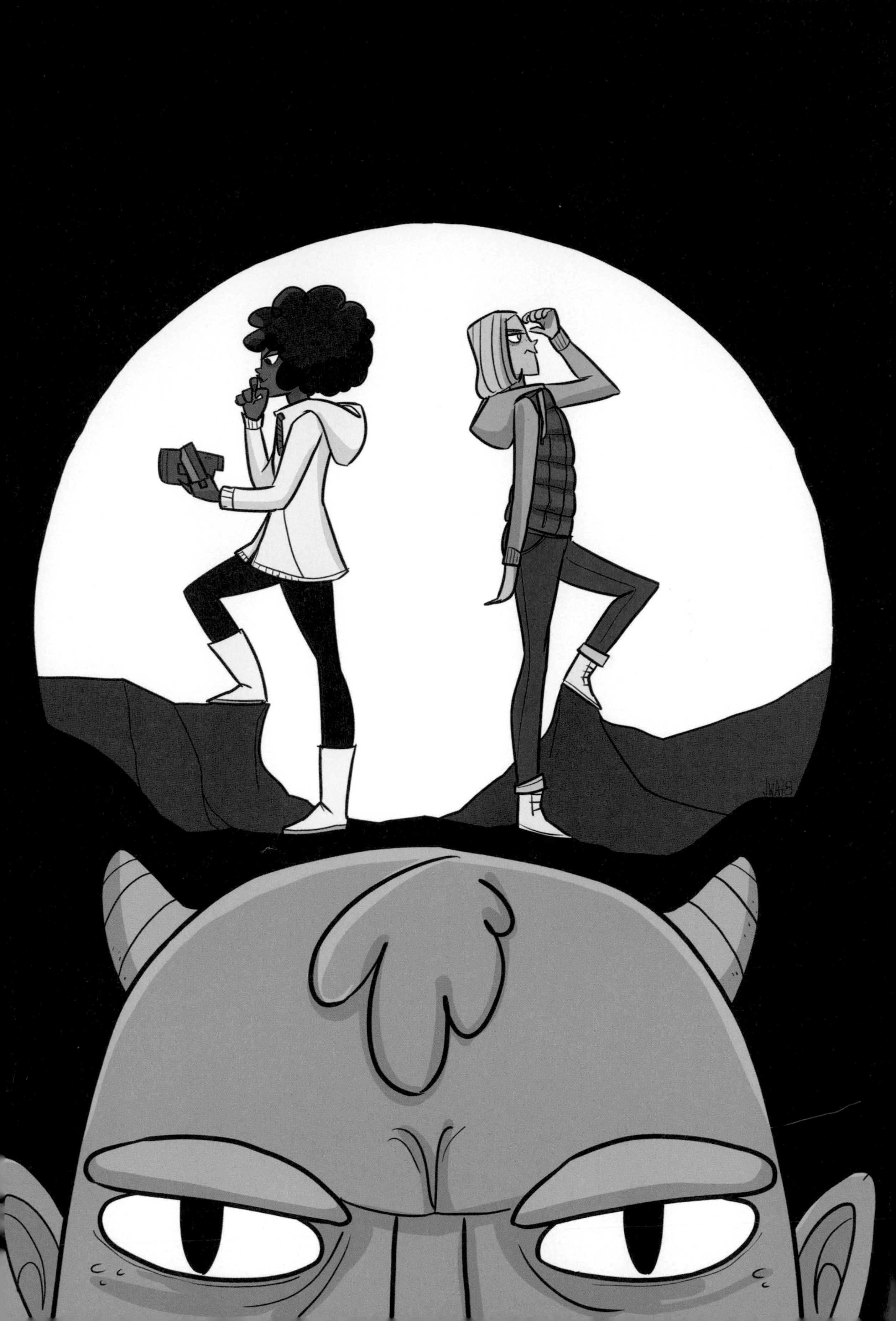

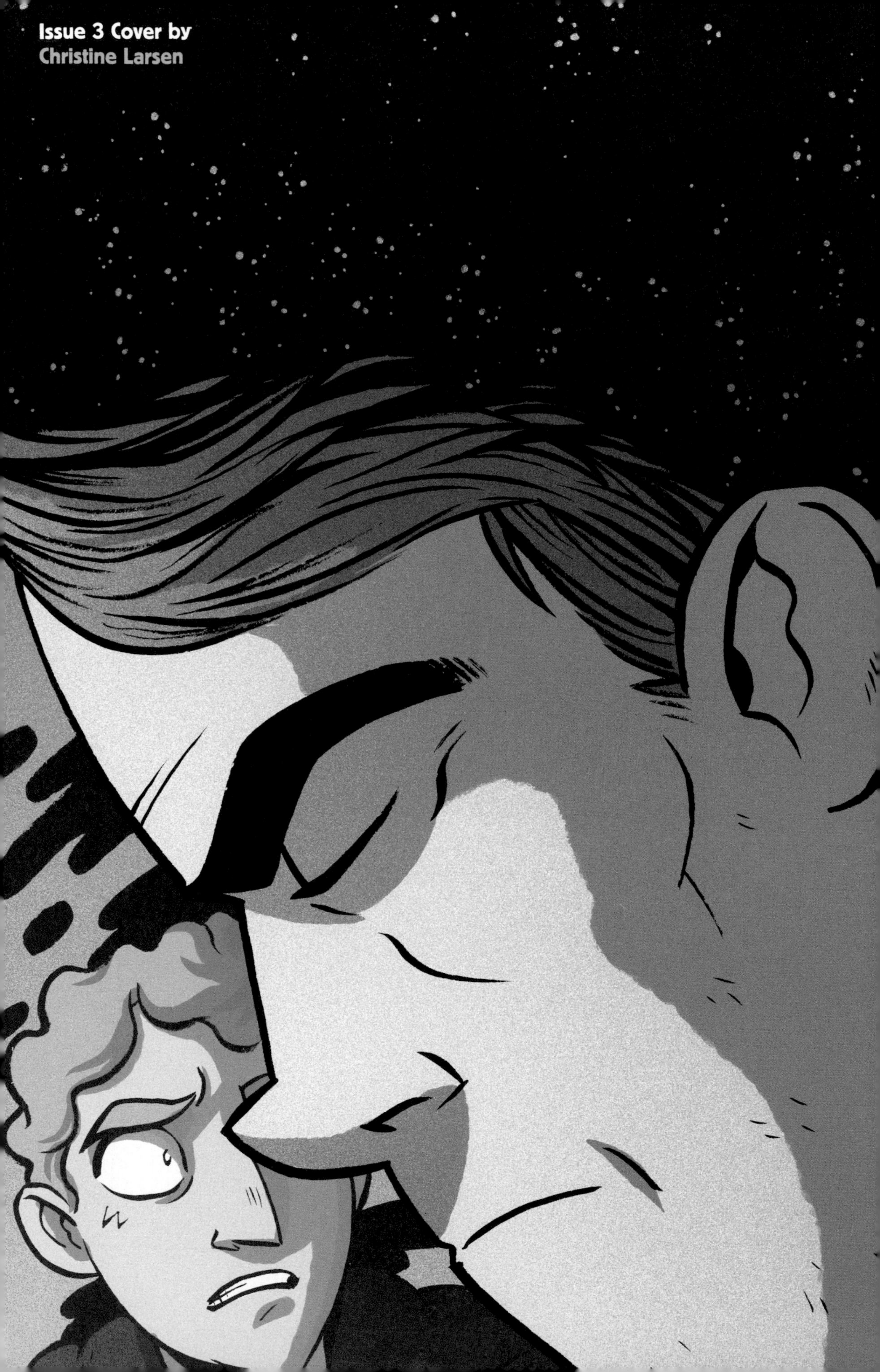

Issue 3 Cover by
Christine Larsen

Issue 3 Subscription Cover by
John Allison

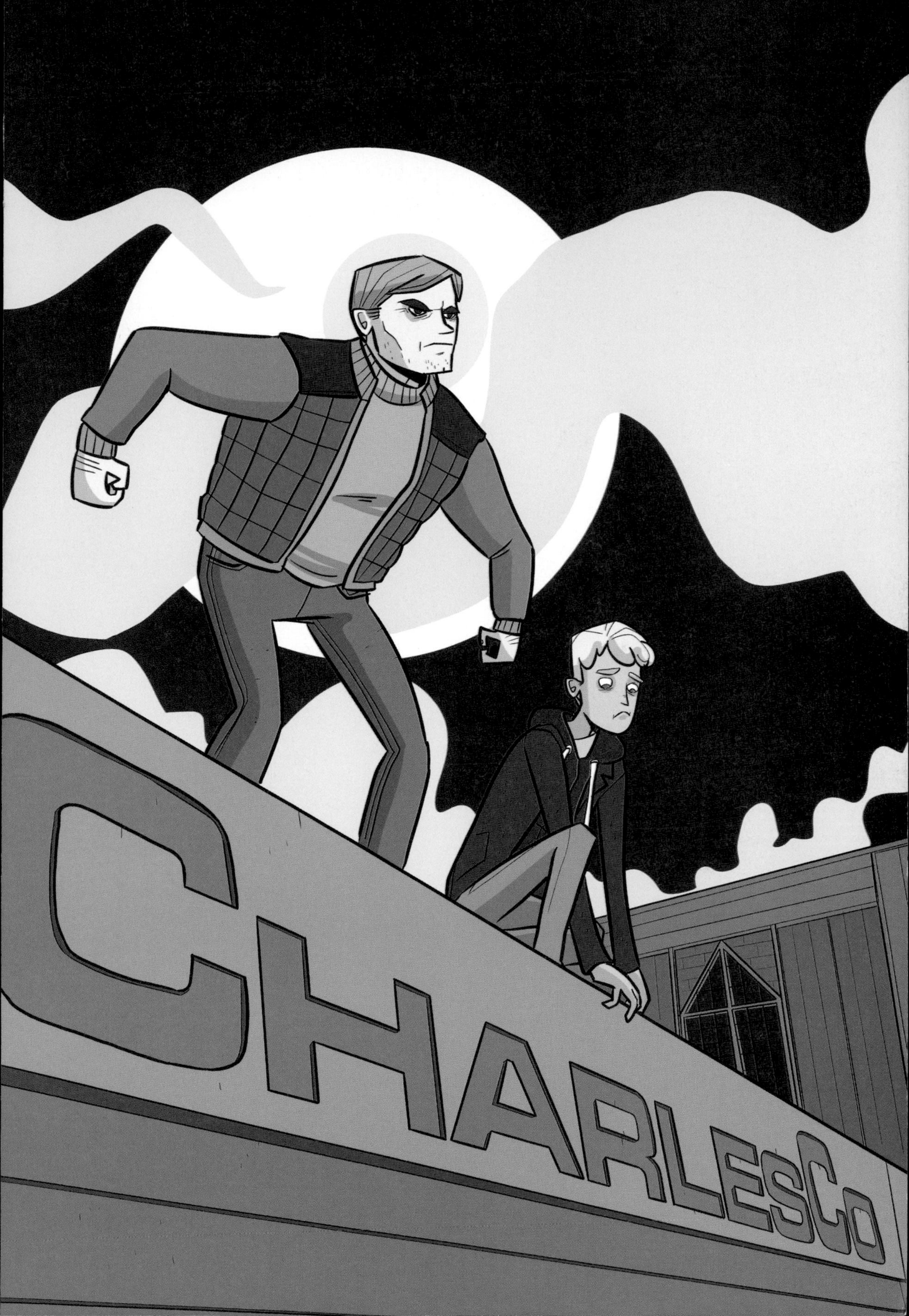
CHARLESCO

Issue 4 Cover by
Christine Larsen

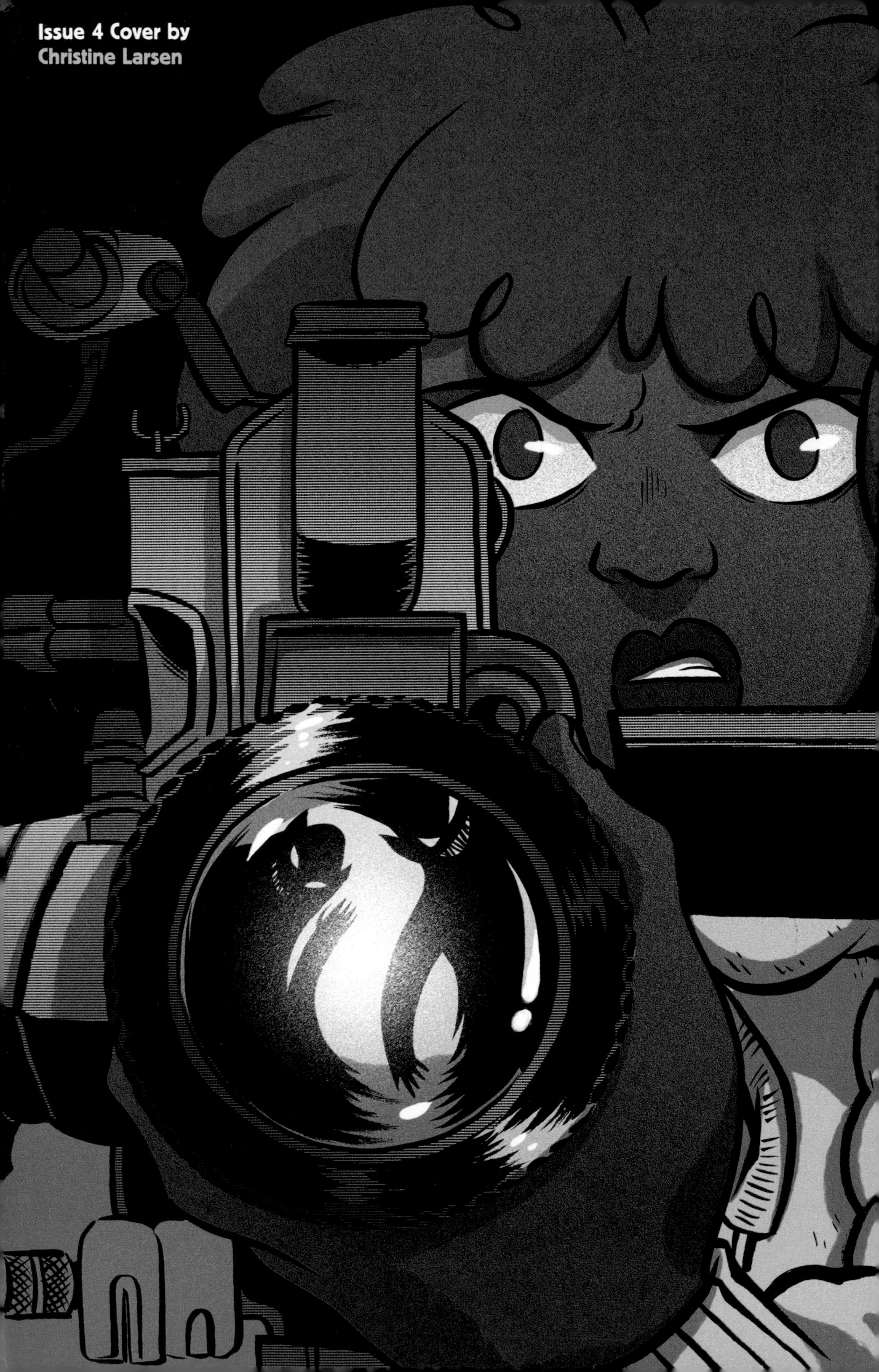

Issue 4 Subscription Cover by
John Allison

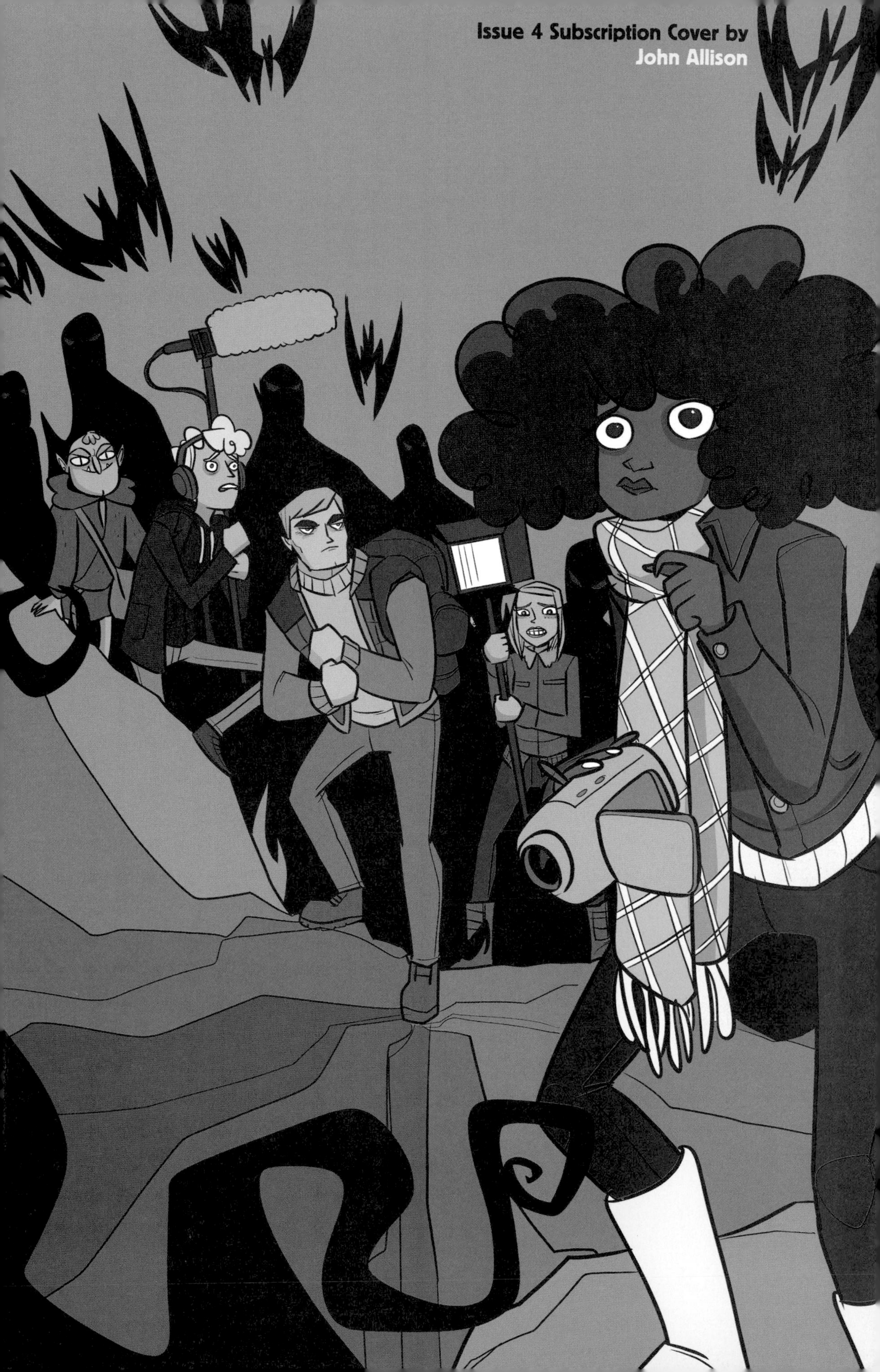

DISCOVER
ALL THE HITS

STEVENSON · ELLIS · WATTERS · ALLEN
LUMBERJANES
BEWARE THE KITTEN HOLY
NEW YORK TIMES BESTSELLING SERIES

Allison + Treiman + Cogar
GIANT DAYS
VOLUME ONE

From a writer of Disney's Moana
RIBON • FISH • PEER
SLAM!
VOLUME ONE

Hope Larson • Brittney Williams • Sarah Stern
GOLDIE VANCE
"Scoot over Nancy Drew..." —Los Angeles Times
Volume One

JAMES TYNION IV • RIAN SYGH • WALTER BAIAMONTE
THE BACKSTAGERS

TYSON HESSE'S
DIESEL
IGNITION

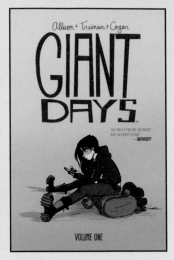

Lumberjanes
Noelle Stevenson, Shannon Watters, Grace Ellis, Brooklyn Allen, and Others
Volume 1: Beware the Kitten Holy
ISBN: 978-1-60886-687-8 | $14.99 US
Volume 2: Friendship to the Max
ISBN: 978-1-60886-737-0 | $14.99 US
Volume 3: A Terrible Plan
ISBN: 978-1-60886-803-2 | $14.99 US
Volume 4: Out of Time
ISBN: 978-1-60886-860-5 | $14.99 US
Volume 5: Band Together
ISBN: 978-1-60886-919-0 | $14.99 US

Giant Days
John Allison, Lissa Treiman, Max Sarin
Volume 1
ISBN: 978-1-60886-789-9 | $9.99 US
Volume 2
ISBN: 978-1-60886-804-9 | $14.99 US
Volume 3
ISBN: 978-1-60886-851-3 | $14.99 US

Jonesy
Sam Humphries, Caitlin Rose Boyle
Volume 1
ISBN: 978-1-60886-883-4 | $9.99 US
Volume 2
ISBN: 978-1-60886-999-2 | $14.99 US

Slam!
Pamela Ribon, Veronica Fish, Brittany Peer
Volume 1
ISBN: 978-1-68415-004-5 | $14.99 US

Goldie Vance
Hope Larson, Brittney Williams
Volume 1
ISBN: 978-1-60886-898-8 | $9.99 US
Volume 2
ISBN: 978-1-60886-974-9 | $14.99 US

The Backstagers
James Tynion IV, Rian Sygh
Volume 1
ISBN: 978-1-60886-993-0 | $14.99 US

Tyson Hesse's Diesel: Ignition
Tyson Hesse
ISBN: 978-1-60886-907-7 | $14.99 US

Coady & The Creepies
Liz Prince, Amanda Kirk, Hannah Fisher
ISBN: 978-1-68415-029-8 | $14.99 US

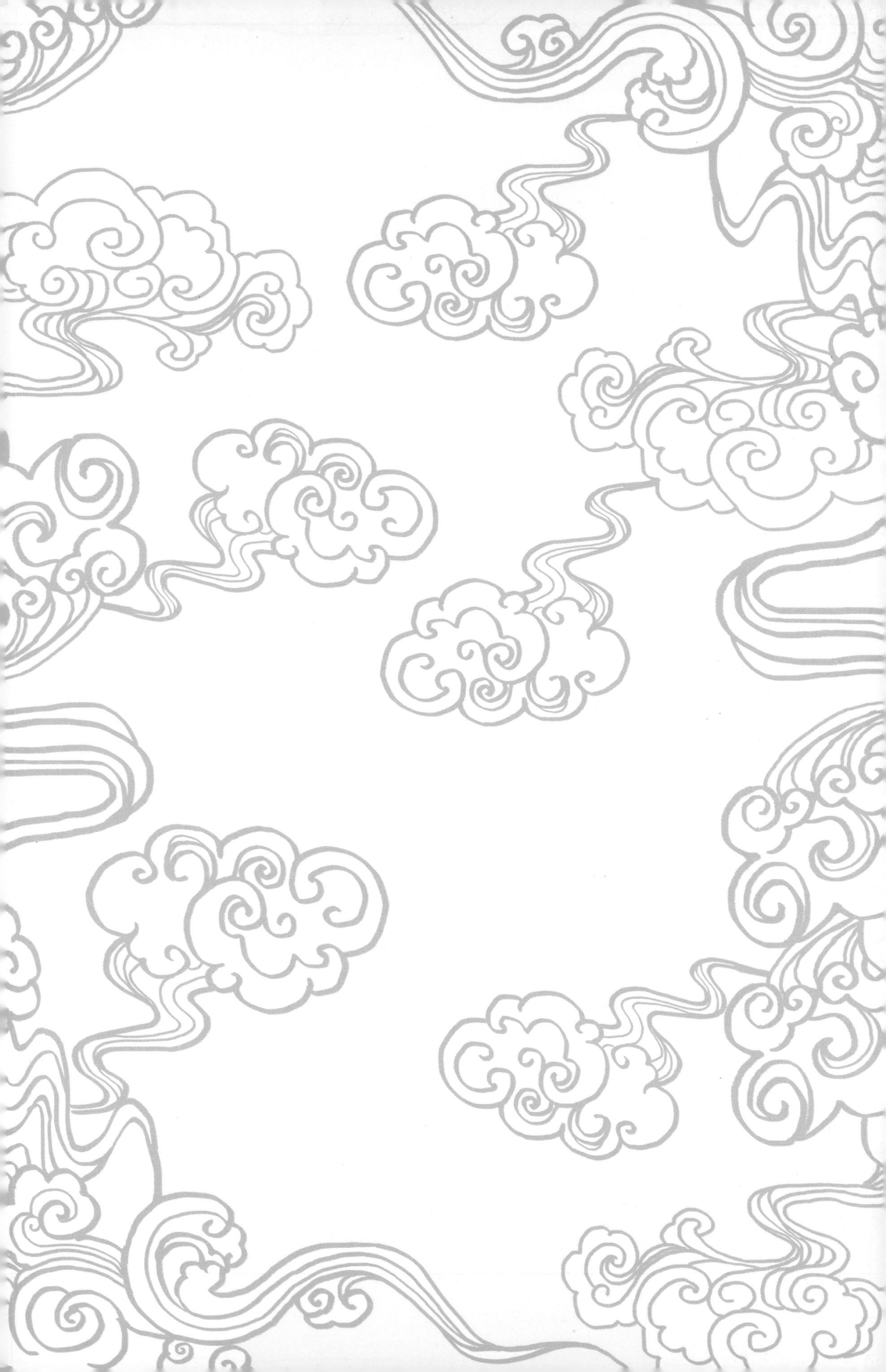

"The unique and otherworldly mystery, as well as the mystery of the characters themselves, makes this not only another Allison hit, but something new, exciting and inevitably rewarding for anyone looking for a new series to immerse themselves in."
—Big Comic Page

"*By Night* glows in the midst of many of the other comics on the shelves."
—ComicBuzz

There's something strange going on in Spectrum, South Dakota.

Home to high school best friends Jane Langstaff and Heather Meadows, Spectrum is a boomtown that's long since stopped booming, with nothing to show for its former glory but the abandoned Charleswood Estate, Charlesco's dwindling sprocket millions, and the story of the disappeared industrialist who founded the place…But deep within Charleswood, unbeknownst to anyone, there is a device called the Eidolon, which can open up a door to an otherworldly dimension. And Heather and Jane are about to go knocking.

Eisner Award nominee John Allison (*Giant Days, Scary Go Round*), and artist Christine Larsen (*Adventure Time*) invite you beyond the Eidolon, to a world of bizarre creatures and fantastical, hilarious adventure.

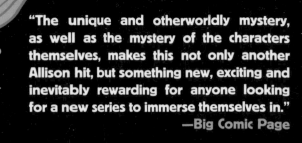

BOOM! BOX™

$14.99 US • **$18.99** CA • **£10.99** UK
ISBN: 978-1-68415-282-7

51499

9 781684 152827

WWW.BOOM-STUDIOS.COM